100 Excel VBA Simulations

Dr. Gerard M. Verschuuren

100 Excel VBA Simulations

Using Excel VBA to Model Risk, Investments, Genetics, Growth, Gambling, and Monte Carlo Analysis

I. TABLE OF CONTENTS

II. INSTRUCTIONS

All simulations in this book are supported by files that you can download from the following website: http://www.genesispc.com/download/100VBAsimulations.zip.

I assume that you are already familiar with many Excel features, including graphs or charts. In this book, I will only explain in more detail those features that are very helpful when you do what-if-analysis with simulations. For more basic features of Excel, I would refer you to some learning tools that you can find on www.mrexcel.com/microsoft-office-visual-learning.html.

If you want to create simulations exclusively with Excel functions and formulas, without using VBA, I recommend another book: http://genesispc.com/tocsimulations100.htm.

This book is not about the basics of Visual Basic (VBA) either. It only uses VBA to make simulations faster, better, and more user-friendly. If you want to learn VBA from the bottom up, I would recommend my interactive CD-ROM: http://genesispc.com/tocvba2013CD.htm. Yet, here are a few basic rules for using VBA:

- To start a new command line in VBA, use ENTER.
- Never use ENTER inside a command line. (In this book lines may wrap to the next line, but in VBA that is not allowed.)
- A colon (:) can separate amd combine several commands on the same line
- Use an apostrophe (') for a comment after, or at the end of, a command line.
- To create shortcuts in Excel for a macro (or *Sub* in VBA), you need the *Developers* tab (if that tab is missing, go to File Options | Macros | Options | Shift + a character.
- Files with macros open with the message "Enable Content." If you find that annoying place such files in a so-called *Trusted Location*: Files | Options | Trust Center | Trust Center Setting | Trusted Locations.
- To open VBA, you can use this shortcut: ALT F11.
- On the VBA screen, choose: Insert | Module.
- I always use *Option Explicit* in VBA: Tools | Options | Require Variable Declaration.
- This means you always have to declare variables with a *Dim* statement.
- There are value type variables such as integer, double, string (see Appendix) and object type variables (Range, Sheet). The latter require the *Set* keyword.
- Type a *dot* (.) after an object such as Range or Chart in order to get access to its properties and methods.
- It is wise to use consistent indentation to make your code more readable and checkable.
- A *With* statement allows us to refer to it later with just a simple dot (.), followed by a property or method.
- Formulas are always strings in VBA, so they should be inside double quotes ("..."). If there are double quotes inside those double quotes, they should be ""...""".
- To split a long string into several lines, you use endquotes-space-ampersand-space-underscore-enter-openquotes.
- To interrupt running code, use *Ctrl + Break*.
- If your VBA code ever runs into trouble (and it will!), make sure you stop the Debugger before you can run the code again. You do so by clicking the *Reset* button:

-

I. GAMBLING

Chapter 1: The Die Is Cast

What the simulation does

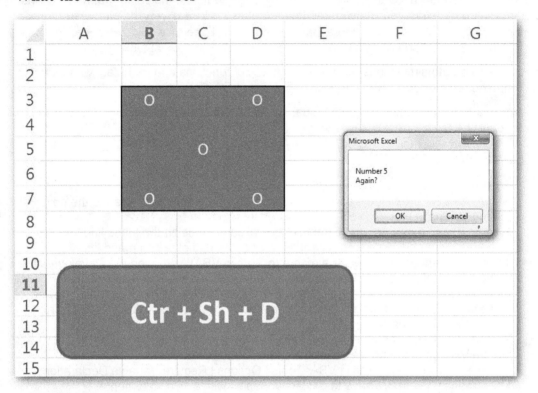

We start with a very simple case of simulation—casting a die. The code generates a random number. According to that outcome, the colored die shows the appropriate number of eyes at their proper locations. Each time the random number changes, the die adjusts accordingly. The code stops when you hit the number 6.

What you need to know

Excel has a volatile function called RAND. On each recalculation, this function generates a new random number between 0 and 1. The equivalent of RAND in VBA is *Rnd*. In addition to these two operators, later versions of Excel also let you use RANDBETWEEN, which returns a random integer between two integers. Instead of using RANDBETWEEN, you can always use a more complicated formula. If you want numbers between 1 and 6, for instance, you multiply by 6, round the number down by using the INT function, and then add 1 to the end result. More in general: =INT((high-low+1)*RAND()+low). In VBA, you must replace RAND with *Rnd*.

Finally, we need to regulate which eyes should pop up for each new random number. This is done by using the *IIf* function in VBA. This function is a "decision maker," which determines whether a specific eye should be on or off.

GoTo allows the code to jump to a specific label—in this case called *Again*, followed by a colon. *GoTo* lets you jump forward or backward in code.

A *MsgBox* can just have an OK button, or a combination of OK, Cancel, Yes, and No. In case there is more than one option, an IF statement has to check what the users decided to click on.

What you need to do

```
Sub Dice()
   Dim i As Integer
Again:      'this is called a label that we use at the end to go back to
   i = Int(Rnd * 6) + 1
   Range("B3") = IIf(i > 1, "O", "")
   Range("D3") = IIf(i > 3, "O", "")
   Range("B5") = IIf(i = 6, "O", "")
   Range("C5") = IIf(i = 1 Or i = 3 Or i = 5, "O", "")
   Range("D5") = IIf(i = 6, "O", "")
   Range("B7") = IIf(i > 3, "O", "")
   Range("D7") = IIf(i > 1, "O", "")
   If i = 6 Then Exit Sub
   If MsgBox("Number " & i & vbCr & "Again?", vbOKCancel) = vbOK Then GoTo
Again
End Sub
```

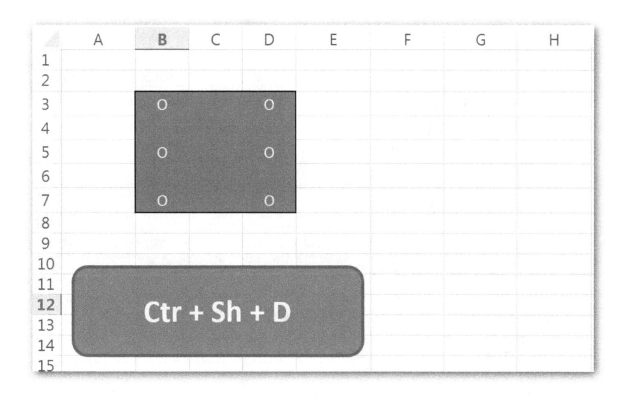

Chapter 2: Casting Six Dice

What the simulation does

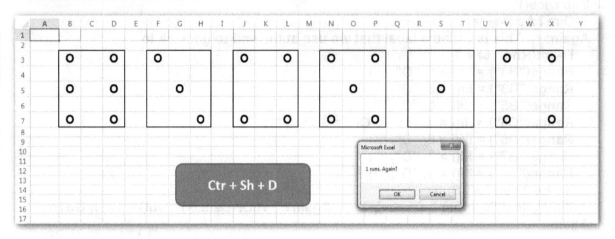

This time we have six different dice. Each die "listens" to a random number in VBA. The settings for each die are similar to what we did in simulation 1.

There is not much new on this sheet. The main difference is that we need 6 different cells with a RAND function in order to control the six die displays. This is done with a *For*-loop in VBA, running from 0 to 5 (or 1 to 6).

When there are at least 3 dice in a row with six eyes, all dice get marked at the same time.

What you need to know

A variable of the *Variant* type can hold an array of items. We fill the array here by using the *Array* function in VBA. This array starts at 0 (that's why the *For*-loop runs from 0 to 5 instead of from 1 to 6). Notice that cell rows and columns always start at 1 (not 0).

VBA can use almost all Excel functions by calling them with *WorksheetFunction*. In this case we use Excel's COUNTBLANK function.

The use of *Range* and *Cells* in VBA can be very powerful, but can also be rather confusing at first sight (see Appendix). *Range("A1")* is equivalent to *Cells(1,1)*, but the latter one is more flexible in loops because we can use a loop variable for the row and/or the column position. Sometimes, they are combined: *Range(Cells(1,1),Cells(10,2))* would refer to A1:B10.

Another important tool in VBA is *Offset*, with which you can specify the row offset and the column offset. For instance, *Range("A1").Offset(2,2)* would evaluate to cell C3.

Don't confuse *End Sub* with *Exit Sub*. Each *Sub* must close with *End Sub*. But if you want to prematurely end the *Sub* routine, you must use *Exit Sub*.

What you need to do

```vba
Sub Dice()
    Dim vArr As Variant, i As Integer, r As Integer, n As Integer, iSix As Integer, oRange As Range
    Sheet1.Cells.Interior.ColorIndex = 0
    vArr = Array("B3", "F3", "J3", "N3", "R3", "V3")
Again:
    Sheet1.Cells = ""
    iSix = 0
    For r = 0 To 5
        Set oRange = Range(Range(vArr(r)), Range(Range(vArr(r)).Offset(4, 2).Address))
        With oRange
            i = Int(Rnd * 6) + 1
            .Cells(1, 1) = IIf(i > 1, "O", "")
            .Cells(1, 3) = IIf(i > 3, "O", "")
            .Cells(3, 1) = IIf(i = 6, "O", "")
            .Cells(3, 2) = IIf(i = 1 Or i = 3 Or i = 5, "O", "")
            .Cells(3, 3) = IIf(i = 6, "O", "")
            .Cells(5, 1) = IIf(i > 3, "O", "")
            .Cells(5, 3) = IIf(i > 1, "O", "")
            If WorksheetFunction.CountBlank(.Cells) = 9 Then iSix = iSix + 1
        End With
    Next r
    n = n + 1
    If iSix >= 3 Then
        Cells.Interior.Color = vbYellow
        MsgBox "3x6 or more! After " & n & " runs."
        Exit Sub
    End If
    If MsgBox(n & " runs. Again?", vbOKCancel) = vbOK Then GoTo Again
End Sub
```

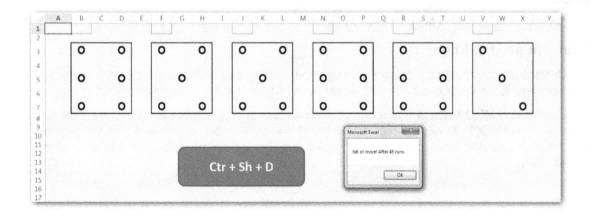

Chapter 3: Roulette Machine

What the simulation does

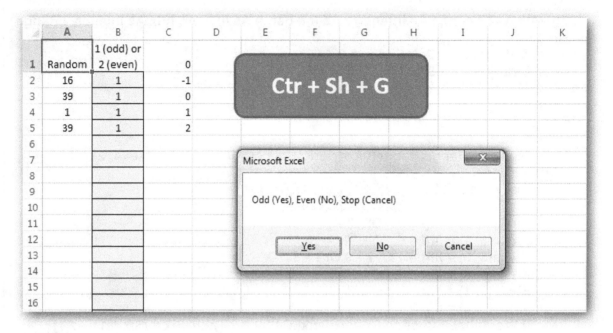

Most people believe that if they keep consistently betting "odd," the ball will most certainly land on an odd number sometime soon. This is called "the law of averages" which says, the longer you wait for a certain random event, the more likely it becomes.

Do not believe it! Try it out in this "real life" simulation and find out how the casino makes money on people who think that way. You may initially gain but eventually lose.

The code clears previous results in the columns A:C when you start the code. Column A simulates a roulette with 1,000 random numbers between 1 and 36. In column B, the code types 1 if you confirm an odd number through the *MsgBox*, expecting the next number to be odd—otherwise 2 for even.

Column C keeps track of the score: it adds 1, when your prediction was correct—otherwise it subtracts 1.

Once you hit *Cancel*, a *MsgBox* tells you whether you won or lost, and with which score.

What you need to know

CurrentRegion represents the entire range bounded by any combination of blank rows and blank columns. So in the above case, that would be A1:C5, and in the case below A1:C11.

Excel has a MOD function that returns the remainder after a number is divided by a divisor. For instance, =MOD(3, 2) returns the remainder of the division 3/2, which is 1. VBA, however, uses the *Mod* operator, which does basically the same. So the syntax would be: *3 Mod 2*, which also returns 1.

What you need to do

```
Sub Guess()
   Dim r As Long, iGuess As Integer, vGuess As Variant, oRange As Range
   Range("A1").CurrentRegion.Offset(1, 0).Delete
   Do
      r = Range("A1").CurrentRegion.Rows.Count + 1
      vGuess = MsgBox("Odd (Yes), Even (No), Stop (Cancel)", vbYesNoCancel)
      Select Case vGuess
         Case 6: Cells(r, 2) = 1
         Case 7: Cells(r, 2) = 2
         Case 2: GoTo Report
      End Select
      Cells(r, 1) = Int(Rnd * 50) + 1
      Cells(r, 3) = IIf(Cells(r, 1) Mod 2 = Cells(r, 2) Mod 2, Cells(r - 1, 3) + 1, Cells(r - 1, 3)
- 1)
   Loop
Report:
   Set oRange = Cells(Range("A1").CurrentRegion.Rows.Count, 3)
   MsgBox "You " & IIf(oRange < 1, "lost", "won") & " with a score of " & oRange
End Sub
```

	A	B	C
1	Random	1 (odd) or 2 (even)	0
2	16	1	-1
3	39	1	0
4	1	1	1
5	39	1	2
6	41	1	3
7	36	1	2
8	3	1	3
9	21	1	4
10	44	1	3
11	40	1	2
12			
13			
14			

Ctr + Sh + G

Microsoft Excel

You won with a score of 2

OK

Chapter 4: An X-O Game

What the simulation does

	A	B	C	D	E	F	G	H	I	J
1					X					
2		X								
3		O	O							
4			X	O						
5	O		X			Lost				
6		Lost	Lost							
7										

Ctrl + Sh + I

This is a game with two players who "choose" X or O randomly. They win when a row or column has the same entries. As soon as a row or column has different entries, the word "lost" gets displayed. As soon as all 5 entries in a row or column are the same, the game is won. A *MsgBox* displays the endresult and keeps track of previous results during the game.

What you need to know

Option Explicit at the beginning of the code requires that all variables are explicitly declared as of a certain type with a *Dim* statement. This is a safe way to prevent you from misspelling a variable farther down in your code.

Do-loops run an unspecified number of times *until* a certain condition kicks in or *while* that condition persists.

To keep track of previous results, we need a *global* variable. Local variables are declared inside a *Sub*, but global variables need to be declared at the top of the *Module*. They retain information until the file is closed.

We also use the *Timer* of VBA. The *Timer* counts the number of seconds since midnight on your machine. This way we can pause a process for a short time. *DoEvents* prevents that the system is blocked during that time period.

	A	B	C	D	E	F
1	O	X	X	O	O	Lost
2	X	X	O	O	O	Lost
3	O	X	O	X		Lost
4	O	X	O	O	X	Lost
5	X	X	X		X	
6	Lost		Lost	Lost	Lost	
7						
8						
9						

Microsoft Excel

X won 1
O won 0
in 3 games.

OK

What you need to do

```vba
Option Explicit
Dim iO As Integer, iX As Integer, iTotal As Integer

Sub IntelligentGame()
    Dim oBoard As Range, bPlayer As Boolean, i As Integer, oCell As Range
    Dim iRow As Integer, iCol As Integer, iTime As Long
    Set oBoard = Range(Cells(1, 1), Cells(5, 5))
    With oBoard
        .Cells(1.1).CurrentRegion.Clear
        .BorderAround , xlThick : .Cells.HorizontalAlignment = xlCenter
        Do
            bPlayer = Not bPlayer
            Do
                iRow = WorksheetFunction.RandBetween(1, 5)
                iCol = WorksheetFunction.RandBetween(1, 5)
                If .Cells(iRow, iCol) = "" Then
                    .Cells(iRow, iCol) = IIf(bPlayer, "X", "O"): Exit Do
                End If
            Loop
            iTime = Timer + 1
            Do Until Timer > iTime
                DoEvents
            Loop
            For i = 1 To 5
                If WorksheetFunction.CountIf(.Rows(i).Cells, "X") >= 1 And
WorksheetFunction.CountIf(.Rows(i).Cells, "O") >= 1 Then .Cells(i, 6) = "Lost"
                If WorksheetFunction.CountIf(.Columns(i).Cells, "X") >= 1 And
WorksheetFunction.CountIf(.Columns(i).Cells, "O") >= 1 Then .Cells(6, i) = "Lost"
            Next i
            If WorksheetFunction.CountIf(.Cells(1, 1).CurrentRegion.Cells, "Lost") = 10
Then MsgBox "No winner": Exit Do
            For i = 1 To 5
                If WorksheetFunction.CountIf(.Rows(i).Cells, "X") = 5 Then MsgBox "X is the
winner.": iX = iX + 1: Exit Do
                If WorksheetFunction.CountIf(.Rows(i).Cells, "O") = 5 Then MsgBox "O is the
winner.": iO = iO + 1: Exit Do
                If WorksheetFunction.CountIf(.Columns(i).Cells, "X") = 5 Then MsgBox "X is
the winner.": iX = iX + 1: Exit Do
                If WorksheetFunction.CountIf(.Columns(i).Cells, "O") = 5 Then MsgBox "O is
the winner.": iO = iO + 1: Exit Do
            Next i
            If WorksheetFunction.CountBlank(oBoard) = 0 Then MsgBox "No winner": Exit
Do
        Loop
    End With
    iTotal = iTotal + 1
    MsgBox "X won " & iX & vbCr & "O won " & iO & vbCr & "in " & iTotal & " games."
End Sub
```

Chapter 5: A Slot Machine

What the simulation does

	A	B	C	D	E	F	G	H	I	J	K	L	M	N	O	P	Q	R	S	T	U
1		run			0					cumulative		game						average score			
2		20			1	-2	2	-1		-1		20		Game 1	1			0.9			
3					2	-2	2	-1		-1				Game 2	5						
4					3	-2	1	2		1				Game 3	-1						
5					4	-2	0	2		0				Game 4	2						
6					5	-1	0	0		-1				Game 5	1						
7					6	0	1	2		3				Game 6	4			Ctr + Sh + R			
8					7	-2	0	2		0				Game 7	0						
9					8	-2	-1	0		-3				Game 8	5						
10					9	1	1	0		2				Game 9	0						
11					10	1	1	-1		1				Game 10	1						
12					11	0	1	1		2				Game 11	5						
13					12	-1	0	2		1				Game 12	-1						
14					13	2	-2	0		0				Game 13	1						
15					14	-1	0	2		1				Game 14	-1						
16					15	-1	1	-1		-1				Game 15	-1						
17					16	0	-1	1		0				Game 16	-2						
18					17	-2	-2	2		-2				Game 17	0						
19					18	-2	2	1		1				Game 18	2						
20					19	0	2	1		3				Game 19	-1						
21					20	-2	0	0		-2				Game 20	-2						

This spreadsheet makes 20 runs for each game (columns F:H). Each run creates 3 random numbers between -2 and +2, and then calculates the cumulative total in column J. After 20 runs, a new game starts.

The results for each game are recorded in columns N and O. After 20 games, the average score features in cell R3. At any moment, the user can cancel further runs and a *MsgBox* reports what the average score was in X games of 20 runs. Then the process can start all over with run 1 for game 1.

What you need to know

To make all of this possible, we need a *Do*-loop for the runs inside a *Do*-loop for the games. Besides we added a *Timer* loop so the results come in gradually

To make the code more understandable, we used *Range Names* here that were assigned in Excel. The range name "games," for instance, refers to the range $N$2:$N$21.

The VBA function *FormatNumber* lets you determine the number of decimals by specifying the second argument.

Instead of using RANDBETWEEN(-2,2), we can use also: *-2 + Int(Rnd * 5)*.

What you need to do

```
Option Explicit

Sub Run()
  Dim iRun As Integer, iGame As Integer, pTime As Long
  Range(Cells(2, 1), Cells(21, 18)).ClearContents
  Do
    iRun = iRun + 1
    Do
      iGame = iGame + 1
      With Range("Runs")
        .Cells(iGame, 1) = iGame
        .Cells(iGame, 2) = -2 + Int(Rnd * 5)
        .Cells(iGame, 3) = -2 + Int(Rnd * 5)
        .Cells(iGame, 4) = -2 + Int(Rnd * 5)
        Range("cumsums").Cells(iGame, 1).FormulaR1C1 = "=SUM(RC[-4]:RC[-2])"
      End With
      pTime = Timer + 0.5
      Do While Timer < pTime
        DoEvents
      Loop
    Loop Until iGame = 20
    Range("run") = iGame
    iGame = 0
    Range("game") = iRun
    Range("games").Cells(iRun, 1) = "Game " & iRun
    Range("gamescores").Cells(iRun, 1) = Range("cumsums").Cells(20, 1)
    Range("avgscore").Formula = "=average(gamescores)"
    If iRun = 20 Then Exit Do
  Loop Until MsgBox("New run?", vbOKCancel) = vbCancel
  MsgBox "Average of " & FormatNumber(Range("avgscore"), 1) & " in " & iRun & "
games of 20 runs"
End Sub
```

	run	0				cumulative	game		average score	
	20	1	1	2	-2	1	20	Game 1	-3	-0.8
		2	2	2	-1	3		Game 2	-1	
		3	-2	1	-2	-3		Game 3	0	
		4	1	0	2	3		Game 4	-3	
		5	-2	-1	1	-2		Game 5	-4	
		6	-1	-1	-2	-4		Game 6	-2	
		7	-2	2	1	1		Game 7	-2	
		8	0	0	0	0		Game 8	3	
		9	2	0	1	3		Game 9	-5	
		10	-1	-1	-1	-3		Game 10	1	
		11	-1	-2	1	-2		Game 11	4	
		12	2	-1	0	1		Game 12	-2	
		13	2	1	0	3		Game 13	1	
		14	2	-1	-2	-1		Game 14	2	
		15	2	0	1	3		Game 15	-3	
		16	1	-1	2	2		Game 16	-4	
		17	-1	-1	-1	-3		Game 17	0	
		18	1	2	-2	1		Game 18	2	
		19	2	1	2	5		Game 19	0	
		20	1	-1	0	0		Game 20	0	

Ctr + Sh + R

Microsoft Excel

Average of -0.8 in 20 games of 20 runs

OK

Chapter 6: Gamblers' Ruin

What the simulation does

	A	B	C	D	E	F	G	H	I	J	K	L
1	0			Average	Min	Max	SD	Final				
2	1			9.58	-2	24	7.74881		17			
3	0			-0.24	-5	4	1.87552		1			
4	1			1.04	-3	5	1.63867		-1			
5	2			6.44	0	10	2.19881		5			
6	3			7.04	-3	15	4.56362		7			
7	4			-11.14	-22	0	5.49016		-15			
8	3			-0.54	-5	4	1.76624		-1			
9	2			7.84	0	17	4.94356		15			
10	1			-7.38	-15	0	3.54418		-11			
11	0			-5.46	-13	2	4.85428		-7			
12	1			-4.76	-15	3	4.81605		-13			
13	0			-3.62	-10	4	3.41648		3			
14	-1			0.06	-5	5	2.12165		3			
15	-2			1.78	-3	8	2.73614		-1			
16	-1			2.4	-4	7	2.69305		5			
17	-2			-1.8	-6	4	2.75241		3			
18	-1			-2.7	-8	2	2.83021		-3			
19	-2			-13.22	-25	0	7.64963		-15			
20	-1			-2.94	-9	2	2.48153		-5			
21	0			-5.26	-10	0	2.33385		-9			
22	1			-1.26	-8	5	2.86962		1			
23	2											
24	3								-1			

Microsoft Excel

8 runs with average above 0
Average of final scores: -1.00

OK

This sheet simulates what may happen to people who are addicted to gambling. When we run the code, we are asked how many chances we want in column A to go for odd or even. We simulate a 50% probability for either choice. If the choice was correct, the count in column A goes up by 1, otherwise it goes down by 1. All this is done on a new sheet.

Next we simulate that this addicted player repeats the game for some twenty more times. This is done with a *Data Table* in D:H (see Appendix). In its top row, we calculate average, minimum, maximum, standard deviation, and the final score (in column H). At the end, we calculate how often the player had a positive final score, and how often a negative one. Most of the work goes into the conditional formatting bars.

What you need to know

Usually a *Data Table* has *have* a formula in the first cell—which would be cell C1 in our case. Based on that formula, a *Data Table* typically uses a row input of variables and a column input of variables to recalculate the formula placed at its origin. It does so by filling the table cells with a formula that has the following syntax: {=TABLE(row-input, col-input)}.

In this case we use a *Data Table* merely to trick Excel into simulating 20 (or many more) iterations of column A. We do so by not placing a formula at the origin, but by leaving the row-input argument empty, and having the col-input argument refer to an empty cell somewhere outside the table. Yes, that does the trick!

By using *Worksheet.Add* we create a new worksheet either before (1st argument) or after (2nd argument after the comma) the *Activesheet*, which is the sheet we are currently on.

An *InputBox* provides users to provide their own input for variables or questions.

What you need to do

```
Sub Gambling()
   Dim oWS As Worksheet, iRow As Long
   iRow = InputBox("How many rows?", , 100)
   Set oWS = Worksheets.Add( , ActiveSheet)
   Range("A1") = 0
   Range(Cells(2, 1), Cells(iRow, 1)).Formula = "=IF(RAND()>0.5,A1+1,A1-1)"
   Range("D1") = "Average": Range("D2").Formula = "=AVERAGE(A:A)"
   Range("E1") = "Min": Range("E2").Formula = "=MIN(A:A)"
   Range("F1") = "Max": Range("F2").Formula = "=MAX(A:A)"
   Range("G1") = "SD": Range("G2").Formula = "=STDEV(A:A)"
   Range("H1") = "Final": Range("H2").Formula = "=" & Cells(iRow, 1).Address(False,
False)
   Range(Range("C2"), Range("H22")).Table , Range("B2")

   Dim oRange As Range, oFormat As FormatCondition
   Set oRange = Range(Range("D2"), Range("D22"))
   Set oFormat = oRange.FormatConditions.Add(xlCellValue, xlLess, "=0")
   oFormat.Interior.Color = 13551615

   'Conditional Formatting with Bars (only in later versions of Excel)
   Dim oBar As Databar
   Set oRange = Range(Range("H2"), Range("H22"))
   oRange.ColumnWidth = 15
   Range("H24").Formula = "=AVERAGE(" & oRange.Address & ")"
   Set oBar = oRange.FormatConditions.AddDatabar
   oBar.MinPoint.Modify newtype:=xlConditionValueAutomaticMin
   oBar.MaxPoint.Modify newtype:=xlConditionValueAutomaticMax
   oBar.BarFillType = xlDataBarFillGradient
   oBar.Direction = xlContext
   oBar.NegativeBarFormat.ColorType = xlDataBarColor
   oBar.BarBorder.Type = xlDataBarBorderSolid
   oBar.NegativeBarFormat.BorderColorType = xlDataBarColor
   oBar.AxisPosition = xlDataBarAxisAutomatic
   oBar.BarColor.Color = 13012579
   oBar.NegativeBarFormat.Color.Color = 5920255
   ActiveWindow.Zoom = 130

   Dim sMsg As String
   sMsg = WorksheetFunction.CountIf(Columns(4), ">0") & " runs with average above
0"
   sMsg = sMsg & vbCr & "Average of final scores: " & FormatNumber(Range("H24"),
2)
   MsgBox sMsg
End Sub
```

Chapter 7: Lottery Numbers

What the simulation does

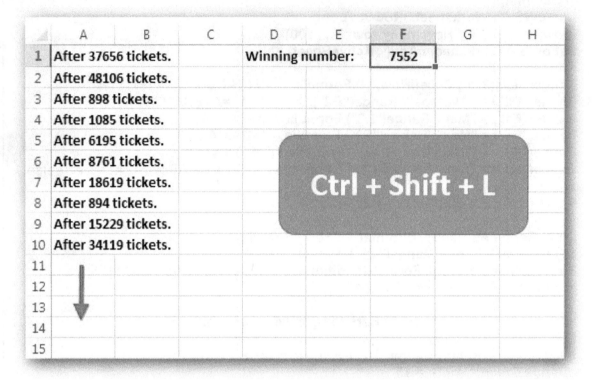

Each time we run this macro, the code creates a 4-digit random number in cell F1. Then it tries to match that number by creating new 4-digit random numbers until the two numbers match.

After each match, it plots in column A how many times—how many "tickets"—it took to find a match. The simulation keeps doing this until we hit the No-button in the *MsgBox*.

What you need to know

Each random digit is generated by *Int(Rnd * 10)*. The *Int* function always rounds down to the nearest integer (0 – 9). But because this digit has to be incorporated in the 4-digit lottery number, we need also the *CStr* function which converts the number into a *String*.

To "string" things together, we always need [space][ampersand][space] between the individual strings that need to be "stringed" together.

Do-loops are perfect when we don't know ahead of time how many loops we need. The loop can be stopped by adding a *While* or *Until* condition on the *Do*-line or the *Loop*-line. Another possibility is—which we did here—using an *IF*-statement. If the condition of the *If*-statement kicks in, we perform an *Exit Do* (not to be confused with an *Exit Sub*), which takes us to the line after the *Loop*-statement.

What you need to do

```vba
Option Explicit

Sub Lottery()
   Dim sNumber As String, sGuess As String, i As Integer, j As Long, n As Long
   Range("A1").EntireColumn.Clear
   If MsgBox("New winning number?", vbYesNo) = vbYes Then
      sNumber = ""
      For i = 1 To 4
         sNumber = sNumber & CStr(Int(Rnd * 10))
      Next i
      Range("F1") = "'" & sNumber
   Else
      sNumber = Range("F1")
   End If
   Do
      For i = 1 To 4
         sGuess = sGuess & CStr(Int(Rnd * 10))
      Next i
      n = n + 1
      If CStr(sNumber) = CStr(sGuess) Then
         j = j + 1
         Cells(j, 1) = "After " & n & " tickets."
         n = 0
         If MsgBox("Another run?", vbYesNo, sGuess) = vbNo Then Exit Do
      End If
      sGuess = ""
   Loop
End Sub
```

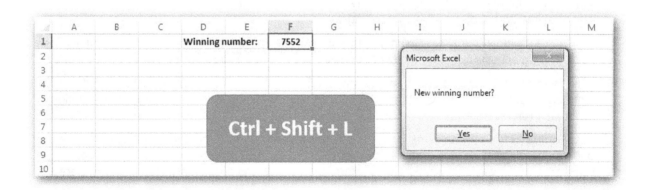

Chapter 8: Win or Lose?

What the simulation does

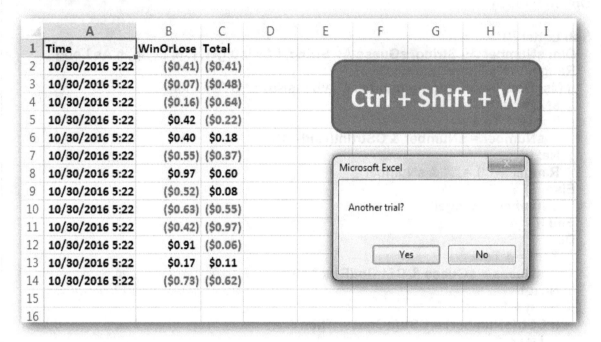

After each trial, the macro plots the current time in Column A, then a random win or lose amount of money in column B, and a cumulative total of what has been won or lost so far in column C.

When we decide to quit, a *MsgBox* reports to us how much we have won or lost in total after an X number of trials.

What you need to know

The *Now* function returns the serial number of the current date and time. If the cell format was *General* before the function was entered, Excel changes the cell format so that it matches the date and time format of your regional settings.

AutoFit widens the *EntireColumn* to its widest entry. It does so for the entire sheet if you use *Cells*, or for a specific range on the sheet that you specify—for instance, *Cells(1,1)*.

FormulaR1C1 uses a row and column notation—for instance, R1C1—instead of the more common notation of A1. To use this notation also in Excel itself, you can go here: File | Options | Formulas | R1C1 reference style.

FormulaR1C1 can have relative or absolute references. Here are some examples: *RC* refers to the same row and column number as where the cell itself is located; *R1C1* refers to a cell in row 1 and column 1 (which is A1); *R[-1]C[1]* refers to 1 row up and 1 column to the right of where the reference is located (see Appendix).

FormatCurrency does something similar to what *FormatNumber* does. It lets you specify the number of decimals in the 2nd argument, but it also adds a currency symbol (which is a non-numeric entity).

What you need to do

```
Sub WinOrLose()
  Dim i As Long, sMsg As String
  Columns("A:C").ClearContents
  Range("A1") = "Time": Range("B1") = "WinOrLose": Range("C1") = "Total"
  For i = 2 To 1000
    Cells(i, 1) = Now
    Cells(i, 2) = FormatCurrency(1 - 2 * Rnd, 2)
    Cells(i, 3).FormulaR1C1 = "=SUM(R2C2:RC2)"
    Cells.EntireColumn.AutoFit
    If MsgBox("Another trial?", vbYesNo) = vbNo Then Exit For
  Next i
  With Cells(i, 3)
    If .Value >= 0 Then sMsg = "you WON: " Else sMsg = "you LOST: "
    MsgBox "After " & i - 1 & " trials " & sMsg & FormatCurrency(Cells(i, 3), 2)
  End With
End Sub
```

	A	B	C	D	E	F	G	H	I
1	Time	WinOrLose	Total						
2	10/30/2016 5:22	($0.41)	($0.41)						
3	10/30/2016 5:22	($0.07)	($0.48)						
4	10/30/2016 5:22	($0.16)	($0.64)						
5	10/30/2016 5:22	$0.42	($0.22)				Ctrl + Shift + W		
6	10/30/2016 5:22	$0.40	$0.18						
7	10/30/2016 5:22	($0.55)	($0.37)						
8	10/30/2016 5:22	$0.97	$0.60						
9	10/30/2016 5:22	($0.52)	$0.08			Microsoft Excel			
10	10/30/2016 5:22	($0.63)	($0.55)						
11	10/30/2016 5:22	($0.42)	($0.97)			After 13 trials you LOST: ($0.62)			
12	10/30/2016 5:22	$0.91	($0.06)						
13	10/30/2016 5:22	$0.17	$0.11						
14	10/30/2016 5:22	($0.73)	($0.62)			OK			
15									
16									

Chapter 9: A Letter Game

What the simulation does

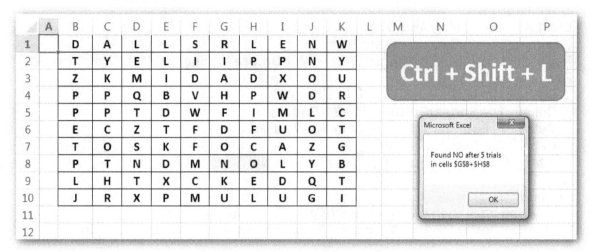

The macro asks you first whether you want to use the 1st or the 2nd sheet. The 2nd sheet uses "weighting"; the weight of each character is assigned in column O. Then the macro asks which word should be found; don't make this more than 2 characters long, for that could be a very time-consuming search.

In a *Do*-loop with two nested *For*-loops, the code scans all numbers in B1:K10 until it finds the word you are looking for. Obviously, that goes faster with "weighted" characters.

What you need to know

	A	B	C	D	E	F	G	H	I	J	K	L	M	N	O	P	Q	R
1		D	O	N	O	O	G	H	O	A	A		0	A	4			
2		I	L	O	E	O	N	O	O	L	O		4	B	3			
3		O	C	D	I	N	E	I	D	H	O		7	C	2			
4		I	A	F	G	E	N	N	G	O	M		9	D	3			
5		N	N	M	N	F	E	N	O	N	G		12	E	5			
6		A	N	O	M	B	N	M	J	N	O		17	F	2			
7		O	D	O	M	H	M	N	O	O	N		19	G	2			
8		M	N	B	O	E	H	M	N	N	E		21	H	3			
9		O	I	M	A	N	N	N	D	N	O		24	I	4			
10		F	A	O	F	N	A	C	N	O	H		28	J	2			
11													30	K	1			
12													31	L	2			
13													33	M	3			
14													36	N	20	N + O are heavily		
15													56	O	20	weighted		
16													76	P	3			

All capitals have an ASCI number between 65 and 90. The Excel function CHAR returns the corresponding letter. Column M totals the scores in column O cumulatively. So cell M2 has this formula: =SUM(O1:$O$1). Now VLOOKUP can find a random number between 0 and 70 in column M, and then return the corresponding letter from column N. VLOOKUP always searches *vertically*, from top to bottom, in the *first* column of a table and then finds a corresponding value in a column to the right, specified by a *number*. So we need a lookup column of cumulative values before column N. Besides, VLOOKUP looks for the previous value in an *ascending* order.

What you need to do

```
Option Explicit

Sub Letters()
   Dim sWord As String, oRange As Range, c As Integer, r As Integer, n As Integer,
sFormula As String
   Application.Calculation = xlCalculationManual
   If MsgBox("Equal chars (Y) or weighted chars (N)?", vbYesNo) = vbYes Then
      Sheet1.Activate
      sFormula = "=CHAR(RANDBETWEEN(65,90))" '65-90 are the capitals
   Else
      Sheet2.Activate
      sFormula = "=VLOOKUP(RANDBETWEEN(0,70),$M$1:$N$26,2)"
   End If
   Set oRange = Range("B1:K10")
   oRange.ClearContents: oRange.Interior.ColorIndex = 0
   sWord = InputBox("Which 2-letter word?", , "NO")
   sWord = UCase(Left(sWord, 2))
   oRange.Cells.Formula = sFormula
   With oRange
      Do
         Sheet1.Calculate
         n = n + 1
         For r = 1 To .Rows.Count
            For c = 1 To .Columns.Count
                If .Cells(r, c) = Left(sWord, 1) Then
                   If c < .Columns.Count Then
                      If .Cells(r, c + 1) = Right(sWord, 1) Then Exit Do
                      'so this loop stops when it finds one (the 1st) case
                   End If
                End If
            Next c
         Next r
      Loop Until MsgBox("Trial " & n & ": not found! Try again?", vbYesNo) = vbNo
      .Range(.Cells(r, c - 1), .Cells(r, c)).Interior.Color = vbYellow
      MsgBox "Found " & sWord & " after " & n & " trials" & vbCr & _
            "in cells " & .Cells(r, c).Address & "+" & .Cells(r, c + 1).Address
   End With
End Sub
```

Chapter 10: A Three-Way Circuit

What the simulation does

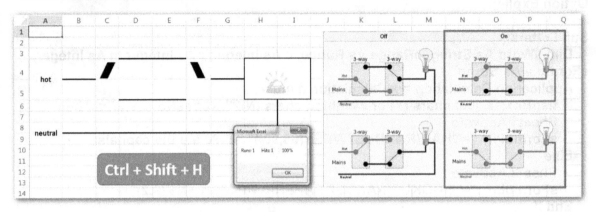

This sheet has a simulation of a three-way circuit. It is, for example, used when a light is regulated by two switches. Either switch can turn the light on or off, but the connections have to be in a certain way, as explained in the diagrams to the right.

The position of the switches in column C and F is regulated randomly by either showing the switch with a black font or hiding it with a white font.

What you need to know

This time we declare *Boolean* variables, which can only be either True(1) or False (0).

In an *IF*-statement we use a combination of *And* and *Or* operators.

Like *FormatCurrency*, the *FormatPercent* function has a 2nd argument for the number of decimals, and it adds the %-sign as a non-numeric entity.

This is ON:

This is OFF:

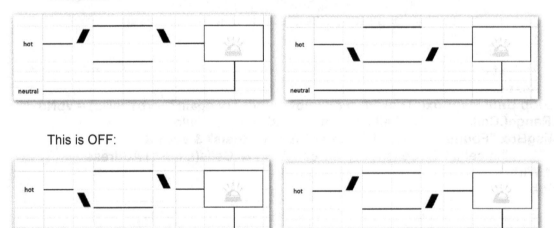

What you need to do

```
Option Explicit

Sub Hits()
   Dim b1 As Boolean, b2 As Boolean, b3 As Boolean, b4 As Boolean
   Dim iHit As Integer, n As Integer, sMsg As String
   Do
     If Rnd > 0.5 Then
        Range("C4").Font.Color = vbBlack:   Range("C5").Font.Color = vbWhite
        b1 = True: b2 = False
     Else
        Range("C4").Font.Color = vbWhite:   Range("C5").Font.Color = vbBlack
        b1 = False: b2 = True
     End If
     If Rnd > 0.5 Then
        Range("F4").Font.Color = vbBlack:   Range("F5").Font.Color = vbWhite
        b3 = True: b4 = False
     Else
        Range("F4").Font.Color = vbWhite:   Range("F5").Font.Color = vbBlack
        b3 = False: b4 = True
     End If
     n = n + 1
     If (b1 And b3) Or (b2 And b4) Then iHit = iHit + 1
     sMsg = sMsg & "Runs: " & n & vbTab & "Hits: " & iHit & vbTab &
FormatPercent(iHit / n, 0) & vbCr
     MsgBox sMsg
   Loop Until MsgBox("Again?", vbYesNo) = vbNo
End Sub
```

Chapter 11: Flocking Behavior

What the simulation does

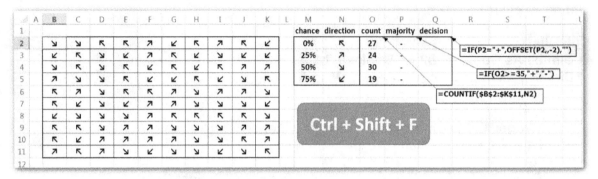

Flocking behaviorr is the behavior exhibited when a group of birds, called a flock, are foraging or in flight. There are clear parallels with the shoaling behavior of fish, the swarming behavior of insects, and herd behavior of land animals. It is considered the emergence of collective behavior arising from simple rules that are followed by individuals and does not involve any central coordination

Scientists have demonstrated a similar behavior in humans. In their studies, people exhibited the behavioral pattern of a "flock": If a certain percentage of the flock changes direction, the others follow suit. In experiments, when one person was designated as a "predator" and everyone else was supposed to avoid him or her, the human flock behaved very much like a school of fish.

What you need to know

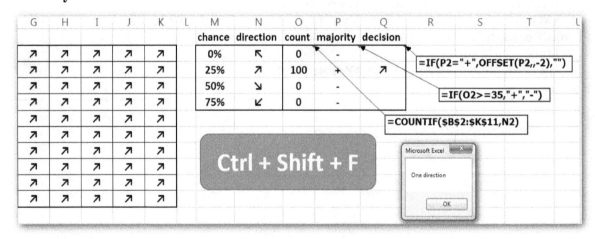

We assume that all animals (100) start randomly in one of four different directions (M2:N5). Once animals with a certain direction happen to gain a certain percentage (say, 35%), all the other animals follow suit.

In the range B2:K11 we place a VLOOKUP function that finds in M2:M5 a random number between 0 and 1, and then returns the corresponding direction arrow. Once column O registers a count over 35, all cells in B2:K11 display that arrow, and the count becomes 100. In other words, the flock has "decided" in which direction to fly or to swim.

What you need to do

```
Option Explicit

Sub FlockBehavior()
   Dim oRange As Range, i As Integer, bWon As Boolean, pTime As Double
   Set oRange = Range("B2:K11")
   oRange.ClearContents
   Do
      oRange.Formula = "=VLOOKUP(RAND(),$M$2:$N$5,2)"
      oRange.Formula = oRange.Value
      pTime = Timer + 0.5 'Timer: secs since midnight; pause by .5 seconds
      Do While Timer < pTime
         DoEvents
      Loop
      For i = 1 To 4
         If Range("O1").Offset(i, 0) >= 35 Then bWon = True: Exit For
      Next i
   Loop Until bWon = True
   If bWon Then oRange = WorksheetFunction.VLookup("+", Range("$P$2:$Q$5"), 2,
0)
   MsgBox "One direction"
End Sub
```

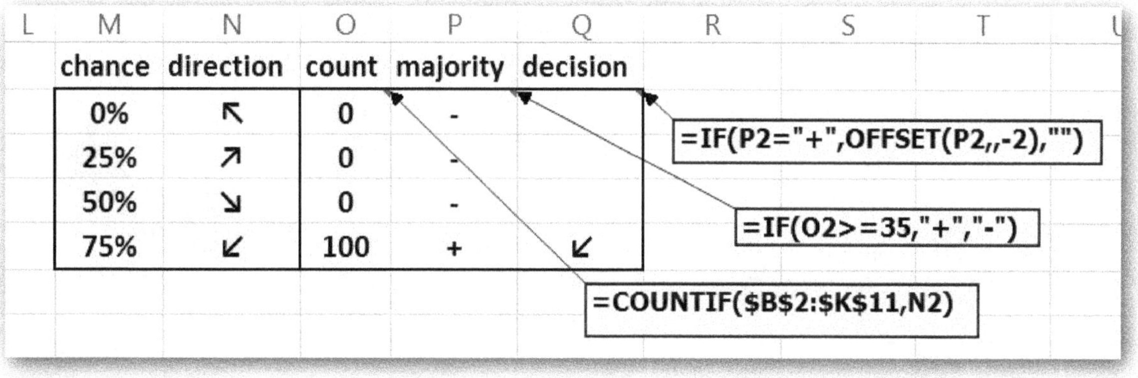

L	M	N	O	P	Q	R	S	T
	chance	direction	count	majority	decision			
	0%	↖	0	-				
	25%	↗	0	-				
	50%	↘	0	-				
	75%	↙	100	+	↙			

=IF(P2="+",OFFSET(P2,,-2),"")

=IF(O2>=35,"+","-")

=COUNTIF($B$2:$K$11,N2)

II. STATISTICS

Chapter 12: Samples

What the simulation does

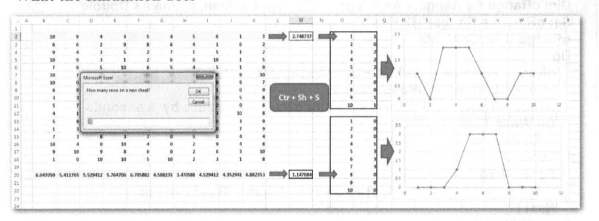

The simulation first asks how many rows we want to plot on a new sheet. Each cell in that range—in the above case range B2:K18—holds a random number between 0 and 10. Columns O and P hold two frequency tables. The top one calculates frequencies for row 2, which are the values for a sample of 10 cases. The bottom one calculates frequencies for row 20, which holds the averages of each column based on a sample of 17x10=170 cases.

It is to be expected that the frequency curve for the large sample resembles more of a normal distribution than the curve for the small sample of 10 cases. Below is the result of 25 rows.

What you need to know

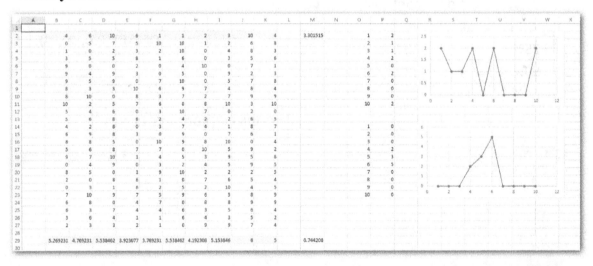

The FREQUENCY function is a so-called array function. That means in Excel, you have to select multiple cells at once and accept the formula with Ctrl + Shift + Enter (on a Mac: Command + Return). In VBA you do this by using the *FormulArray* property of a range of cells.

We also added two *ChartObjects* to the code and the sheet. They are numbered in the order they were created: 1 and 2. Notice that *SetSourceData* is followed by a space—yes, every minute detail counts in VBA!

What you need to do

```
Option Explicit

Sub Samples()
    Dim oWS As Worksheet, iRow As Long, oRange As Range, oChart As Chart
    iRow = InputBox("How many rows on a new sheet?", , 25) + 2
    Set oWS = Worksheets.Add(, ActiveSheet)
    Range(Cells(2, 2), Cells(2, 11)).Formula = "=INT(RAND()*11)"
    Range(Cells(2, 2), Cells(2, 11)).Interior.Color = vbYellow
    Cells(2, 13).Formula = "=STDEV(B2:K2)"
    Range(Range("A2"), Cells(iRow, 11)).Table , Range("A1")
    Set oRange = Range(Cells(iRow + 2, 2), Cells(iRow + 2, 11))
    oRange.FormulaR1C1 = "=AVERAGE(R[-2]C:R[-" & iRow & "]C)"
    oRange.Interior.Color = vbYellow
    Cells(iRow + 2, 13).FormulaR1C1 = "=STDEV(RC[-11]:RC[-2])"
    Range("O2:O11").Formula = "=ROW(A1)"
    Range("P2:P11").FormulaArray = "=FREQUENCY(B2:K2,O2:O11)"
    Range("O14:O23") = "=ROW(A1)"
    Range("P14:P23").FormulaArray = "=FREQUENCY(" & oRange.Address &
",O14:O23)"

    Range("O2:P11").Select
    oWS.Shapes.AddChart2(240, xlXYScatterLines).Select
    ActiveChart.SetSourceData oWS.Range("O2:P11")
    ActiveChart.HasTitle = False
    oWS.ChartObjects(1).Top = Range("R2").Top
    oWS.ChartObjects(1).Left = Range("R2").Left
    oWS.ChartObjects(1).Width = 300
    oWS.ChartObjects(1).Height = 150

    Range("O14:P23").Select
    oWS.Shapes.AddChart2(240, xlXYScatterLines).Select
    ActiveChart.SetSourceData oWS.Range("O14:P23")
    ActiveChart.HasTitle = False
    oWS.ChartObjects(2).Top = Range("R14").Top
    oWS.ChartObjects(2).Left = Range("R14").Left
    oWS.ChartObjects(2).Width = 300
    oWS.ChartObjects(2).Height = 150
    Range("A1").Select
End Sub
```

Chapter 13: A Normal Distribution

What the simulation does

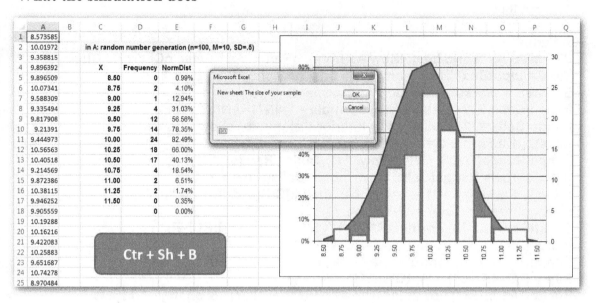

The macro places a new distribution on a new sheet with a number of rows in column A that you the user chose in a *MsgBox*, based on a mean and SD of our choosing as well. Column C has the number of bins chosen, column D the frequencies for each bin, and column E what the corresponding normal distribution values would be.

What you need to know

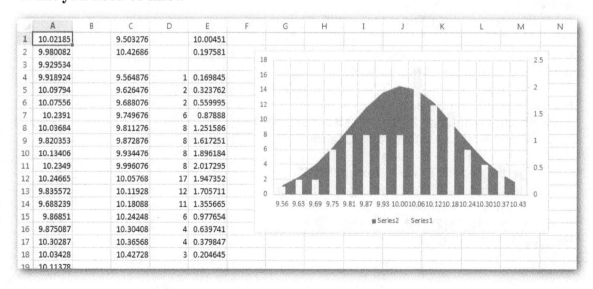

The function NORMINV (or NORM.INV, if available) in column A returns the inverse of the normal cumulative distribution for the specified mean and standard deviation. The function NORMDIST in E returns the normal distribution for the specified mean and standard deviation.

By replacing the *Formula* property of a range with its *Value* property, we are mimicking a *Paste Special* procedure for values—so that things don't keep recalculating.

The Chart has two cases of a *FullSeriesCollection*, 1 and 2.

What you need to do

```
Option Explicit

Sub Bins()
   Dim iSize As Integer, pMean As Double, pSD As Double, iBins As String, oWS As
Worksheet
   iBins = 15
   iSize = InputBox("New sheet: The size of your sample:", , 100)
   pMean = InputBox("New sheet: The mean of your sample:", , 10)
   pSD = InputBox("New sheet: The SD of your sample:", , 0.2)
   Set oWS = Worksheets.Add(, ActiveSheet)
   Range(Cells(1, 1), Cells(iSize, 1)).Formula = "=NORMINV(RAND()," & pMean & "," &
pSD & ")"
   Range(Cells(1, 1), Cells(iSize, 1)).Formula = Range(Cells(1, 1), Cells(iSize, 1)).Value
   Range("C1").Formula = "=MIN(A:A)"
   Range("C2").Formula = "=MAX(A:A)"
   Range(Cells(4, 3), Cells(3 + iBins, 3)).Formula = "=$C$1+(ROW(A1))*(ROUND(($C$2-
$C$1)/(" & iBins & "),4))"
   Range(Cells(4, 4), Cells(3 + iBins, 4)).FormulaArray = "=FREQUENCY(A:A," &
Range(Cells(4, 3), Cells(3 + iBins, 3)).Address & ")"
   Range("E1") = WorksheetFunction.Average(Columns(1))
   Range("E2") = WorksheetFunction.StDev(Columns(1))
   Range(Cells(4, 5), Cells(3 + iBins, 5)).FormulaR1C1 = "=NORMDIST(RC[-
2],R1C5,R2C5,FALSE)"


   Range("C4:E18").Select
   oWS.Shapes.AddChart2(240, xlXYScatterLines).Select
   With ActiveChart
      .SetSourceData Range("C4:E18")
      .HasTitle = False
      .FullSeriesCollection(1).ChartType = xlColumnClustered
      .FullSeriesCollection(2).ChartType = xlArea
      .FullSeriesCollection(2).AxisGroup = 2
      ActiveChart.Axes(xlCategory).TickLabels.NumberFormat = "#,##0.00"
   End With
   Cells(1, 1).Select
End Sub
```

Chapter 14: Distribution Simulations

What the simulation does

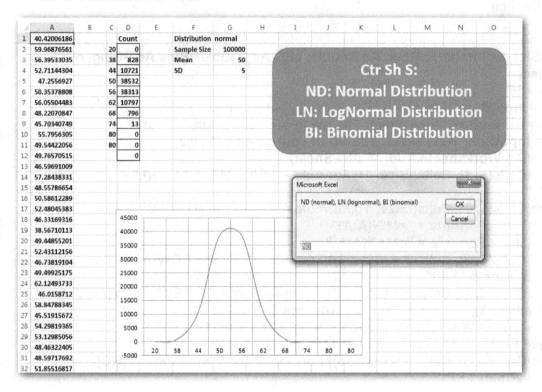

This macro simulates 3 types of distributions: Normal, LogNormal, or Binomial.

What you need to know

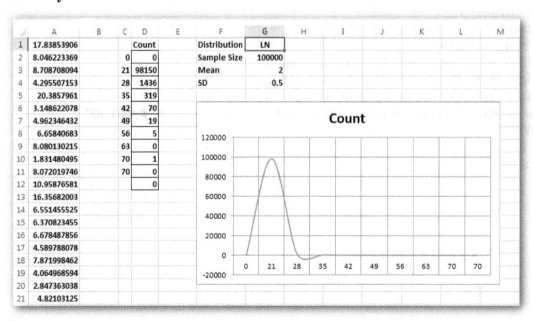

A *Select Case* statement in VBA lets us regulate specifics for each case (ND, LN, or BI).

What you need to do

```vba
Sub Simulation()
    Dim sChoice As String, n As Long, pOne As Double, pTwo As Double, i As Long
    Dim arr() As Variant, sFormula As String, oRange As Range, oWS As Worksheet
    Dim pMin As Double, pMax As Double, oChart As Chart
    sChoice = InputBox("ND (normal), LN (lognormal), BI (binomial)", , "ND")
    n = InputBox("How many numbers?", , 100000)
    If n > 1000000 Then MsgBox "The max is 1000000": Exit Sub
    Set oWS = Worksheets.Add(, ActiveSheet)
    Select Case UCase(sChoice)
        Case "ND":
            pOne = InputBox("What is the mean?", , 50)
            pTwo = InputBox("What is the standard deviation?", , 5)
            sFormula = "=NORM.INV(RAND()," & pOne & "," & pTwo & ")"
        Case "LN":
            pOne = InputBox("What is the mean?", , 2)
            pTwo = InputBox("What is the standard deviation?", , 0.5)
            sFormula = "=LOGNORM.INV(RAND()," & pOne & "," & pTwo & ")"
        Case "BI":
            pOne = InputBox("What is the probability?", , 0.5)
            pTwo = InputBox("How many trials?", , 50)
            sFormula = "=BINOM.INV(" & pTwo & "," & pOne & ",RAND())"
        Case Else: MsgBox "Not a valid option": Exit Sub
    End Select
    Set oRange = Range(Cells(1, 1), Cells(n, 1))
    oRange.Formula = sFormula :    oRange.Formula = oRange.Value
    Cells(1, 4) = "Count"
    Cells(2, 3).Formula = "=MIN(A:A)-MOD(MIN(A:A),10)" : pMin = Cells(2, 3)
    Cells(11, 3).Formula = "=MAX(A:A)+10-MOD(MAX(A:A),10)" : pMax = Cells(11, 3
    For i = 3 To 10
        Cells(i, 3) = pMin + i * Round((pMax - pMin) / 10, 0)
    Next i
    Set oRange = Range(Cells(2, 4), Cells(12, 4))
    oRange.FormulaArray = "=FREQUENCY(A:A," & Range(Cells(2, 3), Cells(11,
3)).Address & ")"
    oRange.Cells.Borders.LineStyle = xlContinuous :   Cells.EntireColumn.AutoFit
    Cells(1, 6) = "Distribution": Cells(1, 7) = sChoice
    Cells(2, 6) = "Sample Size": Cells(2, 7) = n :  Cells(3, 6) = "Mean": Cells(3, 7) = pOne
    Cells(4, 6) = "SD": Cells(4, 7) = pTwo
    Set oRange = oWS.Range(Cells(1, 3), Cells(11, 4))
    Set oChart = Charts.Add
    oChart.HasLegend = False:    oChart.ChartType = xlLine
    oChart.FullSeriesCollection(1).Smooth = True
    oChart.SetSourceData oRange:    oChart.PlotBy = xlColumns
    oChart.Axes(xlCategory).HasMajorGridlines = True
    oChart.Location xlLocationAsObject, oWS.Name
    Sheet1.ChartObjects(1).Left = 125:    Sheet1.ChartObjects(1).Top = 250
    Sheet1.ChartObjects(1).Chart.HasTitle = False:    Cells(1, 1).Select
End Sub
```

Chapter 15: Discrete Distributions

What the simulation does

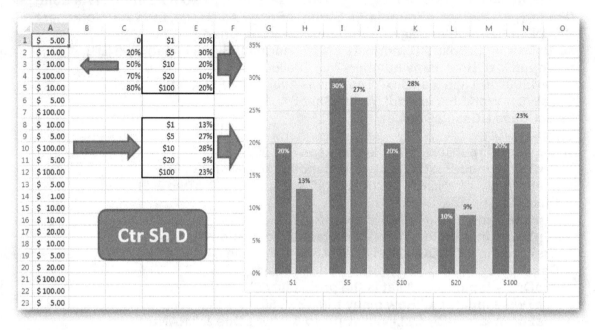

Let's pretend you are a persistent, but very systematic, gambler. You decide ahead of time how to spend your different kinds of banknotes, which is specified in range D1:E5. The first columns in the chart display these settings as well.

Then the macro lets the machine determine one hundred times, in column A, when and which kind of banknotes to use and in which order. This is a random process, but within the margins set in D1:E5. The results are shown in the second columns of the chart.

Although the process is random, it follows a discrete distribution which comes always very close to what you would expect.

What you need to know

For the Range E1:E5, the macro creates random percentages, which together should make for 100%. That requires some math manipulation. Then we need the function VLOOKUP to use these percentages to find the corresponding type of banknote.

However, VLOOKUP always searches *vertically*, from top to bottom, in the *first* column of a table, and then finds a corresponding value in a column to the right, specified by a *number*. So we need a lookup column before D1:D5 in order to determine the type of banknote to use. Besides, VLOOKUP looks for the previous value in an *ascending* order, so it would find $1 for all percentages between 0% and 60%, $5 between 60% and 80%, and $100 for percentages greater than or equal to 98%.

Therefore, we need cumulative totals in the first column (C), starting at 0%. The third column (E) is now redundant, but is still needed for the chart to the right in order to show the expected frequencies—versus the randomly generated frequencies.

What you need to do

```
Option Explicit

Sub Distribution()
   Dim i As Integer, arr() As Integer, n As Integer
   ReDim arr(4)
   n = WorksheetFunction.RandBetween(0, 60)
   arr(0) = n - (n Mod 5)
   n = WorksheetFunction.RandBetween(0, 100 - arr(0))
   arr(1) = n - (n Mod 5)
   n = WorksheetFunction.RandBetween(0, 100 - (arr(0) + arr(1)))
   arr(2) = n - (n Mod 5)
   n = WorksheetFunction.RandBetween(0, 100 - (arr(0) + arr(1) + arr(2)))
   arr(3) = n - (n Mod 5)
   arr(4) = 100 - (arr(0) + arr(1) + arr(2) + arr(3))
   For i = 0 To 4
      Cells(i + 1, 5) = FormatPercent(arr(i) / 100, 0)
   Next i
   Range("C2:C5").Formula = "=SUM($E$1:E1)"
   Range("A1:A100").Formula = "=VLOOKUP(RAND(),$C$1:$D$5,2)"
End Sub
```

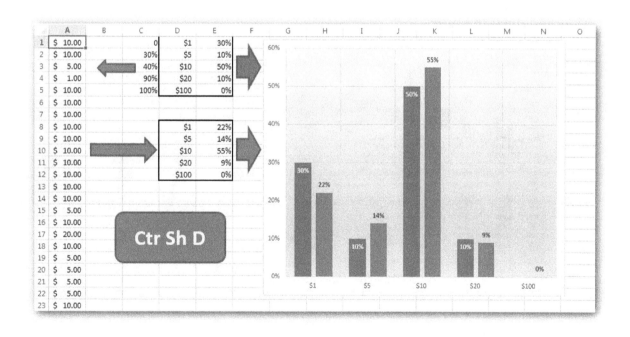

Chapter 16: Peaks

What the simulation does

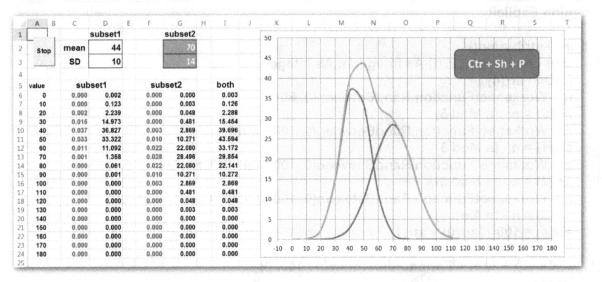

Here we are dealing with a population (in I) that is composed of two sub-populations (in D and G). As long as the two subpopulations have the same mean, even with different standard deviations, the entire population may look nicely symmetrical. But when the mean of one subpopulation changes, the symmetrical curve may easily lose its symmetry and may even become *bi-modal*. The macro simulates this by looping with a timer.

What you need to know

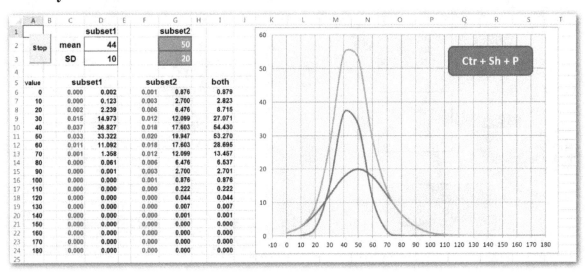

We have a global variable again to stop the macro: *bStopMacro*. Stopping the macro is done with a *CommandButton* on the sheet: Developer | Design Mode | Insert | Command Button | View Code (don't forget to click the Design Mode button OFF when you are done). The VBA code behind the button is very simple. Most of the work is done in the *Module*.

The *UBound* function of an array returns the index of the last array element.

What you need to do

In a module:

```
Option Explicit

Dim bStopMacro As Boolean
'Place Commandbutton on the sheet to run the next Sub

Sub StopLooping()
   bStopMacro = True
End Sub

Sub Peaks() 'Ctr + Sh + P
   Dim vMeans As Variant, vSDs As Variant, i As Integer, j As Integer, pTime As
Double
   vMeans = Array(40, 50, 60, 70, 80, 90, 100)
   vSDs = Array(14, 16, 18, 20)
   For i = 0 To UBound(vMeans)
      Range("G2") = vMeans(i)
      For j = 0 To UBound(vSDs)
         Range("G3") = vSDs(j)
         pTime = Timer + 1
         Do
            DoEvents
         Loop Until Timer > pTime
         If bStopMacro Then bStopMacro = False: Exit Sub
      Next j
   Next i
   If MsgBox("Start again?", vbYesNo) = vbYes Then Peaks
End Sub
```

On the sheet that has the commandButton1:

```
Option Explicit

Private Sub CommandButton1_Click()
   StopLooping
   Cells(1, 1).Select
End Sub
```

Chapter 17: Confidence Margins

What the simulation does

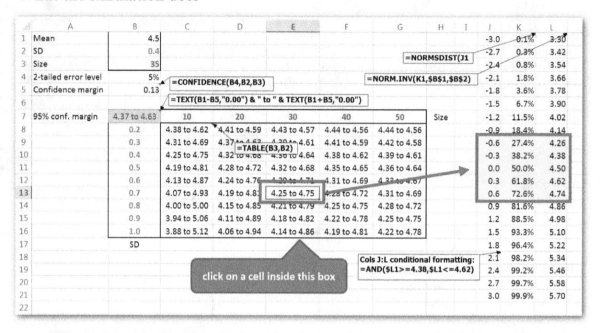

This sheet is actually done with Excel functions and formulas as mentioned in the inserted comments. The function CONFIDENCE in Excel returns the confidence interval for a population mean, using a normal distribution. It works best for sample sizes over 32.

In this case we used a 2-tailed error level of 5% (2.5% for each tail), which equates to a 95% confidence level. This means we have a 95% confidence that the vales we found in this sample lie actually between the two values mentioned in the *Data Table* (which equates to the mean plus the confidence margin and the mean minus the confidence margin). Notice how confidence margins depend heavily on sample size and standard deviation.

The only thing VBA does on this sheet is following which cell the user clicks on inside the *Data Table*.

What you need to know

Instead of using a *Module*, the VBA code is on the sheet itself: *SelectionChange* (see the screen shot on the next page). This is a *Sub* that kicks in whenever the user selects another cell on that sheet.

Instead of using a regular *For*-loop, we used a *For-Each*-loop that scans every single cell in a range of cells. The *Boolean* variable *bFound* always starts as 0 (False) until it is set to 1 (True).

We also applied conditional formatting by adding a *FormatCondition* to the collection of *FormatConditions*, starting at 1. In this case we used a formula for this condition as shown in the VBA code which marks the correct range in columns J:L with a certain color.

Because adding to the *FormatConditions* keeps literally adding the same condition again and again, the macro deletes all conditions earlier in the code first.

What you need to do

```
Option Explicit

Private Sub Worksheet_SelectionChange(ByVal Target As Range)
    Dim oRange As Range, sFormula As String, pLower As Double, pUpper As Double
    Dim oCell As Range, bFound As Boolean
    For Each oCell In Range("B8:G16")
        If oCell = ActiveCell Then bFound = True: Exit For
    Next oCell
    If bFound = False Then Exit Sub

    Set oRange = Range("J1:L21")
    oRange.FormatConditions.Delete
    pLower = Left(ActiveCell, 4)
    pUpper = Right(ActiveCell, 4)
    sFormula = "=and($L1>=" & pLower & ",$L1<=" & pUpper & ")"
    oRange.FormatConditions.Add xlExpression, , sFormula
    oRange.FormatConditions(1).Interior.Color = vbYellow
End Sub
```

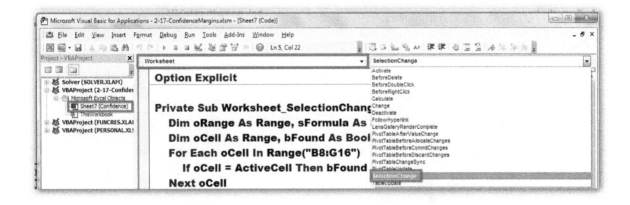

Chapter 18: Sample Size and Confidence Interval

What the simulation does

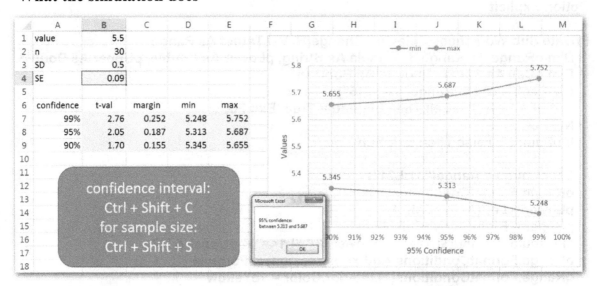

This sheet has two macros. The first macro (see above) simply asks for input variables and calculates confidence intervals.

The second macro (see below) calculates how many cases you would need in your sample in order to reach a specific margin limit.

What you need to know

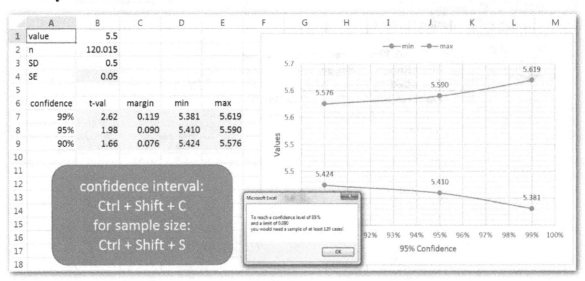

The *WorksheetFunction T_Inv_2T* returns the t-value of the Student t-distribution as a function of the probability and the degrees of freedom. The degrees of freedom are the number of cases minus 1. The t-value works for all sample sizes, even under 32.

The Standard Error (SE) is the Standard Deviation (SD) divided by the SQRT of the number of cases. So the confidence margin is the Standard Error times the t-value.

The 2nd macro uses Excel's *GoalSeek* tool that allows you to alter data in formulas to get a specific result that you want to reach by changing a specific value (here B2, in the 2nd argument).

What you need to do

```
Option Explicit

Sub ConfidenceIntervall()
   Dim pValue As Double, iCases As Long, pSE As Double, pPerc As Double
   Dim pTInv As Double, pMin As Double, pMax As Double, pMargin As Double
   On Error Resume Next
   pValue = InputBox("Which value?", , 5.5)
   iCases = InputBox("How many cases?", , 30)
   pSE = InputBox("SD", , 0.5) / Sqr(iCases)
   pPerc = InputBox("Confidence", , 0.95)
   pTInv = WorksheetFunction.T_Inv_2T(1 - pPerc, iCases - 1)
   pMargin = pSE * pTInv
   pMin = FormatNumber(pValue - pMargin, 3)
   pMax = FormatNumber(pValue + pMargin, 3)
   MsgBox pPerc * 100 & "% confidence: " & vbCr & "between " & pMin & " and " &
pMax
End Sub


Sub SampleSize()
   Dim pConf As Double, pGoal As Double, iRow As Integer, sAddr As String, sMsg
As String
   pConf = InputBox("Which confidence level?", , 0.95)
   iRow = WorksheetFunction.Match(0.95, Range("A7:A9"))
   sAddr = Range("C7:C9").Cells(iRow, 1).Address
   pGoal = InputBox("Which limit do you want to reach?", , 0.09)
   Range(sAddr).GoalSeek pGoal, Range("B2")
   sMsg = "To reach a confidence level of " & FormatPercent(pConf, 0) & vbCr
   sMsg = sMsg & "and a limit of " & FormatNumber(pGoal, 3) & vbCr
   sMsg = sMsg & "you would need a sample of at least " &
FormatNumber(Range("B2"), 0) & " cases!"
   MsgBox sMsg
   Range("B2") = 30 : Calculate
   End Sub
```

Chapter 19: Random Repeats

What the simulation does

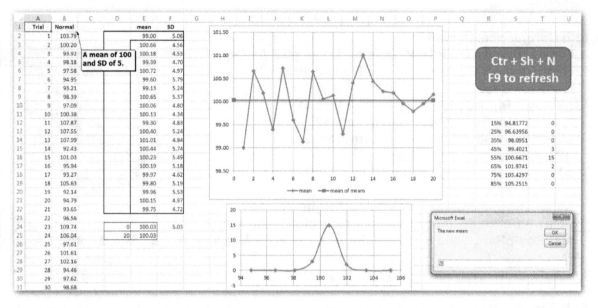

This time we are going to simulate several runs in order to check as to whether the normal distribution we tried to simulate earlier did come out the way we would expect.

In column B the macro simulates a series of 100 random numbers—not equally but *normally* distributed, with a mean of 100 and a SD of 10. In the range D2:F22, it simulates 20 repeats of this random number generation, with a *Data Table*, so we end up with 20 x 100 = 2,000 trials (which is still a very modest number for statistical standards). As it turns out, the mean of means oscillates around 100 (cell E24) and the mean of SDs stays more or less around 10 (cell F24).

The top graph plots the mean values as found in 20 runs (E2:E22). Even the frequency distribution of all the means, calculated in range R12:T19, creates a rather *normal* distribution with a bell shape in the lower graph, although the number of cases is still very modest in statistical terms.

What you need to know

The 100 sequential numbers in column A were calculated by using the ROW function. This function returns the row number of the cell the function happens to be in—so ROW() in A10 would return 10. If you provide a cell reference as an argument, it returns the row number of that specific cell reference—so ROW(B25) in cell A10 (or in cell B1) would always return 25.

The VBA code copies the first sheet to a new sheet, but mean and SD can be changed. It also asks whether you want to replace formulas with values. If you do, F9 will not recalculate anything, and the *Data Table* will no longer work.

The average line in the graph is based on cells D24:E25.

This time we decided to also add a so-called error-handler, in case something goes (unexpectedly) wrong. It works with *On Error GoTo [label]* at the beginning, and at the end, after *Exit Sub*, a label like "Trap" or so and a *MsgBox* that uses information from the *Err* object (see Appendix).

What you need to do

```
Option Explicit

Sub NewSample()
    Dim oWS As Worksheet, oRange As Range, oChart As ChartObject
    Dim pMean As Double, pSD As Double
    On Error GoTo Trap
    pMean = InputBox("The new mean on a new sheet:", , 50)
    pSD = InputBox("The new SD:", , 10)
    Set oWS = ActiveSheet
    oWS.Copy , Sheets(Sheets.Count)
    Set oRange = ActiveSheet.Range("A1").CurrentRegion.Offset(1, 0)
    oRange.Columns(2).Formula = "=NORMINV(RAND()," & pMean & "," & pSD & ")"
    If MsgBox("Keep formulas for F9?", vbYesNo) = vbNo Then
        oRange.Columns(2).Formula = oRange.Columns(2).Value
    End If
    Range("B2").Comment.Text "A mean of " & pMean & " and SD of " & pSD & "."
    Set oChart = ActiveSheet.ChartObjects("Chart 2")
    oChart.Chart.Axes(xlCategory).MinimumScale = Round(Range("S12"), 1)
    oChart.Chart.Axes(xlCategory).MaximumScale = Round(Range("S19"), 1)
    Range("A1").Select
    Exit Sub
Trap:
    MsgBox "There was an error: " & Err.Description
End Sub
```

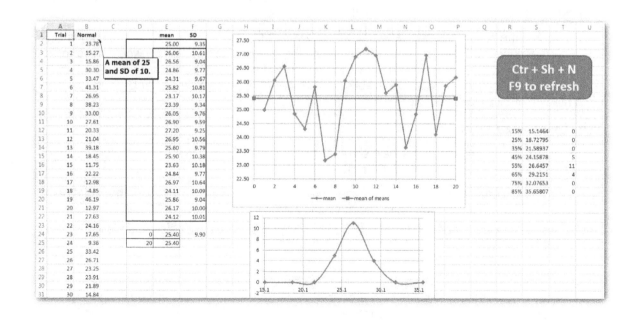

Chapter 20: Flipping a Fair Coin?

What the simulation does

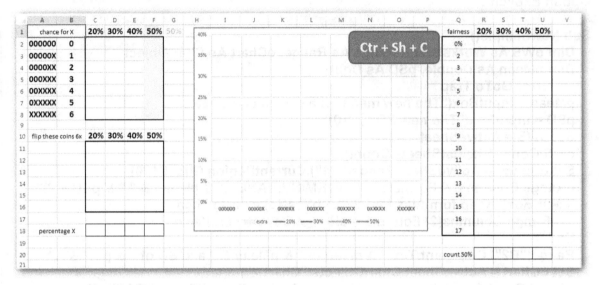

This simulation is about flipping a coin six times, calculating how often we hit six times "tails" (0), five times, and so on (column A). The most likely outcome is 3x "heads" (X) and 3x "tails" (0)—actually 31% of all cases (column F). The center curve in the graph is a "bell-shaped" curve that represents this situation. Going more to the left or to the right under the bell-shaped curve, the chances decrease dramatically, but they will never become 0.000000000000.

Events with random outcomes have the property that no particular outcome is known in advance. However, in the aggregate, the outcomes occur with a specific frequency. When we flip a "fair" coin, we do not know how it will land, but if we flip the coin millions of times, we know that it will land heads up (X) very close to 50% of the time—unless...

Unless... the coin is not "fair" and has a "preference" for lower X percentages (columns C:E and the other curves in the graph). To determine whether a coin is fair or not, we would need to flip a coin millions of times. In this simulation we only simulated some 100 coin tosses. In the situation shown on the next page, we would probably declare the fair coin unfair (column U). It is clear we need many more flips for a reliable verdict.

What you need to know

Place a copy of the sheet on a new sheet after (2nd argument) the last one in the collection of *Sheets* so far—that is, *Sheets(Sheets.Count)*.

In order to create a normal distribution for a binary situation—such as yes/no, correct/defect, heads/tails, success/failure—we need the function BINOMDIST (or BINOM.DIST). It returns a binomial distribution probability for problems with a fixed number of tests or trials, when the outcomes of any trial are either success or failure, when trials are independent, and when the probability of success is constant throughout the experiment.

The *Formula* property of a range requires a string, so the formula property is set with an equal sign (=) to a string that starts with a double quote, followed by another equal sign (=), and ending with a double quote. If there is another string inside this string, we need two double quotes instead of one.

What you need to do

```
Option Explicit

Sub Coins()
    Dim oWS As Worksheet
    Set oWS = ActiveSheet
    oWS.Copy , Sheets(Sheets.Count)
    Range("C2:G8,C11:F16,C18:F18,R2:U18,R20:U20").ClearContents
    Range("A1").Select
    MsgBox "The chances for X (head) if the coin is 20 to 50% fair:"
    Range("C2:G8").Formula = "=BINOMDIST($B2,6,C$1,0)"
    MsgBox "Flip these coins 6 times randomly:"
    Range("C11:F16").Formula = "=IF(RAND()<=C$10,""X"",""0"")"
    MsgBox "Here are the chances of X for each coin:"
    Range("C18:F18").Formula = "=COUNTIF(C11:C16,""X"")/6"
    MsgBox "Then we repeat these calculations 17 times:"
    Range("R2:U2").Formula = "=C18"
    Range("Q2:U18").Table , Cells(100, 100)
    MsgBox "How often did we hit 50% chance of head vs. tail?"
    Range("R20:U20").Formula = "=COUNTIF(R2:R18,0.5)"
End Sub
```

Chapter 21: Simulation of Sick Cases

What the simulation does

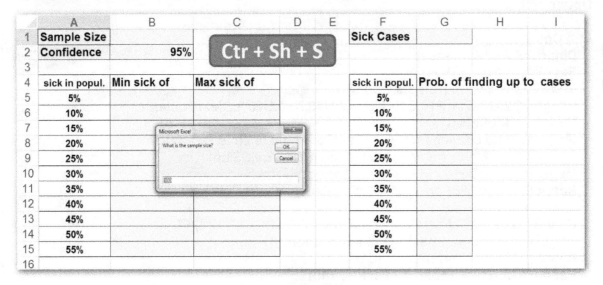

If a certain percentage of people is sick in the population (column A), we can find out with a 95% confidence how many in a sample of 100 persons will be sick, either as a minimum (column B) or as a maximum (column C) based on that confidence level.

We can also calculate what the probability is of finding up to a certain number of sick cases (column G), given a certain sample size (B1).

We can vary the sample size (B1) as well as the number of sick cases (G1) by answering both InputBox questions. The confidence level can be manually adjusted on the sheet.

The macro simulates all of this on the sheet.

What you need to know

One of the functions we need in column G is BINOMDIST (or BINOM.DIST) again. As explained in the previous Chapter, it returns a binomial distribution probability for problems with a fixed number of tests or trials, when the outcomes of any trial are either success or failure, when trials are independent, and when the probability of success is constant throughout the experiment.

The other crucial function is BINOM.INV (which replaces CRITBINOM in pre-2010 versions. It has 3 arguments: the number of trials, the probability of a success on each trial, and the criterion value (alpha).

The function IFERROR is also quite recent (ISERROR could be used in earlier versions, but is a bit mpore involved). If there is an error in a certain BINOMDIST calculation, it should display an empty string—which calls for four double quotes (a string inside a string).

What you need to do

```
Option Explicit

Sub SickCases()
    Dim iSize As Integer, iSick As Integer
    iSize = InputBox("What is the sample size?", , 100)
    Range("B1") = iSize
    Range("B5:B15").Formula = "=BINOM.INV($B$1,$A5,1-$B$2)"
    Range("C5:C15").Formula = "=BINOM.INV($B$1,$A5,$B$2)"
    iSick = InputBox("How many sick cases?", , iSize / 4)
    Range("G1") = iSick
    Range("G5:G15").Formula = "=IFERROR(1-BINOMDIST(G$1,$B$1,$F5,TRUE),"""")"
    If MsgBox("Empty calculated cells?", vbYesNo) = vbYes Then
        Range("B1") = ""
        Range("B5:B15") = ""
        Range("C5:C15") = ""
        Range("G1") = ""
        Range("G5:G15") = ""
    End If
End Sub
```

	A	B	C	D	E	F	G	H	I	J
1	Sample Size	100				Sick Cases	25			
2	Confidence	95%		Ctr + Sh + S						
3										
4	sick in popul.	Min sick of 100	Max sick of 100			sick in popul.	Prob. of finding up to 25 cases			
5	5%	2	9			5%	0.00%			
6	10%	5	15			10%	0.00%			
7	15%	9	21			15%	0.30%			
8	20%	14	27			20%	8.75%			
9	25%	18	32			25%	44.65%			
10	30%	23	38			30%	83.69%			
11	35%	27	43			35%	97.89%			
12	40%	32	48			40%	99.88%			
13	45%	37	53			45%	100.00%			
14	50%	42	58			50%	100.00%			
15	55%	47	63			55%	100.00%			
16										

Chapter 22: Unbiased Sampling

What the simulation does

	A	B	C	D	E	F	G	H	I	J	K	L	M	N	O	P	Q	R	S	T	U
1	mere random			0.25 of random			only 10 codes							10 weighted area codes							
2																					
3	area code	random		area code	25%		area code	rand	10		cumul.	area code	weight	bar		sample of 10 weighted					
4	206	0.007		906	TRUE		201	0.18	843		0	201	1	+		213	++++		1 +		
5	570	0.009		515	TRUE		202	0.913	225		1	202	4	++++		206	+		2 ++		
6	664	0.010		401	TRUE		203	0.197	828		5	203	2	++		201	+		3 +++		
7	412	0.021		831	TRUE		204	0.554	530		7	204	1	+		207	++++		4 ++++		
8	850	0.023		425	TRUE		205	0.867	268		8	205	1	+		219	++				
9	626	0.029		609	TRUE		206	0.088	906		9	206	1	+		206	+				
10	801	0.032		606	TRUE		207	0.554	540		10	207	4	++++		202	++++				
11	910	0.033		773	TRUE		208	0.973	205		14	208	3	+++		219	++				
12	268	0.033		956	TRUE		209	0.837	308		17	209	1	+		207	++++				
13	281	0.035		832	TRUE		210	0.035	935		18	210	1	+		203	++				
14	785	0.035		660	TRUE		212	0.32			19	212	1	+							
15	506	0.037		600	TRUE		213	0.171			20	213	4	++++							
16	284	0.037		215	TRUE		214	0.815			24	214	2	++							
17	712	0.040		202	TRUE		215	0.635			26	215	1	+							
18	803	0.041		225	TRUE		216	0.375			27	216	1	+							
19	500	0.044		504	TRUE		217	0.7			28	217	1	+							
20	972	0.047		775	TRUE		218	0.858			29	218	4	++++							
21	404	0.049		876	TRUE		219	0.474			33	219	2	++							
22	614	0.060		902	TRUE		224	0.425			35	224	1	+							
23	517	0.062		709	TRUE		225	0.155			36	225	1	+							
24	767	0.075		718	TRUE		228	0.845			37	Total									
25	519	0.079		340	TRUE		240	0.346													
26	228	0.085		456	TRUE		248	0.577													
27	920	0.086		562	TRUE		254	0.559						Ctr + Sh + R							
28	881	0.088		403	TRUE		256	0.402													
29	882	0.089		514	TRUE		264	0.415													
30	224	0.089		435	TRUE		267	0.437													

When taking samples, the problem is that some are more likely to be chosen than others—so we call them biased samples. Unbiased sampling requires some bias-proof techniques. Therefore, we need the unbiased verdict of mathematical tools.

In this simulation, we use four different techniques to select telephone area codes at random. Technique #1 assigns a random number, sorts by that number, and then takes the first or last N cases. Technique #2 selects $X\%$ of the area codes randomly. Technique #3 produces N cases randomly. Technique #4 "weighs" each area code (say, depending on population density) and then performs a *weighted* sampling of N cases.

The simulation scrolls through these four different techniques of unbiased sampling.

What you need to know

Case #1 sorts the random numbers after their formulas have been changed into values. The *Sort* method has many optional arguments. The 1st argument specifies the first sort field, either as a range name (String) or *Range* object; it determines the values that need to be sorted. The 2nd argument determines the sort order—by default *xlAscending*.

Case #4 may need some more explanation. In column K, we calculate the cumulative total of all previous weights. So area code 202 (in L5) is four times included in that total. In column O, we multiply the grand total (K24) with a random number between 0 and 1, and then we look up that value in range K4:L24 and determine its corresponding area code. In other words, the second area code, 202, can be found through the random numbers between >=1 and <5; this amounts to 4 chances of being picked (4x more than the first area code, 201).

What you need to do

```
Option Explicit

Sub RandomSelect()
   Dim oRange As Range, iSize As Integer
   If MsgBox("Sort all areacodes randomly", vbYesNo) = vbNo Then Exit Sub
   Range("B4:B270").Formula = "=RAND()"
   Range("B4:B270").Formula = Range("B4:B270").Value
   Range("A4:B270").Sort Range("B4")


   If MsgBox(Range("E3") & " sample from column D?", vbYesNo) = vbNo Then Exit
Sub
   Range("E4:E270").Formula = "=RAND()<$E$3"
   Range("E4:E270").Formula = Range("E4:E270").Value
   Range("D4:E270").Sort Range("E4"), xlDescending


   If MsgBox("Random selection of " & Range("I3"), vbYesNo) = vbNo Then Exit Sub
   Range("H4:H270").Formula = "=RAND()"
   Range("H4:H270").Formula = Range("H4:H270").Value
   iSize = Range("I3")
   Range(Range("I4"), Cells(3 + iSize, 9)).Formula =
"=INDEX($G$4:$G$270,RANK(H4,$H$4:$H$270))"


   If MsgBox("Weighted sample of 10", vbYesNo) = vbNo Then Exit Sub
   Range("P4:P13").Formula = "=VLOOKUP($K$24*RAND(), $K$4:$L$24, 2)"
   Range("Q4:Q13").Formula = "=VLOOKUP(P4,$L$4:$N$23,3,0)"

End Sub
```

K	L	M	N	O	P	Q	R	S	T	U
			10 weighted area codes							
cumul.	area code	weight	bar		sample of 10 weighted					
0	201	1	+		213	++++		1	+	
1	202	4	++++		206	+		2	++	
5	203	2	++		201	+		3	+++	
7	204	1	+		207	++++		4	++++	
8	205	1	+		219	++				
9	206	1	+		206	+				
10	207	4	++++		202	++++				
14	208	3	+++		219	++				
17	209	1	+		207	++++				
18	210	1	+		203	++				
19	212	1	+							
20	213	4	++++							
24	214	2	++							
26	215	1	+							
27	216	1	+							
28	217	1	+							
29	218	4	++++							
33	219	2	++							
35	224	1	+							
36	225	1	+							
37	Total									

Chapter 23: Transforming a LogNormal Distribution

What the simulation does

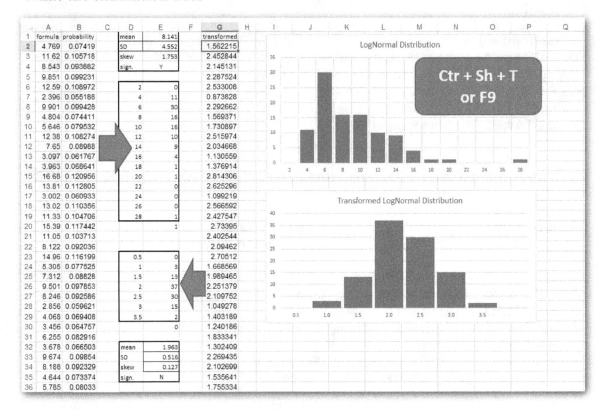

Column A holds 100 random values based on a lognormal distribution with a mean of 2 and a Standard Deviation of 0.5. Column B shows the probability of each value. In column G, the lognormally distributed values are transformed by taking their natural logarithm.

In columns D:E, we calculate the mean and SD plus their frequencies—first of the values in A, then for the transformed values in G. We also calculate if and how skewed they are.

It turns out that the transformed lognormal distribution comes close to a normal distribution.

What you need to know

The function LOGNORM.INV allows us to create a series of values that have a lognormal distribution: =LOGNORM.INV(RAND(),2,0.5).

In cell E3 (and E34) we use the SKEW function, but nested inside a TEXT function, so we can use a formatted result in the *MsgBox*: =TEXT(SKEW(A:A), "0.000"). Skewness characterizes the degree of asymmetry of a distribution around its mean.

In cell E4 (and E35) we use a thumb rule as to whether a distribution is significantly skewed or not. The formula is for E4 as follows: =IF(E3>(2*SQRT(6/COUNT(A:A))),"Y","N")

What you need to do

```
Option Explicit

Sub TransformLogNormal()
    Dim oWS As Worksheet
    Set oWS = ActiveSheet
    oWS.Copy , Sheets(Sheets.Count)
    Range("A2:A101").Clear: Range("B2:B101").Clear: Range("G2:G101").Clear
    If MsgBox("Create a random LogNormal Distribution?", vbYesNo) = vbNo Then
        Application.DisplayAlerts = False
        Sheets(Sheets.Count).Delete
        Application.DisplayAlerts = True
        Exit Sub
    End If
    Range("A2:A101").Formula = "=LOGNORM.INV(RAND(),2,0.5)"
    Range("B2:B101").Formula = "=LOGNORM.DIST(A2,$E$1,$E$2,TRUE)"
    If MsgBox("Transform the data?", vbYesNo) = vbNo Then Exit Sub
    Range("G2:G101").Formula = "=LN(A2)"
    MsgBox "Lognormal is " & IIf(Range("E4") = "Y", "", "not ") & _
            "significantly skewed: " & Range("E3") & vbCr & "After transformation " & _
            IIf(Range("E35") = "Y", "slightly ", "no longer ") & _
            "skewed: " & Range("E34") & ""
End Sub
```

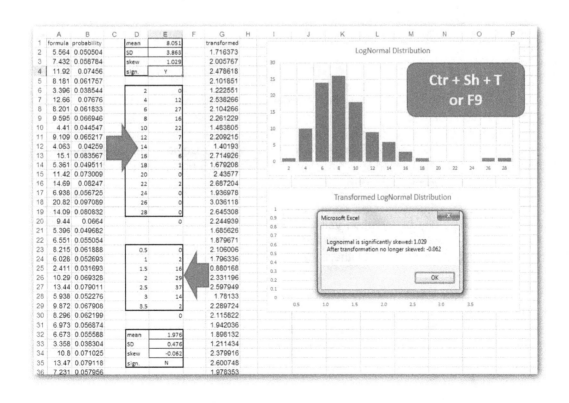

Chapter 24: Outlier Detection

What the simulation does

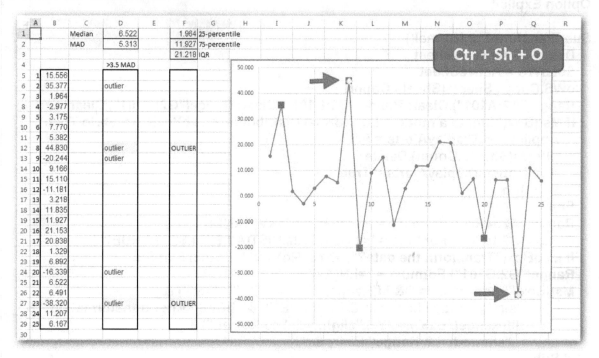

Outliers are defined as numeric values in any random data set that have an unusually high deviation from either the statistical mean or the median value. In other words, these numbers are relatively extreme. It requires sound statistics—not intuition—to locate them. A rather simple rule is that all values outside a range of three times the standard deviation around the mean could be considered outliers—provided they follow a normal distribution.

What you need to know

In this simulation, however, we will use a more robust statistical detection of outliers by calculating the deviation for each number, expressed as a "modified Z-score," and testing it against a predefined threshold. Z-scores stand for the amount of standard deviation relative to the statistical median (in D1). MAD (in D2) stands for Median Absolute Deviation. Any number in a data set with the absolute value of modified Z-scores exceeding 3.5 times MAD is considered an outlier. Column D shows the outcome.

In the 1970's the famous statistician John Tukey decided to give the term outlier a more formal definition. He called any observation value an outlier if it is smaller than the first quartile (F1) minus 1.5 times the *IQR* (F3), or larger than the third quartile (F2) plus 1.5 times the *IQR*. The Inter-Quartile Range, *IQR*, is the width of the interval that contains the middle half of the data. Column F shows the outcome.

The graph to the right shows the observed values marked with a *square* shape if it is an outlier according to the first method, or with a *diamond* shape if it is an outlier according to the second method. Most of the time, the first method detects more outliers than the second one.

What you need to do

```
Option Explicit

Sub Outliers()
    Dim oWS As Worksheet
    Set oWS = ActiveSheet
    oWS.Copy , Sheets(Sheets.Count)
    Range("B5:B29").Formula = "=NORMINV(RAND(),30,15)*(1-2*RAND())"
    Range("D5:D29").Formula = "=IF(ABS(D$1-B5)>(3.5*D$2), ""outlier"", """")"
    Range("F5:F29").Formula = "=IF(OR(B5>($F$2+1.5*$F$3),B5<($F$1-
1.5*$F$3)),""OUTLIER"","""")"
    Range("D5:D29,F5:F29").FormatConditions.Add xlExpression, ,
"=AND($D5=""outlier"",$F5=""OUTLIER"")"
    Range("D5:D29,F5:F29").FormatConditions(1).Interior.Color = vbYellow
End Sub
```

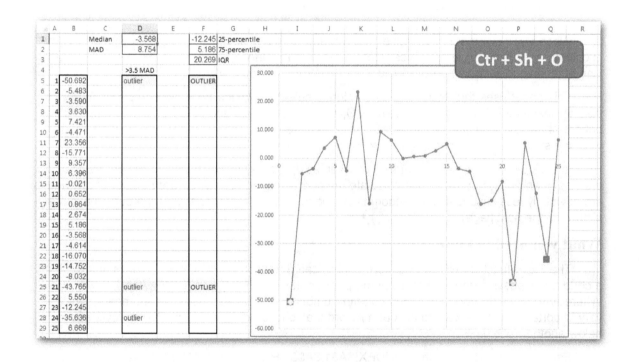

Chapter 25: Bootstrapping

What the simulation does

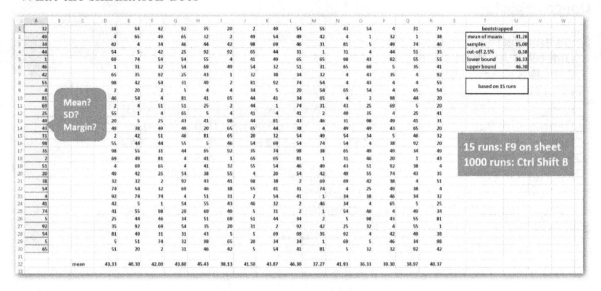

When you have a series of values that are not normally distributed—say, 30 values such as in column A—it is not so simple to calculate a mean, a median, a SD, or a margin. You need some kind of technique such as bootstrapping.

This sheet uses that technique by randomly selecting values from the sample in A. We do that, for instance, 15 times: first in column D, then in column E, and so on until column R. At the bottom of each column we calculate the average. Based on these averages, we are able to know what the statistical parameters are that we were looking for.

In the VBA code, we do all of this, not 15 times, but 1,000 times by storing the results of each drawing in an array, from which we calculate the bootstrapping results. Larger number of drawings are obviously less susceptible to random fluctuations. A *MsgBox* reports what the outcome is (see picture on the next page).

What you need to know

The Excel function INDEX is a more sophisticated version of VLOOKUP. It looks in a table at a certain row position and a certain column position. It uses this syntax: *INDEX(table, row#, col#)*. Whereas VLOOKUP works only with column numbers, INDEX also uses row numbers, which is very important when we want to look at a record that is located a certain number of rows above or below another record.

Each cell in D1:R30 has this: =INDEX($A$1:$A$30,ROWS($A$1:$A$30)*RAND()+1)

In cell U2 is the mean of means: =AVERAGE(D32:R32)

In cell U3 is the number of samples: =COUNT(D32:R32)

In cell U4 is the 2.5% cut off: =U3*0.025

In cell U5 is the lower bound: =SMALL($D$32:$R$32,ROUNDUP($U$4,0))

In cell U6 is the upper bound: =LARGE($D$32:$R$32,ROUNDUP($U$4,0)):

What you need to do

```vba
Option Explicit

Sub BootStrap()
   Dim i As Long, r As Long, j As Long, oRange As Range, sMsg As String
   Dim pValue As Double, pMean As Double, pSE As Double, iCutOff As Integer, pMargin As Double
   Dim arrMeans() As Double, arrValues() As Double
   r = Range("A1").CurrentRegion.Rows.Count
   Set oRange = Range(Cells(1, 1), Cells(r, 1))
   ReDim arrMeans(1 To 1000)
   For j = 1 To 1000
      ReDim arrValues(1 To r)
      For i = 1 To r
         arrValues(i) = WorksheetFunction.Index(oRange, r * Rnd() + 1)
      Next i
      arrMeans(j) = WorksheetFunction.Average(arrValues)
   Next j
   iCutOff = WorksheetFunction.RoundUp(100 * 0.025, 0)
   pMean = Format(WorksheetFunction.Average(arrMeans), "0.00")
   pSE = Format(WorksheetFunction.StDev_S(arrMeans), "0.00")
   pMargin = Format(pSE * WorksheetFunction.T_Inv_2T(0.05, r - 1), "0.00")
   sMsg = "Based on 1000 runs:" & vbCr
   sMsg = sMsg & "Mean of the arrMeans: " & pMean & vbCr
   sMsg = sMsg & "SE of the arrMeans: " & pSE & vbCr
   sMsg = sMsg & "Margin at 95%: " & pMargin & vbCr
   sMsg = sMsg & "Lower Bound: " & pMean - pMargin & vbCr
   sMsg = sMsg & "Upper Bound: " & pMean + pMargin
   MsgBox sMsg
End Sub
```

Microsoft Excel

Based on 1000 runs:
Mean of the arrMeans: 41.44
SE of the arrMeans: 4.64
Margin at 95%: 9.49
Lower Bound: 31.95
Upper Bound: 50.93

OK

Chapter 26: Bean Machine Simulation

What the simulation does

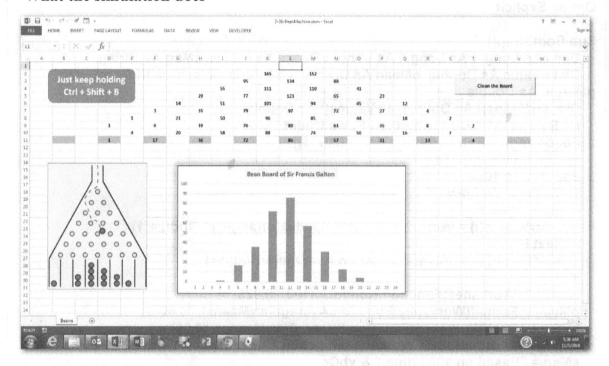

The Galton board, also known as a quincunx or bean machine, is a device for statistical experiments named after English scientist Sir Francis Galton. It consists of an upright board with evenly spaced nails (or pegs) driven into its upper half, where the nails are arranged in staggered order, and a lower half divided into a number of evenly-spaced rectangular slots. The front of the device is covered with a glass cover to allow viewing of both nails and slots. In the middle of the upper edge, there is a funnel into which balls can be poured, where the diameter of the balls must be much smaller than the distance between the nails. The funnel is located precisely above the central nail of the second row so that each ball, if perfectly centered, would fall vertically and directly onto the uppermost point of this nail's surface.

Each time a ball hits one of the nails, it can bounce right or left. For symmetrically placed nails, balls will bounce left or right with equal probability. This process therefore gives rise to a binomial distribution of in the heights of heaps of balls in the lower slots. If the number of balls is sufficiently large, then the distribution of the heights of the ball heaps will approximate a normal distribution.

What you need to know

This sheet simulates this process. All you have to do is keep holding the keys Ctrl + Shift + B down, and the slots will fill as to be expected. If you want to start all over, with an empty board, just hit the command button in the top right corner. In the beginning, the distribution may be not be very "normal" (see picture below), but that will soon change.

What you need to do

Place in a Module:

```
Option Explicit

Sub Beans()
   Dim oStart As Range, oPrev As Range, oNext As Range, c As Integer, r As Integer
   Set oStart = Range("L1")
   oStart.Interior.ColorIndex = 15
   Set oPrev = oStart
   For r = 1 To 10
      If Rnd > 0.5 Then c = c + 1 Else c = c - 1
      Set oNext = oStart.Cells.Offset(r, c)
      oNext = oNext + 1
      oNext.Interior.ColorIndex = 15
      oPrev.Interior.ColorIndex = 0
      Set oPrev = oNext
   Next r
End Sub
```

Place on Sheet1:

```
Option Explicit

Private Sub CommandButton1_Click()
   Range("A1:X11").ClearContents
   Range("L1").Select
End Sub
```

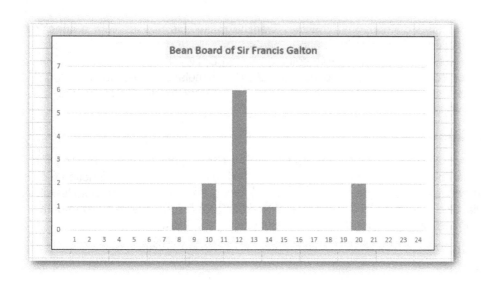

Chapter 27: Correlated Distributions

What the simulation does

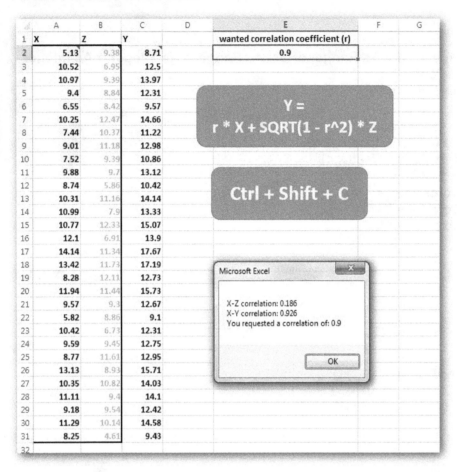

When you create multiple distributions, you may want to make this happen with a specific correlation coefficient between them. This simulation does so for you. In columns A:B, the macro creates two sets of normally distributed values in columns A and B. However, we want these two sets (X and Z) to be correlated as requested by cell E2. This simulation does so by using a transformation with the formula mentioned above. Then, in a *MsgBox*, it compares the old correlation coefficient with the new one.

What you need to know

When there are not 2 but 3 sets involved, you could hit Ctrl + Shift + D, which does the following. It performs the so-called Cholensky decomposition with a customized array function (see VBA-code), and then converts your three sets of values by using the array function results with another array formula like this: =MMULT(A2:C31,TRANSPOSE(F8:H10)). MMULT returns the matrix product of two arrays, with one of them transposed by using the TRANSPOSE function.

What you need to do

```
Sub Correlation()
   Dim oRange As Range
   Sheet2.Select
   Set oRange = Range("A2:C31"): oRange.ClearContents
```

```vba
    MsgBox "First randomized values for X, Y, and Z"
    oRange.Formula = "=ROUND(NORMINV(RAND(),10,2),2)"
    Set oRange = Range("F8:H10"): oRange.ClearContents
    MsgBox "Now the Cholensky Decomposition in F8:H10"
    oRange.FormulaArray = "=Cholenksy(F3:H5)" 'see function below
    Set oRange = Range("J2:L31"): oRange.ClearContents
    MsgBox "Now the matrix manipulation in J2:L31"
    oRange.FormulaArray = "=MMULT(A2:C31,TRANSPOSE(F8:H10))"
End Sub


Sub Decomposition()
    Dim oRange As Range
    Sheet2.Select
    Set oRange = Range("A2:C31"): oRange.ClearContents
    MsgBox "First randomized values for X, Y, and Z"
    oRange.Formula = "=ROUND(NORMINV(RAND(),10,2),2)"
    Set oRange = Range("F8:H10"): oRange.ClearContents
    MsgBox "Now the Cholensky Decomposition in F8:H10"
    oRange.FormulaArray = "=Cholenksy(F3:H5)" 'see function below
    Set oRange = Range("J2:L31"): oRange.ClearContents
    MsgBox "Now the matrix manipulation in J2:L31"
    oRange.FormulaArray = "=MMULT(A2:C31,TRANSPOSE(F8:H10))"
End Sub


Function Cholenksy(oMatrix As Range) 'partially borrowed from Kurt Verstegen
    Dim i As Integer, j As Integer, k As Integer, N As Integer
    Dim arrMatrix() As Double, arrLower() As Double, pValue As Double
    N = oMatrix.Columns.Count
    ReDim arrMatrix(1 To N, 1 To N) :    ReDim arrLower(1 To N, 1 To N)
    For i = 1 To N
        For j = 1 To N
            arrMatrix(i, j) = oMatrix(i, j).Value :        arrLower(i, j) = 0
        Next j
    Next i
    For i = 1 To N
        For j = 1 To N
            pValue = arrMatrix(i, j)
            For k = 1 To i - 1
                pValue = pValue - arrLower(i, k) * arrLower(j, k)
            Next k
            If i = j Then
                arrLower(i, i) = Sqr(pValue)
            ElseIf i < j Then
                arrLower(j, i) = pValue / arrLower(i, i)
            End If
        Next j
    Next i
    Cholenksy = WorksheetFunction.Transpose(arrLower)
End Function
```

Chapter 28: Sorted Random Sampling

What the simulation does

	A	B	C	D	E	F	G	H	I	J	K	L	M	N	O
1	0.70276	1				lot size	25								
2	0.2685					sample size	15			Ctrl + Shift + N					
3	0.79245	3													
4	0.06474				hide with white font										
5	0.02099								random, no duplicates, sorted						
6	0.40036	6		1	1	18									
7	0.08491			2	3	21									
8	0.35094	8		3	6	22									
9	0.54029	9		4	8	23									
10	0.13669			5	9	24									
11	0.078			6	12										
12	0.71064	12		7	13										
13	0.76911	13		8	15										
14	0.02006			9	16										
15	0.51336	15		10	17										
16	0.94128	16			0	10	20	30	40	50	60	70	80	90	
17	0.29696	17													

Sheet1 of this simulation takes random samples from values in column A—but without any duplicates, and in a sorted order, based on a specific lot size and sample size. It does so by sampling numbers in column A, then manipulates them in column B (see picture on the next page), and displays them orderly in E6:N15. Sheet2 does something similar, but this time with dates.

What you need to know

	C	D	E	F	G	H	I	J	K	L	M	N	O	P
1	13-Feb-10			lot size	50									
2	9-Mar-10			sample size	25		Ctrl + Shift + D							
3	20-Mar-10													
4	25-Mar-10						random positions							
5	1-Apr-10		1	3	25	41								
6	3-Apr-10		2	6	26	43								
7	5-Apr-10		3	7	27	46								
8	13-Apr-10		4	15	28	47								
9	28-Apr-10		5	17	29	49								
10	29-Apr-10		6	18	30									
11	25-May-10		7	19	32									
12	19-Aug-10		8	21	33									
13	27-Aug-10		9	22	38									
14	29-Aug-10		10	24	40									
15	27-Sep-10			0	10	20	30	40	50	60	70	80	90	
16	22-Oct-10													
17	24-Nov-10					look up dates at random positions								
18	30-Nov-10		1	20-Mar-10	19-Apr-11	17-Mar-12								
19	19-Dec-10		2	3-Apr-10	25-Apr-11	17-May-12								
20	14-Jan-11		3	5-Apr-10	29-Apr-11	16-Jul-12								
21	23-Feb-11		4	27-Sep-10	30-Apr-11	17-Jul-12								
22	6-Mar-11		5	24-Nov-10	5-May-11	4-Sep-12								
23	22-Mar-11		6	30-Nov-10	7-May-11									
24	4-Apr-11		7	19-Dec-10	18-Jul-11									
25	19-Apr-11		8	23-Feb-11	30-Jul-11									
26	25-Apr-11		9	6-Mar-11	9-Dec-11									
27	29-Apr-11		10	4-Apr-11	10-Jan-12									
28	30-Apr-11			0	10	20	30	40	50	60	70	80	90	

Sheet2 has an extra secret: two hidden rows before column C. The hidden columns A and B do the same work as they did on sheet1. In F18:O27 it finds the dates corresponding to F5:O14.

What you need to do

```
Option Explicit

Sub Numbers()
    Dim iLot As Integer, iSample As Integer
    Sheet1.Select
    Range("A1:B100,E6:N15").ClearContents
    iLot = InputBox("Lot size (max of 100)", , 25): If iLot > 100 Then Exit Sub
    iSample = InputBox("Sample size (max of 100)", , 15): If iLot > 100 Then Exit Sub
    Range("G1") = iLot: Range("G2") = iSample
    Range("A1:A100").Formula = "=IF(ROW(A1)>$G$1,"""",RAND())"
    Range("B1:B100").Formula =
"=IF(A1="""","""",IF(RANK(A1,$A$1:$A$101)>$G$2,"""",ROW(A1)))"
    Range("E6:N15").Formula =
"=IF($D6+E$16>$G$2,"""",SMALL($B$1:$B$100,$D6+E$16))"
    Do
        Calculate
    Loop Until MsgBox("Again?", vbYesNo) = vbNo
End Sub


Sub Dates()
    Dim iLot As Integer, iSample As Integer
    Sheet2.Select
    Range("A1:B100,F5:O14,F18:O27").ClearContents
    iLot = InputBox("Lot size (max of 100)", , 25): If iLot > 100 Then Exit Sub
    iSample = InputBox("Sample size (max of 100)", , 15): If iLot > 100 Then Exit Sub
    Range("G1") = iLot: Range("G2") = iSample
    Range("A1:A100").Formula = "=IF(ROW(A1)>$G$1,"""",RAND())"
    Range("A1:A100").EntireColumn.Hidden = True
    Range("B1:B100").Formula =
"=IF(A1="""","""",IF(RANK(A1,$A$1:$A$100)>$G$2,"""",ROW(A1)))"
    Range("B1:B100").EntireColumn.Hidden = True
    Range("F5:O14").Formula =
"=IF($E5+F$15>$G$2,"""",SMALL($B$1:$B$100,$E5+F$15))"
    Range("F18:O27").Formula =
"=IF($E5+F$15>$G$2,"""",SMALL($B$1:$B$100,$E5+F$15))"
    Do
        Calculate
    Loop Until MsgBox("Again?", vbYesNo) = vbNo
End Sub
```

	A	B	C	D	E
1	=IF(ROW(A1)>$G$1,"",RAND())	=IF(A1="","",IF(RANK(A1,$A$1:$A$101)>$G$2,"",ROW(A1)))			
2	=IF(ROW(A2)>$G$1,"",RAND())	=IF(A2="","",IF(RANK(A2,$A$1:$A$101)>$G$2,"",ROW(A2)))			
3	=IF(ROW(A3)>$G$1,"",RAND())	=IF(A3="","",IF(RANK(A3,$A$1:$A$101)>$G$2,"",ROW(A3)))			
4	=IF(ROW(A4)>$G$1,"",RAND())	=IF(A4="","",IF(RANK(A4,$A$1:$A$101)>$G$2,"",ROW(A4)))			
5	=IF(ROW(A5)>$G$1,"",RAND())	=IF(A5="","",IF(RANK(A5,$A$1:$A$101)>$G$2,"",ROW(A5)))			
6	=IF(ROW(A6)>$G$1,"",RAND())	=IF(A6="","",IF(RANK(A6,$A$1:$A$101)>$G$2,"",ROW(A6)))		1	=IF($D6+E$16>$G$2,"",SMALL($B$1:$B$100,$D6+E$16))
7	=IF(ROW(A7)>$G$1,"",RAND())	=IF(A7="","",IF(RANK(A7,$A$1:$A$101)>$G$2,"",ROW(A7)))		2	=IF($D7+E$16>$G$2,"",SMALL($B$1:$B$100,$D7+E$16))
8	=IF(ROW(A8)>$G$1,"",RAND())	=IF(A8="","",IF(RANK(A8,$A$1:$A$101)>$G$2,"",ROW(A8)))		3	=IF($D8+E$16>$G$2,"",SMALL($B$1:$B$100,$D8+E$16))

Chapter 29: Frequencies

What the simulation does

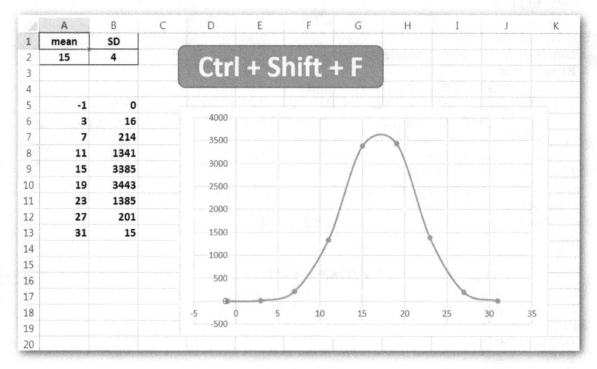

There is not much new in this simulation. It asks for a specific mean and SD, loops for a specific amount of runs, creates a frequency table, and then replaces the chart with a new one.

What you need to know

	A	B	C	D	E	F	G	H
1	**mean**	**SD**						
2	**20**	**4**						
3								
4								
5	4	1						
6	8	15						
7	12	207						
8	16	1378						
9	20	3378						
10	24	3372						
11	28	1421						
12	32	217						
13	36	11						
14								

Ctrl + Shift + F

Microsoft Excel

After 10000 runs:
Mean = 20.040
SD = 4.023

OK

What you need to do

```
Option Explicit

Sub Frequencies()
  Dim pMean As Double, pSD As Double, pArr() As Double, i As Long
  ActiveSheet.Shapes(2).Delete
  pMean = InputBox("Mean", , Cells(2, 1))
  pSD = InputBox("SD", , Cells(2, 2))
  Cells(2, 1) = pMean: Cells(2, 2) = pSD
  Cells(5, 1) = pMean - 4 * pSD
  Cells(6, 1) = pMean - 3 * pSD
  Cells(7, 1) = pMean - 2 * pSD
  Cells(8, 1) = pMean - 1 * pSD
  Cells(9, 1) = pMean
  Cells(10, 1) = pMean + 1 * pSD
  Cells(11, 1) = pMean + 2 * pSD
  Cells(12, 1) = pMean + 3 * pSD
  Cells(13, 1) = pMean + 4 * pSD
  For i = 1 To InputBox("Runs", , 10000)
    ReDim Preserve pArr(i)
    pArr(i) = WorksheetFunction.Norm_Inv(Rnd, pMean, pSD)
  Next i
  pMean = WorksheetFunction.Average(pArr)
  pSD = WorksheetFunction.StDev_S(pArr)
  Range("B5:B13") = WorksheetFunction.Frequency(pArr, Range("$A$5:$A$13"))
  Range("A5:B13").Select
  ActiveSheet.Shapes.AddChart2(240, xlXYScatterSmooth).Select
  ActiveChart.SetSourceData Range("A5:B13"):    ActiveChart.HasTitle = False
  Range("A1").Select
  MsgBox "After " & i - 1 & " runs:" & vbCr & "Mean = " & _
        FormatNumber(pMean, 3) & vbCr & "SD = " & FormatNumber(pSD, 3)
End Sub
```

III. MONTE CARLO SIMULATIONS

Chapter 30: The Law of Large Numbers

What the simulation does

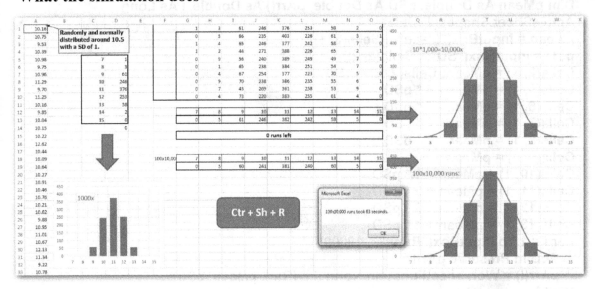

This is an example of a Monte Carlo simulation. Why are they called *Monte Carlo* simulations? The name came up in the 1940s when Los Alamos physicists John von Neumann, Stanislaw Ulam, and Nicholas Metropolis were working on nuclear weapon research during the Manhattan Project in the Los Alamos National Laboratory. They were unable to solve their problems using conventional, deterministic mathematical methods. Then one of them, Stanisław Ulam, had the idea of using random simulations based on random numbers. The Monte Carlo simulations required for the Manhattan Project were severely limited by the computational tools at the time. Nowadays we have Excel!

Currently, the technique is used by professionals in such widely disparate fields as finance, project management, energy, manufacturing, engineering, research and development, insurance, and transportation. Monte Carlo simulation furnishes you as a decision-maker with a range of possible outcomes and the probabilities they will occur for any choice of action. Always run at least 1,000 iterations of Monte Carlo models to reduce the risk of random impact.

What you need to know

This simulation shows the effect of large numbers. Column A contains "only" 1,000 numbers (plotted in the chart lower left). Then we run the results of those 1,000 numbers 10 more times in a *Data Table*, which makes for 10,000 cases (plotted in the chart top right). Finally we let VBA loop through these results some 100 times, and average them again. Row 15 keeps track of how many runs have not been executed yet. The outcome of these 1,000,000 runs in total is plotted in the third chart (lower right).

Notice how all three charts change during execution, but the third one stays rather stable.

Needless to say that this is a time consuming process—mostly because of cell manipulation on the sheet, for the use of arrays in VBA is comparatively fast. When all the runs are completed (probably after some 60 seconds), a *MsgBox* shows the time needed for completion, which depends partly on the processing speed of your machine.

What you need to do

```
Option Explicit

Sub Repeating()
   Dim i As Integer, vArr As Variant, arrTotals() As Long
   Dim iRepeats As Integer, n As Integer, iTime As Long
   iTime = Timer
   Range("G19:O19").ClearContents
   iRepeats = InputBox("How many repeats?", , 100)
   Cells(1, 1).Select
   ReDim arrTotals(1 To 9)
   For i = 1 To iRepeats
     ActiveSheet.Calculate
     vArr = Range("G13:O13")
     For n = 1 To UBound(vArr, 2)
        arrTotals(n) = arrTotals(n) + Int(vArr(1, n))
        Range("G19:O19").Cells(1, n) = Int(arrTotals(n) / i)
        Range("G15") = iRepeats - i & " runs left"
     Next n
   Next i
   Range("F18") = iRepeats & "x10,000 runs:"
   MsgBox iRepeats & "x10,000 runs took " & Int(Timer - iTime) & " seconds."
End Sub
```

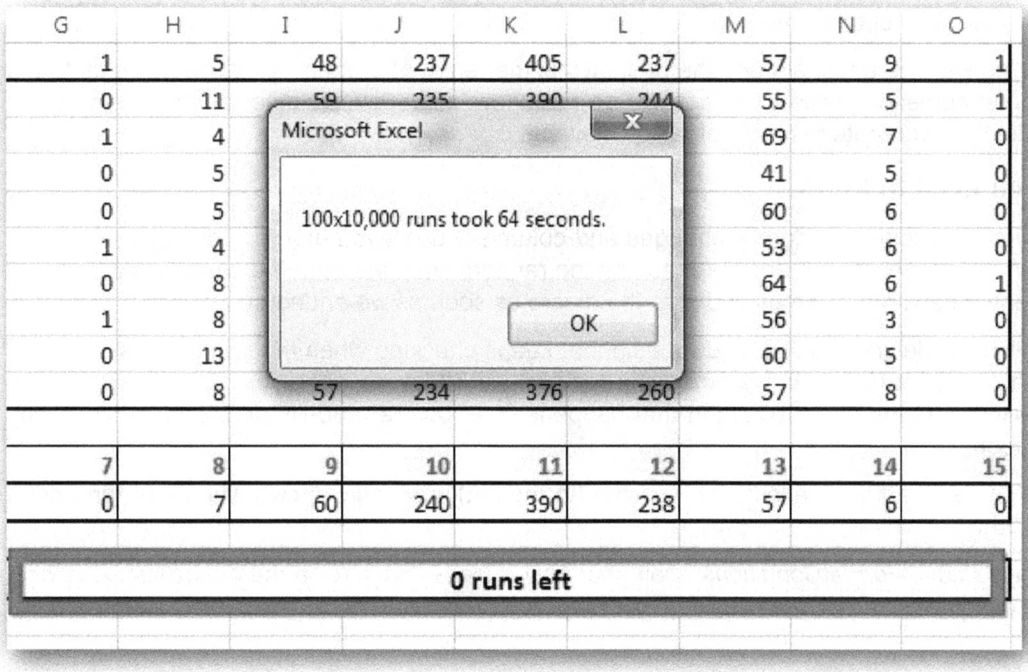

G	H	I	J	K	L	M	N	O
1	5	48	237	405	237	57	9	1
0	11	59	235	390	244	55	5	1
1	4					69	7	0
0	5					41	5	0
0	5					60	6	0
1	4					53	6	0
0	8					64	6	1
1	8					56	3	0
0	13					60	5	0
0	8	57	234	376	260	57	8	0

Microsoft Excel

100x10,000 runs took 64 seconds.

OK

7	8	9	10	11	12	13	14	15
0	7	60	240	390	238	57	6	0

0 runs left

Chapter 31: Brownian Motion

What the simulation does

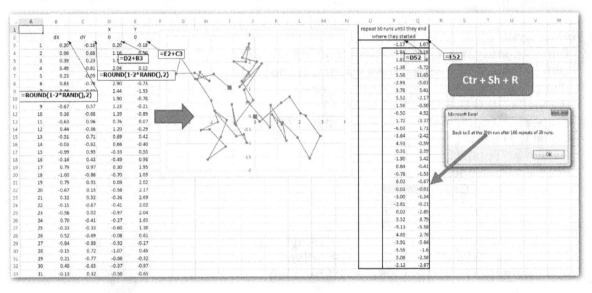

Brownian motion was discovered in the early 1800s by botanist Robert Brown, who noticed under his microscope how grains of pollen appeared to constantly and randomly move in a jittery way on the surface of the water. In his 1905 paper, Albert Einstein hypothesized that Brownian motion was caused by actual atoms and molecules hitting the grains of pollen, impelling them to take a "random walk" on the surface of the liquid. Einstein's work eventually led to the inherently probabilistic nature of quantum mechanics.

This is a simulation of how a grain of pollen—or a molecule, for that matter—takes a "random walk" on the surface of the water.

Dealing with the uncertain and the unknown is the realm of probability, which helps us to put a meaningful numerical value on things we do not know. Although a single random event is not predictable, the aggregate behavior of random events is.

What you need to know

Column B displays random X-changes and column C displays random Y-changes. In D and E, we start at coordinates 0,0 and keep adding the random changes from the previous columns. In P:Q we repeat each run 14 times and stop the macro as soon as we ended up close to 0,0 again.

The VBA code creates this random path, but keeps checking when the end point is the same as the starting point (0,0)—that is when the random walk took us back very close to where we started (within a range of 0.02). When that happens, it stops the process and reports how many runs that took.

The center chart only reflects the first run (to the left), so it only shows when that run ended where it started. See the chart below.

We also used *FormatConditions* again, but only once, for otherwise the macro keeps adding the same condition.

What you need to do

```
Option Explicit

Sub Returning()
   Dim i As Integer, oRange As Range, bBack As Boolean, n As Long
   Range("O3:Q32").Table , Range("N1")
   Range("A1").Select
   Set oRange = Range("P3:Q32")
   'oRange.FormatConditions.Add xlExpression, ,
"=AND(AND($P3>=0,$P3<0.05),AND($Q3>=0,$Q3<0.05))"
   'oRange.FormatConditions(1).Interior.Color = vbYellow
   Do While bBack = False
     Calculate
     For i = 1 To 30
       If oRange.Cells(i, 1) > -0.03 And oRange.Cells(i, 1) < 0.03 Then
         If oRange.Cells(i, 2) > -0.03 And oRange.Cells(i, 2) < 0.03 Then bBack = True:
Exit Do
       End If
     Next i
     n = n + 1
   Loop
   MsgBox "Back to 0 at the " & i & "th run after " & n & " repeats of 30 runs."
End Sub
```

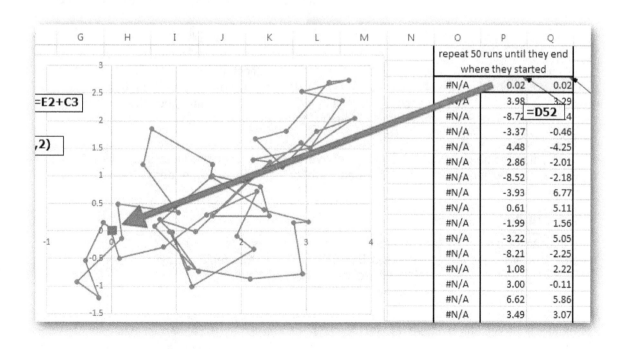

Chapter 32: Ehrenfest Urn

What the simulation does

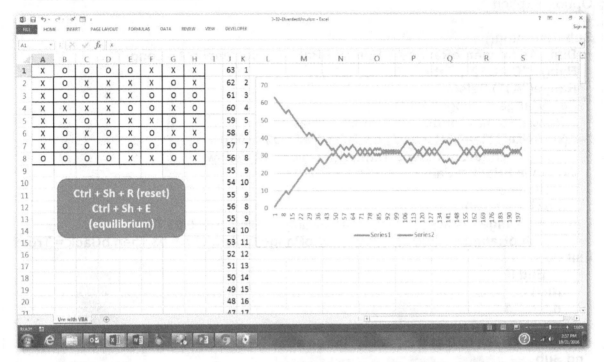

Consider two urns A and B. Urn A contains N marbles and urn B contains none. The marbles are labelled 1,2,...N. At each step of the algorithm, a number between 1 and N is chosen randomly, with all values having equal probability. The marble corresponding to that value is moved to the opposite urn. Hence the first step of the algorithm will always involve moving a marble from A to B.

What will the two urns look like after k steps? If k is sufficiently large, we may expect the urns to have equal populations, as the probabilities of drawing a marble from A or from B become increasingly similar. States in which one urn has many more marbles than the other may be said to be unstable, as there is an overwhelming tendency to move marbles to the urn that contains fewer. This phenomenon is called the "Ehrenfest Urn."

Ehrenfest sometimes used the image of two dogs; the one with fleas gradually infects the other one. In the long-time run, the mean number of fleas on both dogs converges to the equilibrium value.

What you need to know

Instead of using two urns, we use a "board" that has X's at all positions. Each time, at a random row and column position (cells B11 and B12), an X is replaced by an O, or vice-versa. Gradually, we reach an equilibrium where the number of X's and O's have become very similar, albeit with some oscillations of course.

The VBA code finds a random row and column position to replace an X with an O or reversed. It counts the number of X's and Y's after each change and places that number sequentially in row J (for X's) and in row K for O's. These two columns gradually feed the progressing curves in the chart.

One macro feeds the board; the other macro resets the board.

What you need to do

```vba
Option Explicit

Dim i As Integer 'global variable

Sub Equilibrium()
  Dim oRange As Range, iRow As Long, iCol As Integer
  Set oRange = Range("A1").CurrentRegion
  With oRange
    iRow = WorksheetFunction.RandBetween(1, 8)
    iCol = WorksheetFunction.RandBetween(1, 8)
    If .Cells(iRow, iCol) = "X" Then .Cells(iRow, iCol) = "O" Else .Cells(iRow, iCol) = "X"
    Range("J1").Offset(i) = WorksheetFunction.CountIf(oRange, "X")
    Range("K1").Offset(i) = WorksheetFunction.CountIf(oRange, "O")
    i = i + 1
  End With
  Do While i < 200
    Equilibrium
  Loop
End Sub

Sub Reset()
  Dim oRange As Range
  Set oRange = Range("A1").CurrentRegion
  oRange.Cells = "X"
  Columns(10).Clear
  Columns(11).Clear
  i = 0
End Sub
```

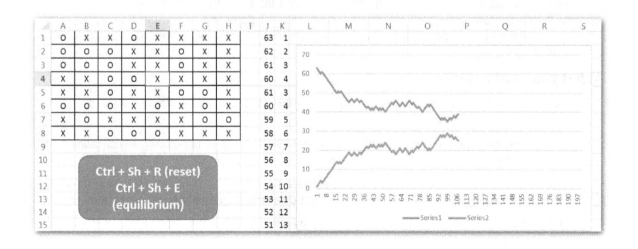

Chapter 33: Random Walk

What the simulation does

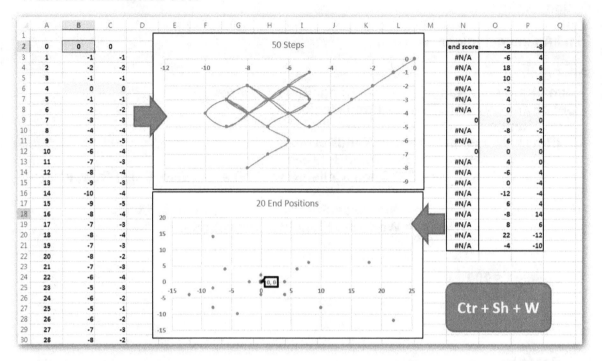

This simulation uses a *random-walk* approach, similar to Brownian motion. Imagine we are leaving home (position 0). Iif we flip a coin and get heads, we go one block north (position +1); if we flip tails, we go one block south (position -1). We keep doing this many times and then check how far we end up being from home. (We may also ask what the probability is that we return to where we started—believe it or not, that probability is 100% if the walk is long enough!).

First we will simulate 50 steps for columns B and C, plotted in the top graph. In the *Data Table* to the right, we repeated all 50 steps 14 times. The columns O and P of the *Data Table* are plotted in the bottom graph.

As it turns out, we could make big "gains" and drift far away from where we started. But not always! If this random-walk were interpreted as a case of gambling, we could encounter many negative, perhaps even huge negative outcomes—"losses" in gambling terms. Random walks are just fascinating.

What you need to know

We do use *FormatConditions* again, but not in the macro, for that would create the same condition over and over again.

In addition, we use the Excel function COUNTIFS (missing in pre-2007), which allows for multiple count criteria: a zero in column B as well as a zero in column C.

In Range N3:N22, we use a formula with a nested NA function. This function returns #N/A. The advantage of doing so is that a curve in the chart does not display #N/A, but just "skips" it.

At the end, the macro can call itself again if so desired.

What you need to do

```
Option Explicit

Sub Walking()
  Dim oRange As Range, i As Integer, sBack As String, sEndScores As String
  Set oRange = Range("B3:C52")
  With oRange
    .Columns(1).ClearContents
    .Columns(2).ClearContents
    .Columns(1).FormulaR1C1 = "=IF(RAND()<0.5,R[-1]C-1,R[-1]C+1)"
    .Columns(2).FormulaR1C1 = "=IF(RAND()<0.5,R[-1]C-1,R[-1]C+1)"
'      .FormatConditions.Add xlExpression, , "=AND($B3=0,$C3=0)"
'      .FormatConditions(1).Interior.Color = vbYellow
  End With
  Range("N3:N21").Formula = "=IF(AND(O3=0,P3=0),0,NA())"
  Set oRange = Range("O2:P21")
'   oRange.FormatConditions.Add xlExpression, , "=AND($O2=0,$P2=0)"
'   oRange.FormatConditions(2).Interior.Color = vbYellow
  sBack = WorksheetFunction.CountIfs(Range("B3:B52"), 0, Range("C3:C52"), 0) & _
          "x back to a position of 0,0 during 1st run"
  sEndScores = WorksheetFunction.CountIfs(Range("O2:O21"), 0, Range("P2:P21"),
0) & _
          "x back to start position 0,0 in 20 runs"
  If MsgBox(sBack & vbCr & sEndScores & vbCr & "Try again?", vbYesNo) = vbYes
Then Walking
End Sub
```

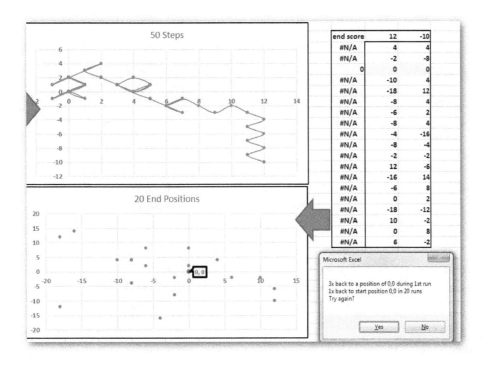

Chapter 34: A Data Table with Memory

What the simulation does

	A	B	C	D	E	F	G	H	I	J
1	0		10%	100						
2	0		11%	105						
3	0		12%	99						
4	0		13%	85						
5	0		14%	93						
6	0		15%	109						
7	0		16%	95						
8	0		17%	104						
9	1		18%	97						
10	0		19%	80						
11	0									

Ctr + Sh + M

Microsoft Excel

Percent	Min	Max
0.11	105	118
0.12	99	114
0.13	85	89
0.14	93	105
0.15	83	109
0.16	95	105
0.17	95	104
0.18	97	107
0.19	80	92

OK

In column A, we randomly choose 1,000 times 0's or 1's, with a chance for 1's based on an *InputBox* (say, 10%, shown in cell C1). The number of 1's is calculated in cell D1, but also for other percentages. This is done by using a *Data Table*. Based on this calculation, the Data Table in columns E and F runs all of this again for the next 9 percentages. When the percentage in C1 has been chosen to be 15%, column C shows the next 9 percentages from 16% to 24%.

A *MsgBox* displays the lowest and highest value. After the first run, these two values are the same, but when you keep running the macro, the difference between the two will begin to rise.

Doing this in Excel with formulas is hard to do, because that requires self-reference, and thus leads to circular reference. This can only be done with iterations ON. VBA can solve this easily.

What you need to know

To prevent the screen from flashing during operations, we can use *Application.ScreenUpdating*. If you set this to False, make sure you set it later back to True.

We use four *Variant* arrays, because they can hold an array or series of values, including the values found in a range of cells. However, this creates a *two*-dimensional array, starting at element 1 (not 0 this time). So in order to address one of its elements, we need *two* indexes, one for each dimension (e.g. *array(1,1)*).

VBA can let you see what is in the array by doing the following: View | Locals Window (see picture to the left). Place a *BreakPoint* in the code after the line you want to check by clicking in the gray margin to the left of it; this creates a brown line. Then click inside the *Sub* and hit the *Run* button; the yellow line indicates where the code has come to a halt. Now the *Locals Window* shows the values of all your variables, including the arrays. Click the *BreakPoint* off, so the code no longer stops there.

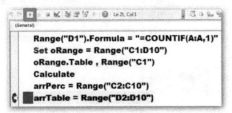

```
Range("D1").Formula = "=COUNTIF(A:A,1)"
Set oRange = Range("C1:D10")
oRange.Table , Range("C1")
Calculate
arrPerc = Range("C2:C10")
arrTable = Range("D2:D10")
```

What you need to do

```
Option Explicit

Sub Memorize()
   Dim oRange As Range, i As Integer, pPercent As Double, sMsg As String
   Dim arrTable As Variant, arrMin As Variant, arrMax As Variant, arrPerc As Variant
   Range("F2:G10").ClearContents
   pPercent = InputBox("The chance for 1's is:", , 0.1)
   If pPercent > 1 Then MsgBox "Must be between 0 and 1": Exit Sub
Again:
   Application.ScreenUpdating = False
   Range("A1:A1000").Formula = "=IF(RAND()<=" & pPercent & ",1,0)"
   Range("C1") = FormatPercent(pPercent, 2)
   For i = 1 To 9
      Range("C2:C10").Cells(i, 1) = pPercent + i / 100
   Next i
   Range("D1").Formula = "=COUNTIF(A:A,1)"
   Set oRange = Range("C1:D10")
   oRange.Table , Range("C1")
   Calculate
   arrPerc = Range("C2:C10")
   arrTable = Range("D2:D10")
   If IsEmpty(arrMin) Then
      arrMin = Range("D2:D10")
      arrMax = Range("D2:D10")
   Else
      For i = 1 To 9
         If arrTable(i, 1) < arrMin(i, 1) Then arrMin(i, 1) = arrTable(i, 1)
         If arrTable(i, 1) > arrMax(i, 1) Then arrMax(i, 1) = arrTable(i, 1)
      Next i
   End If
   sMsg = "Percent" & vbTab & "Min" & vbTab & "Max" & vbCr
   For i = 1 To 9
      sMsg = sMsg & arrPerc(i, 1) & vbTab & arrMin(i, 1) & vbTab & arrMax(i, 1) & vbCr
   Next i
   Application.ScreenUpdating = True
   MsgBox sMsg
   If MsgBox("Keep running?", vbYesNo) = vbYes Then GoTo Again
End Sub
```

Chapter 35: Juror Selection in Court

What the simulation does

	No opinion	No witness	Yes death														Mean	
Candidates 100		Needed 24			qualified 7	6	9	6	4	6	5	12	9	3				
	0.4	0.3	0.6	Juror?														
Juror 1		+	+	0	100 6	100 6	100 4	100 9	100 10	100 2	100 10	100 6	100 4	100 11		100	15
Juror 2		+	+	0	150 10	150 16	150 12	150 8	150 10	150 9	150 14	150 11	150 8	150 6		150	23
Juror 3				0	200 11	200 17	200 18	200 17	200 22	200 15	200 18	200 18	200 16	200 8		200	32
Juror 4	+			0	250 19	250 14	250 12	250 11	250 21	250 9	250 14	250 16	250 15	250 25		250	37
Juror 5		+	+	0	300 19	300 22	300 30	300 22	300 18	300 16	300 23	300 20	300 23	300 21		300	46
Juror 6				0	350 21	350 23	350 28	350 24	350 23	350 28	350 25	350 21	350 24	350 26		350	53
Juror 7			+	0	400 31	400 28	400 37	400 28	400 31	400 31	400 26	400 46	400 25	400 22		400	64
Juror 8	+			0	450 25	450 32	450 25	450 27	450 20	450 31	450 31	450 25	450 36	450 31		450	66
Juror 9			+	0	500 37	500 25	500 25	500 42	500 40	500 30	500 48	500 40	500 37	500 37		500	79
Juror 10	+			0	550 44	550 46	550 40	550 37	550 41	550 43	550 43	550 31	550 34	550 48		550	87
Juror 11	+	+	+	1	600 36	600 44	600 39	600 45	600 42	600 41	600 50	600 37	600 52	600 56		600	94
Juror 12				0	650 46	650 60	650 54	650 31	650 52	650 52	650 46	650 47	650 33	650 54		650	102
Juror 13	+			0	700 47	700 62	700 62	700 59	700 51	700 46	700 53	700 49	700 53	700 52		700	112
Juror 14	+			0	750 48	750 57	750 55	750 47	750 59	750 65	750 48	750 51	750 55	750 60		750	117
Juror 15			+	0	800 62	800 69	800 50	800 54	800 50	800 61	800 55	800 53	800 60	800 60		800	124
Juror 16	+		+	0	850 66	850 60	850 59	850 65	850 49	850 55	850 60	850 53	850 63	850 63		850	131
Juror 17			+	0	900 64	900 75	900 81	900 55	900 67	900 66	900 79	900 71	900 61	900 70		900	144
Juror 18		+	+	0	950 54	950 78	950 73	950 74	950 87	950 73	950 54	950 66	950 65	950 75		950	149
Juror 19			+	0	1000 63	1000 75	1000 76	1000 65	1000 48	1000 70	1000 64	1000 78	1000 68	1000 73		1000	152
Juror 20			+	0													

Ctr + Sh + J

Countries with a juror system in court have to face the fact that they must choose 2x12 jurors from a larger pool of candidates after checking each candidate for certain criteria.

We assume we need 24 jurors (cell E1) from a pool of 100 (cell B1). We also use the following criteria: #1 they have no opinion yet whether the defendant is guilty (column B); #2 they were not witness to the crime (column C); #3 they accept the possibility of the death penalty (column D). These criteria have a probability in the population as shown in range B4:D4. Column E decides whether all three conditions have been met. Cell F4 counts how many in the pool of candidates actually qualified to be a juror in the case.

Finally we run this setup with a *Data Table* repeated 10 times (G:H, I:J, up to Y:Z); each one running pool sizes from 100 to 1000. We average these results in column AC, and we mark pool sizes that meet the needed number of candidates (F2) with Conditional Formatting.

What you need to know

All gray cells have a formula in it. This is done by selecting all cells and implementing Condition Formatting based on this formula: =ISFORMULA(A1).

In the run shown below, a pool of 100 or 150 candidates would not be enough to reach the 24 jurors needed, given the three conditions in B:D and their probabilities. But 200 would! Again, we are dealing with probabilities here, so results may vary!

	No opinion	No witness	Yes death														Mean	
Candidates 100		Needed 24			qualified 11	7	6	6	4	11	6	7	6	8				
	0.4	0.3	0.6	Juror?														
Juror 1	+	+	+	1	100 2	100 9	100 8	100 11	100 5	100 6	100 10	100 6	100 3	100 14		100	15
Juror 2			+	0	150 8	150 5	150 13	150 14	150 11	150 12	150 12	150 7	150 12	150 8		150	22
Juror 3	+			0	200 8	200 9	200 14	200 11	200 11	200 9	200 9	200 12	200 15	200 15		200	28
Juror 4			+	0	250 26	250 11	250 18	250 18	250 19	250 20	250 20	250 17	250 21	250 23		250	40
Juror 5		+		0	300 29	300 18	300 19	300 14	300 18	300 17	300 19	300 15	300 18	300 14		300	43
Juror 6			+	0	350 34	350 26	350 17	350 24	350 24	350 29	350 23	350 25	350 24	350 25		350	54

Ctr + Sh + J

What you need to do

```
Option Explicit

Sub Jurors()
   Dim iCand As Integer, iNeeded As Integer, i As Integer, oRange As Range
   Application.ScreenUpdating = False
   Range("H4,J4, L4, N4, P4, R4, T4,V4,X4,Z4,AC4").EntireColumn.ClearContents
   Set oRange = Range("A5:E1005")
   oRange.ClearContents
   Range("H5:H23").ClearContents
   Application.ScreenUpdating = True
   Range("B1") = InputBox("How many candidates?", , 100)
   Range("E1") = InputBox("How many jurors needed?", , 24)
   With oRange
      .Columns(1).Formula = "=IF(ROW(A1)<=$B$1,TEXT(ROW(A1), ""Juror 0""),"""")"
      .Columns(2).Formula = "=IF(ROW(A1)<=$B$1,IF(RAND()<B$4,""+"",""""),"""")"
      .Columns(3).Formula = "=IF(ROW(B1)<=$B$1,IF(RAND()<C$4,""+"",""""),"""")"
      .Columns(4).Formula = "=IF(ROW(C1)<=$B$1,IF(RAND()<D$4,""+"",""""),"""")"
      .Columns(5).Formula = "=IF(COUNTIF(B5:D5,""+"")=3,1,0)"
   End With
   Application.ScreenUpdating = False
   Range("H4,J4, L4, N4, P4, R4, T4,V4,X4,Z4").Formula = "=SUM($E$5:$E$1005)"
   With Range("G4:R23")
      For i = 2 To 20 Step 2
         .Range(Cells(1, i - 1), Cells(20, i)).Table , Range("B1")
         'to prevent each table from recalculating, replace with values:
         .Range(Cells(1, i - 1), Cells(20, i)).Formula = .Range(Cells(1, i - 1), Cells(20,
i)).Value
      Next i
   End With
   Range("AC5:AC23").Formula =
"=INT(AVERAGE(H5,J5,L5,N5,P5,R5,U5,T5,V5,X5,Z5))"
   Application.ScreenUpdating = True
End Sub
```

Chapter 36: Running Project Costs

What the simulation does

	A	B	C	D	E	F	G	H	I	J	K	L	M	N
1	Estimates	SubProject1	SubProject2	SubProject3	SubProject4	SubProject5	Total		Mean	$ 222,500.00				
2	Max. Costs	$ 30,000	$ 10,000	$ 50,000	$ 80,000	$ 100,000	$270,000		SD	$ 38,783.59				
3	Min. Costs	$ 20,000	$ 5,000	$ 25,000	$ 50,000	$ 75,000	$175,000		Margin	$ 741.67		Ctr Sh P		
4									Z or t 95%	1.96				
5	average	$ 25,007	$ 7,508	$ 37,561	$ 65,034	$ 87,599	$222,709							
6	upper bound	$ 30,631	$ 10,373	$ 51,736	$ 82,035	$ 101,624	$249,662		Runs	10,505				
7	lower bound	$ 19,384	$ 4,643	$ 23,386	$ 48,032	$ 73,574	$195,756							
8														
9		$ 27,844	$ 6,214	$ 37,096	$ 74,914	$ 80,664	$226,731							
10		$ 27,489	$ 9,575	$ 29,187	$ 77,319	$ 78,281	$221,852							
11		$ 21,520	$ 5,564	$ 42,015	$ 77,004	$ 76,754	$222,856							
12		$ 23,322	$ 6,712	$ 45,785	$ 63,180	$ 75,714	$214,712							
13		$ 27,122	$ 7,979	$ 31,165	$ 64,854	$ 89,868	$220,988							
14		$ 20,418	$ 9,102	$ 45,021	$ 53,090	$ 95,954	$223,586							
15		$ 22,779	$ 5,005	$ 29,767	$ 51,469	$ 99,338	$208,358							
16		$ 20,233	$ 9,093	$ 47,584	$ 64,896	$ 90,313	$232,119							
17		$ 24,718	$ 8,861	$ 27,886	$ 56,545	$ 84,625	$202,635							
18		$ 29,822	$ 8,742	$ 45,267	$ 67,222	$ 82,081	$233,134							
19		$ 28,703	$ 6,563	$ 41,287	$ 74,812	$ 90,439	$241,804							
20		$ 27,908	$ 5,245	$ 40,403	$ 75,897	$ 87,206	$236,658							
21		$ 22,862	$ 7,991	$ 49,610	$ 73,157	$ 90,226	$243,825							
22		$ 23,242	$ 7,502	$ 25,363	$ 69,155	$ 86,168	$211,430							
23		$ 25,735	$ 9,688	$ 25,684	$ 60,437	$ 87,421	$208,964							

This Monte Carlo simulation deals with risks we encounter when we have project costs that we anticipate to be between a maximum value and a minimum value for several sub-projects or various products.

Based on 10,500 runs the simulation starts a new sheet and narrows down our risks with a 95% confidence to be between a certain upper- and lowerbound. As usual, results may vary since there is randomness involved. But a Monte Carlo simulation can reduce this risk.

Manually changing maximum and minimum costs in rows 2 and 3 should affect the outcome.

What you need to know

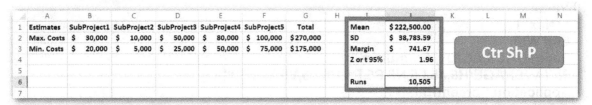

The number of runs (J6) is determined by the values in the cells above it: $((1.96/(margin/mean))\ ^\wedge\ 2) * ((SD/mean)\ ^\wedge\ 2)$

The mean (J1) is: =AVERAGE(G2:G3).

The Standard Deviation (J2) is: =STDEVP(G2:G3,J1).

The Margin (J3) is: =J1/300.

The Z or t value for 95% confidence is approximately 1.96.

What you need to do

```vba
Option Explicit

Sub ProjectCosts()
    Dim i As Integer, iRuns As Long
    Dim oWS As Worksheet, oRange As Range, oCell As Range
    iRuns = Range("J6") 'Formula: ((1.96/(margin/mean)) ^ 2) * ((SD/mean) ^ 2)
    ActiveSheet.Copy , Sheets(Sheets.Count)
    Application.Calculation = xlCalculationManual
    Set oRange = Range(Range("B9"), Range("B9").Cells(iRuns, 5))
    oRange.Formula = "=RAND()*(B$2-B$3)+B$3"
    Set oRange = Range(Range("G9"), Range("G9").Cells(iRuns, 1))
    oRange.Formula = "=SUM(B9:F9)"
    Range("B5:G5").FormulaR1C1 = "=average(R[4]C:R[" & iRuns + 3 & "]C)"
    Range("A5") = "average"
    Range("B6:G6").FormulaR1C1 = "=R[-1]C + 1.96* stdev(R[3]C:R[" & iRuns + 2 & _
"]C)"
    Range("A6") = "upper bound"
    Range("B7:G7").FormulaR1C1 = "=R[-2]C - 1.96* stdev(R[2]C:R[" & iRuns + 1 & _
"]C)"
    Range("A7") = "lower bound"
    Application.Calculation = xlCalculationAutomatic
    Cells.EntireColumn.AutoFit
    MsgBox "Based on " & iRuns & " iterations"
    Range("B5:G7").Formula = Range("B5:G7").Value
    If MsgBox("Delete the calculations that were generated?", vbYesNo) = vbYes Then
        Range(Range("B9"), Range("B9").Cells(iRuns, 6)).ClearContents
    End If
End Sub
```

Chapter 37: Forecasting Profits

What the simulation does

	A	B	C	D	E	F	G	H	I	J	K
1	produced	60,000	=RAND()		demand probabilities						
2	rand#	0.33531318		0.00	20,000	10%					
3	demand	30,000		0.10	30,000	35%					
4	unit cost	$1.50		0.45	40,000	30%					
5	unit price	$4.00		0.75	60,000	25%					
6	unit disposal	$0.20							Ctr Sh P		
7											
8	revenues	$120,000.00									
9	prod. costs	$90,000.00									
10	dispos. Costs	$6,000.00									
11	profit	$24,000.00									
12									production		
13	mean profit	$50,000.00	$70,632.00	$76,690.00	$71,198.00	$66,462.00	$45,850.00		40,000	best profit	
14	SD profits	$0.00	$12,827.36	$28,281.58	$39,776.81	$55,919.21	$55,100.03		60,000	most risky	
15	lower 95%	$50,000.00	$69,836.95	$74,937.09	$68,732.61	$62,996.09	$42,434.86				
16	upper 95%	$50,000.00	$71,427.05	$78,442.91	$73,663.39	$69,927.91	$49,265.14				
17											
18	$24,000.00	20,000	30,000	40,000	50,000	60,000	70,000	units produced			
19	$1.00	$50,000.00	$75,000.00	$58,000.00	-$1,000.00	-$18,000.00	$49,000.00				
20	$2.00	$50,000.00	$75,000.00	$100,000.00	$41,000.00	$150,000.00	$7,000.00				
21	$3.00	$50,000.00	$75,000.00	$58,000.00	-$1,000.00	$24,000.00	$7,000.00				
22	$4.00	$50,000.00	$33,000.00	$16,000.00	$125,000.00	$24,000.00	$133,000.00				

Let's say we are trying to the figure out the optimal amount of production needed in order to maximize our profits. If the demand for this product is regulated by a range of probabilities, then we can determine our optimal production by simulating demand within that range of probabilities and calculating profit for each level of demand.

The simulation uses three tables to set up this calculation. The table top right (E:F) sets up the assumed probabilities of various demand levels. The table top left (A:B) calculates the profit for one trial production quantity. Cell B1 contains the trial production quantity. Cell B2 has a random number. In cell B3, we simulate demand for this product with the function VLOOKUP.

The third table, on the lower left, is a *Data Table* which simulates each possible production quantity (20,000, 30,000, to 70,000) some 1,000 times and calculates profits for each trial number (1 to 1,000) and each production quantity (10,000, etc.).

Finally, row 13 calculates the mean profit for the six different production quantities. In this example, the figures show that a production of 40,000 units results in maximum profits.

The VLOOKUP function in B3 matches the value in B1 with the closest previous match in the first column of table D2:E5; column D has cumulative totals.

In cell A18 starts a *Data Table*. A18 has a link to the profit in B11. Then it uses cell B1 (20,000) for the row input, and an empty cell (say, H12) for the column input.

What you need to know

The VBA code creates each time a new sheet and plots range A13:H16 six times (after recalculation) on this new sheet. At the bottom of the new sheet, it calculates the average for the upper and lower bounds. These averages are essentially based on 6x1,000 runs. A real Monte Carlo simulation would need more iterations, of course.

Setting the *CutCopyMode* fo False is usually wise after a copy operation—otherwise the copied area remains highlighted.

What you need to do

```vba
Sub Profit()
   Dim oData As Worksheet, oWS As Worksheet, oRange As Range, i As Integer
   Sheet1.Activate
   Set oData = ActiveSheet
   Set oWS = Worksheets.Add(, Sheets(Sheets.Count))
   For i = 1 To 30 Step 5
      oData.Calculate
      Set oRange = oData.Range("A13:J16")
      oRange.Copy
      oWS.Cells(i, 1).PasteSpecial xlPasteValues
   Next i
   Application.CutCopyMode = False
   Range("B31:G31").Formula = "=AVERAGE(B3,B8,B13,B18,B23,B28)"
   Range("B32:G32").Formula = "=AVERAGE(B4,B9,B14,B19,B24,B29)"
   oWS.Cells.NumberFormat = "$#,##0.00": oWS.Columns(1).NumberFormat = "0"
   oWS.Cells.EntireColumn.AutoFit
   oWS.Cells(1, 1).Activate
End Sub
```

	A	B	C	D	E	F	G	H	I	J	K
1	mean profit	$50,000.00	$70,296.00	$78,832.00	$68,930.00	$64,446.00	$48,790.00		production		
2	SD profits	$0.00	$13,252.02	$26,840.35	$40,365.88	$55,677.94	$56,517.49		$40,000.00	best profit	
3	lower 95%	$50,000.00	$69,474.63	$77,168.42	$66,428.10	$60,995.05	$45,287.01		$70,000.00	most risky	
4	upper 95%	$50,000.00	$71,117.37	$80,495.58	$71,431.90	$67,896.95	$52,292.99				
5											
6	mean profit	$50,000.00	$71,262.00	$78,370.00	$72,038.00	$63,354.00	$49,000.00		production		
7	SD profits	$0.00	$11,965.22	$28,801.26	$39,751.06	$55,414.09	$56,782.82		$40,000.00	best profit	
8	lower 95%	$50,000.00	$70,520.39	$76,584.88	$69,574.20	$59,919.40	$45,480.56		$70,000.00	most risky	
9	upper 95%	$50,000.00	$72,003.61	$80,155.12	$74,501.80	$66,788.60	$52,519.44				
10											
11	mean profit	$50,000.00	$70,548.00	$77,614.00	$71,576.00	$66,420.00	$50,680.00		production		
12	SD profits	$0.00	$12,935.65	$28,341.95	$40,085.85	$56,625.56	$55,594.93		$40,000.00	best profit	
13	lower 95%	$50,000.00	$69,746.24	$75,857.35	$69,091.45	$62,910.31	$47,234.19		$60,000.00	most risky	
14	upper 95%	$50,000.00	$71,349.76	$79,370.65	$74,060.55	$69,929.69	$54,125.81				
15											
16	mean profit	$50,000.00	$70,716.00	$76,606.00	$70,232.00	$60,582.00	$47,530.00		production		
17	SD profits	$0.00	$12,717.59	$28,274.59	$40,208.29	$54,406.41	$55,806.93		$40,000.00	best profit	
18	lower 95%	$50,000.00	$69,927.76	$74,853.52	$67,739.86	$57,209.86	$44,071.05		$70,000.00	most risky	
19	upper 95%	$50,000.00	$71,504.24	$78,358.48	$72,724.14	$63,954.14	$50,988.95				
20											
21	mean profit	$50,000.00	$70,254.00	$78,790.00	$69,644.00	$61,926.00	$45,472.00		production		
22	SD profits	$0.00	$13,303.55	$27,809.37	$40,192.74	$53,642.11	$55,508.22		$40,000.00	best profit	
23	lower 95%	$50,000.00	$69,429.44	$77,066.36	$67,152.83	$58,601.23	$42,031.56		$70,000.00	most risky	
24	upper 95%	$50,000.00	$71,078.56	$80,513.64	$72,135.17	$65,250.77	$48,912.44				
25											
26	mean profit	$50,000.00	$71,136.00	$77,446.00	$69,728.00	$63,354.00	$45,010.00		production		
27	SD profits	$0.00	$12,145.16	$28,519.58	$39,467.20	$54,482.17	$54,400.18		$40,000.00	best profit	
28	lower 95%	$50,000.00	$70,383.23	$75,678.34	$67,281.80	$59,977.16	$41,638.24		$60,000.00	most risky	
29	upper 95%	$50,000.00	$71,888.77	$79,213.66	$72,174.20	$66,730.84	$48,381.76				
30											
31		$50,000.00	$69,913.61	$76,201.48	$67,878.04	$59,935.50	$44,290.44				
32		$50,000.00	$71,490.39	$79,684.52	$72,837.96	$66,758.50	$51,203.56				

Chapter 38: Uncertainty in Sales

What the simulation does

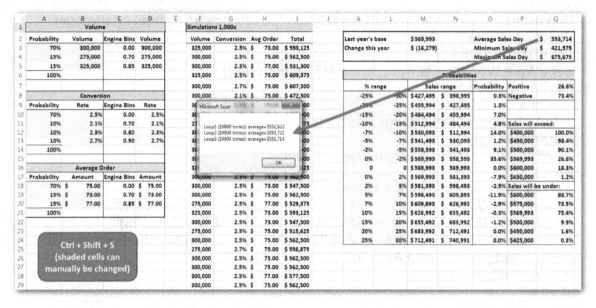

As said before, Monte Carlo simulations are computerized mathematical techniques that allow people to account for risks in quantitative analysis and decision making.

In this case, the decision-maker supplies sales data and probabilities (the shaded cells in columns A and B).

Based on this information, the macro simulates some 10,000 distributions with a range of possible outcomes (center section) and with the probabilities they will occur for any choice of action (right section).

At the end, a *MsgBox* reports for every new trial what the average sales are for each consecutive loop.The results are pretty close to each other.

What you need to know

The situation is basically simple. The major functions we need to achieve such kinds of predictions in this case are RAND, VLOOKUP, COUNT, and COUNTIF. Again we use 1,000 simulations in the center section (F:I) to reach more reliable predictions.

	A	B	C	D	E	F	G	H	I
1		Volume				Simulations 1,000x			
2		Probability	Volume	Engine Bins	Volume		Volume	Conversion	Avg Order	Total
3	0.7	300000	0	=B3	=VLOOKUP(RAND(),$C$3:$D$5,2)	=VLOOKUP(RAND(),$C$10:$D$13,2)	=VLOOKUP(RAND(),$C$18:$D$20,2)	=F3*G3*H3
4	0.15	275000	=C3+A3	=B4	=VLOOKUP(RAND(),$C$3:$D$5,2)	=VLOOKUP(RAND(),$C$10:$D$13,2)	=VLOOKUP(RAND(),$C$18:$D$20,2)	=F4*G4*H4
5	=A6-(SUM(A3:A4))	325000	=C4+A4	=B5	=VLOOKUP(RAND(),$C$3:$D$5,2)	=VLOOKUP(RAND(),$C$10:$D$13,2)	=VLOOKUP(RAND(),$C$18:$D$20,2)	=F5*G5*H5
6	1				=VLOOKUP(RAND(),$C$3:$D$5,2)	=VLOOKUP(RAND(),$C$10:$D$13,2)	=VLOOKUP(RAND(),$C$18:$D$20,2)	=F6*G6*H6
7					=VLOOKUP(RAND(),$C$3:$D$5,2)	=VLOOKUP(RAND(),$C$10:$D$13,2)	=VLOOKUP(RAND(),$C$18:$D$20,2)	=F7*G7*H7
8		Conversion			=VLOOKUP(RAND(),$C$3:$D$5,2)	=VLOOKUP(RAND(),$C$10:$D$13,2)	=VLOOKUP(RAND(),$C$18:$D$20,2)	=F8*G8*H8
9		Probability	Rate	Engine Bins	Rate	=VLOOKUP(RAND(),$C$3:$D$5,2)	=VLOOKUP(RAND(),$C$10:$D$13,2)	=VLOOKUP(RAND(),$C$18:$D$20,2)	=F9*G9*H9
10	0.7	0.025	0	=B10	=VLOOKUP(RAND(),$C$3:$D$5,2)	=VLOOKUP(RAND(),$C$10:$D$13,2)	=VLOOKUP(RAND(),$C$18:$D$20,2)	=F10*G10*H10
11	0.1	0.021	=C10+A10	=B11	=VLOOKUP(RAND(),$C$3:$D$5,2)	=VLOOKUP(RAND(),$C$10:$D$13,2)	=VLOOKUP(RAND(),$C$18:$D$20,2)	=F11*G11*H11
12	0.1	0.023	=C11+A11	=B12	=VLOOKUP(RAND(),$C$3:$D$5,2)	=VLOOKUP(RAND(),$C$10:$D$13,2)	=VLOOKUP(RAND(),$C$18:$D$20,2)	=F12*G12*H12
13	=A14-(SUM(A10:A12))	0.027	=C12+A12	=B13	=VLOOKUP(RAND(),$C$3:$D$5,2)	=VLOOKUP(RAND(),$C$10:$D$13,2)	=VLOOKUP(RAND(),$C$18:$D$20,2)	=F13*G13*H13
14	1				=VLOOKUP(RAND(),$C$3:$D$5,2)	=VLOOKUP(RAND(),$C$10:$D$13,2)	=VLOOKUP(RAND(),$C$18:$D$20,2)	=F14*G14*H14
15					=VLOOKUP(RAND(),$C$3:$D$5,2)	=VLOOKUP(RAND(),$C$10:$D$13,2)	=VLOOKUP(RAND(),$C$18:$D$20,2)	=F15*G15*H15
16		Average Order			=VLOOKUP(RAND(),$C$3:$D$5,2)	=VLOOKUP(RAND(),$C$10:$D$13,2)	=VLOOKUP(RAND(),$C$18:$D$20,2)	=F16*G16*H16
17		Probability	Amount	Engine Bins	Amount	=VLOOKUP(RAND(),$C$3:$D$5,2)	=VLOOKUP(RAND(),$C$10:$D$13,2)	=VLOOKUP(RAND(),$C$18:$D$20,2)	=F17*G17*H17
18	0.7	75	0	=B18	=VLOOKUP(RAND(),$C$3:$D$5,2)	=VLOOKUP(RAND(),$C$10:$D$13,2)	=VLOOKUP(RAND(),$C$18:$D$20,2)	=F18*G18*H18
19	0.15	73	=C18+A18	=B19	=VLOOKUP(RAND(),$C$3:$D$5,2)	=VLOOKUP(RAND(),$C$10:$D$13,2)	=VLOOKUP(RAND(),$C$18:$D$20,2)	=F19*G19*H19
20	=A21-(SUM(A18:A19))	77	=C19+A19	=B20	=VLOOKUP(RAND(),$C$3:$D$5,2)	=VLOOKUP(RAND(),$C$10:$D$13,2)	=VLOOKUP(RAND(),$C$18:$D$20,2)	=F20*G20*H20
21	1				=VLOOKUP(RAND(),$C$3:$D$5,2)	=VLOOKUP(RAND(),$C$10:$D$13,2)	=VLOOKUP(RAND(),$C$18:$D$20,2)	=F21*G21*H21
22					=VLOOKUP(RAND(),$C$3:$D$5,2)	=VLOOKUP(RAND(),$C$10:$D$13,2)	=VLOOKUP(RAND(),$C$18:$D$20,2)	=F22*G22*H22

What you need to do

```vba
Option Explicit

Sub SalesSimulation()
  Dim oRange As Range, oTable As Range, i As Long, n As Long, sMsg As String
  Set oRange = Range("F4").CurrentRegion
  With oRange
    Set oTable = .Offset(2, 0).Resize(.Rows.Count - 2, .Columns.Count)
  End With
  oTable.ClearContents
  n = InputBox("How many runs (1,000 to 100,000)?", , 10000)
  Set oTable = Range(Cells(3, 6), Cells(n, 9)) 'oTable.Offset(0, 0).Resize(n,
Columns.Count)
  oTable.Columns(1).Formula = "=VLOOKUP(RAND(),$C$3:$D$5,2)"
  oTable.Columns(2).Formula = "=VLOOKUP(RAND(),$C$10:$D$13,2)"
  oTable.Columns(3).Formula = "=VLOOKUP(RAND(),$C$18:$D$20,2)"
  oTable.Columns(4).Formula = "=F3*G3*H3"
  Do
    Application.Calculate
    i = i + 1
    sMsg = sMsg & "Loop" & i & " (" & n & " times): average="
    sMsg = sMsg & FormatCurrency(Range("Q2"), 0) & vbCr
    MsgBox sMsg
  Loop Until MsgBox("Run again?", vbYesNo) = vbNo
End Sub
```

	K	L	M	N	O	P	Q
1							
2	Last year's base	569993			Average Sales Day		=AVERAGE(I:I)
3	Change this year	=Q2-M2			Minimum Sales Day		=MIN(I:I)
4					Maximum Sales Day		=MAX(I:I)
5							
6					Probabilities		
7	% range		Sales range		Probability	Positive	=(COUNTIF(I:I,">"&M2)/(COUNT(I:I)))
8	-0.25	-0.3	=$M$2+($M$2*K8)	=$M$2+($M$2*L8)	=(COUNTIF(I:I,"<="&M8)-(COUNTIF(I:I,"<"&N8)))/(COUNT(I:I))	Negative	=(COUNTIF(I:I,"<"&M2)/(COUNT(I:I)))
9	-0.2	-0.25	=$M$2+($M$2*K9)	=$M$2+($M$2*L9)	=(COUNTIF(I:I,"<="&M9)-(COUNTIF(I:I,"<"&N9)))/(COUNT(I:I))		
10	-0.15	-0.2	=$M$2+($M$2*K10)	=$M$2+($M$2*L10)	=(COUNTIF(I:I,"<="&M10)-(COUNTIF(I:I,"<"&N10)))/(COUNT(I:I))		
11	-0.1	-0.15	=$M$2+($M$2*K11)	=$M$2+($M$2*L11)	=(COUNTIF(I:I,"<="&M11)-(COUNTIF(I:I,"<"&N11)))/(COUNT(I:I))	Sales will exceed:	
12	-0.07	-0.1	=$M$2+($M$2*K12)	=$M$2+($M$2*L12)	=(COUNTIF(I:I,"<="&M12)-(COUNTIF(I:I,"<"&N12)))/(COUNT(I:I))	400000	=(COUNTIF(I:I,">"&P12)/(COUNT(I:I)))
13	-0.05	-0.07	=$M$2+($M$2*K13)	=$M$2+($M$2*L13)	=(COUNTIF(I:I,"<="&M13)-(COUNTIF(I:I,"<"&N13)))/(COUNT(I:I))	450000	=(COUNTIF(I:I,">"&P13)/(COUNT(I:I)))
14	-0.02	-0.05	=$M$2+($M$2*K14)	=$M$2+($M$2*L14)	=(COUNTIF(I:I,"<="&M14)-(COUNTIF(I:I,"<"&N14)))/(COUNT(I:I))	500000	=(COUNTIF(I:I,">"&P14)/(COUNT(I:I)))
15	0	-0.02	=$M$2+($M$2*K15)	=$M$2+($M$2*L15)	=(COUNTIF(I:I,"<="&M15)-(COUNTIF(I:I,"<"&N15)))/(COUNT(I:I))	=M2	=(COUNTIF(I:I,">"&P15)/(COUNT(I:I)))
16	0	0	=$M$2+($M$2*K16)	=$M$2	=(COUNTIF(I:I,"<="&M16)-(COUNTIF(I:I,"<"&N16)))/(COUNT(I:I))	600000	=(COUNTIF(I:I,">"&P16)/(COUNT(I:I)))
17	0	0.02	=($M$2+($M$2*K17))	=$M$2+($M$2*L17)	=(COUNTIF(I:I,"<="&M17)-(COUNTIF(I:I,"<"&N17)))/(COUNT(I:I))	650000	=(COUNTIF(I:I,">"&P17)/(COUNT(I:I)))
18	0.02	0.05	=$M$2+($M$2*K18)	=$M$2+($M$2*L18)	=(COUNTIF(I:I,"<="&M18)-(COUNTIF(I:I,"<"&N18)))/(COUNT(I:I))	Sales will be under:	
19	0.05	0.07	=$M$2+($M$2*K19)	=$M$2+($M$2*L19)	=(COUNTIF(I:I,"<="&M19)-(COUNTIF(I:I,"<"&N19)))/(COUNT(I:I))	600000	=(COUNTIF(I:I,"<"&P19)/(COUNT(I:I)))
20	0.07	0.1	=$M$2+($M$2*K20)	=$M$2+($M$2*L20)	=(COUNTIF(I:I,"<="&M20)-(COUNTIF(I:I,"<"&N20)))/(COUNT(I:I))	575000	=(COUNTIF(I:I,"<"&P20)/(COUNT(I:I)))
21	0.1	0.15	=$M$2+($M$2*K21)	=$M$2+($M$2*L21)	=(COUNTIF(I:I,"<="&M21)-(COUNTIF(I:I,"<"&N21)))/(COUNT(I:I))	=M2	=(COUNTIF(I:I,"<"&P21)/(COUNT(I:I)))
22	0.15	0.2	=$M$2+($M$2*K22)	=$M$2+($M$2*L22)	=(COUNTIF(I:I,"<="&M22)-(COUNTIF(I:I,"<"&N22)))/(COUNT(I:I))	500000	=(COUNTIF(I:I,"<"&P22)/(COUNT(I:I)))
23	0.2	0.25	=$M$2+($M$2*K23)	=$M$2+($M$2*L23)	=(COUNTIF(I:I,"<="&M23)-(COUNTIF(I:I,"<"&N23)))/(COUNT(I:I))	450000	=(COUNTIF(I:I,"<"&P23)/(COUNT(I:I)))
24	0.25	0.3	=$M$2+($M$2*K24)	=$M$2+($M$2*L24)	=(COUNTIF(I:I,"<="&M24)-(COUNTIF(I:I,"<"&N24)))/(COUNT(I:I))	425000	=(COUNTIF(I:I,"<"&P24)/(COUNT(I:I)))
25							

Chapter 39: Exchange Rate Fluctuations

What the simulation does

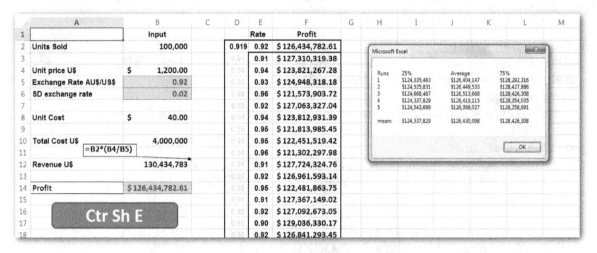

The profit of a certain company depends on a fluctuating exchange rate between the American and Australian dollar—or any other foreign currency. The average profit we predict in cell B14 is based on a fixed exchange rate (B5). But in reality this rate has normally distributed fluctuations with a Standard Deviation shown in cell B6. So we need to simulate such variations.

This simulation is done by using a *Data Table* combined with repeated calculations in arrays operating in the background. First the user is asked how many rows the *Data Table* should have—by default 1,000. The *Data Table* shows what the profits would be for different exchange rates.

The *MsgBox* displays what the average profit would be, plus the 25-percentile and 75-percentile profit values. Then the user has a chance to run the *Data Table* repeatedly. The results of each run are added to the *MsgBox*. When the user decides to stop any further runs, the average and two percentile values are calculated from all these runs. So the end result in the above picture is based on 10 x 1,000 normally distributed calculations.

What you need to know

An essential part of this simulation is the first column of the *Data Table* (column D). It holds this formula: =NORMINV(RAND(),0.92,0.02)—or whatever the fixed numeric values should be. In the macro we change these random settings from formulas to values, so those numbers don't keep changing while the *Data Table* makes its calculations.

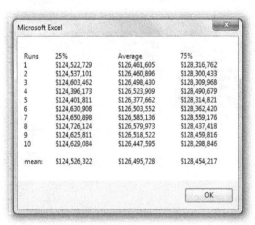

The column input cell of the *Data Table* is the exchange rate value in cell B5.

You also should know that we need variables of the *Double* type for mathematical calculations, but if we want to format them as currency, we need variables of the *String* type as well.

The three arrays we use must be "redimensioned" for a new element each time we run the loop. This is done with a *ReDim* statement, but make sure you include also the *Preserve* keyword, otherwise the array loses its previous contents.

What you need to do

```
Option Explicit

Sub ExchangeRates()
   Dim oRange As Range, iRuns As Long, i As Long, sMsg As String
   Dim arrAvg() As Double, arr25() As Double, arr75() As Double
   Dim pAvg As Double, p25 As Double, p75 As Double 'for the currencies
   Dim sAvg As String, s25 As String, s75 As String 'for the formatted currencies
   Range("D1").CurrentRegion.Offset(1, 0).ClearContents
   iRuns = InputBox("How many runs?", , 1000)
   Range("E2").Formula = "=B5"
   Range("F2").Formula = "=B14"
   Set oRange = Range(Range("D2"), Range("F2").Cells(iRuns, 1))
   oRange.Table , Range("B5")
   sMsg = "Runs" & vbTab & "25%" & vbTab & vbTab & "Average" & vbTab & vbTab &
"75%" & vbCr
   Do
      oRange.Columns(1).Formula = "=NORMINV(RAND(),$B$5,$B$6)"
      oRange.Columns(1).Formula = oRange.Columns(1).Value
      ReDim Preserve arrAvg(i): ReDim Preserve arr25(i): ReDim Preserve arr75(i)
      arrAvg(i) = WorksheetFunction.Average(oRange.Columns(3))
      arr25(i) = WorksheetFunction.Percentile(oRange.Columns(3), 0.25)
      arr75(i) = WorksheetFunction.Percentile(oRange.Columns(3), 0.75)
      sAvg = FormatCurrency(arrAvg(i), 0)
      s25 = FormatCurrency(arr25(i), 0)
      s75 = FormatCurrency(arr75(i), 0)
      sMsg = sMsg & i + 1 & vbTab & s25 & vbTab & sAvg & vbTab & s75 & vbCr
      i = i + 1
   Loop Until MsgBox(sMsg & "Run again?", vbYesNo) = vbNo
   pAvg = WorksheetFunction.Average(arrAvg): sAvg = FormatCurrency(pAvg, 0)
   p25 = WorksheetFunction.Percentile(arr25, 0.25): s25 = FormatCurrency(p25, 0)
   p75 = WorksheetFunction.Percentile(arr75, 0.75): s75 = FormatCurrency(p75, 0)
   sMsg = sMsg & vbCr & "mean:" & vbTab & s25 & vbTab & sAvg & vbTab & s75
   MsgBox sMsg
End Sub
```

IV. GENETICS

Chapter 40: Shuffling Chromosomes

What the simulation does

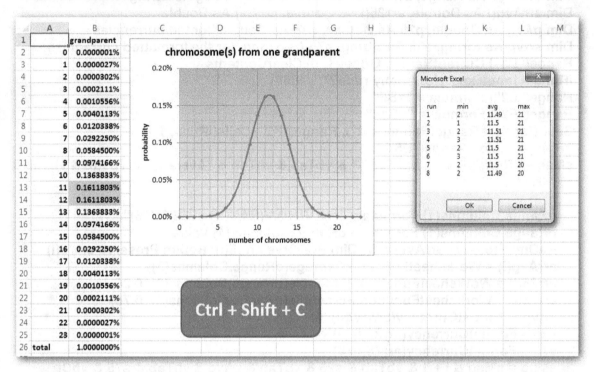

This simulation shows what the probability is that an individual still has chromosomes derived from one particular grandparent. Since we have 23 pairs of chromosomes, on average we have 11 or 12 chromosomes that were handed down to us from one particular grandparent, two generations ago—actually a 16% chance (row 13 and 14). But the outcome can vary between 0 chromosomes or the entire set of 23 chromosomes—but these extremes are very unlikely. Genetics, the science of inheritance of traits and characteristics, is modeled probabilistically.

As an aside, the situation is much more complicated. One problem is that chromosomes do not remain identical during the formation of reproductive cells, but they can exchange parts between the two of a pair—which is called crossing-over or recombination. In this simulation, we stay clear of that issue.

What you need to know

We will also use the new function BINOM.INV in this simulation. There is no pre-2010 version of this function, so if you use a file with this function in 2007, you will get an error message. In Excel 2007, an alternative would be CRITBINOM.

Cells B2:B25 hold this formula: =BINOMDIST(A2,23,0.5,0)/100. BINOMDIST needs to know the number of "successes" (running from 0 to 23 in column A), out of 23 trials (23 chromosomes), with a 50% probability of "success" in each trial, and with a non-cumulative setting in our case. Make sure to divide by 100.

What you need to do

```
Option Explicit

Sub Chromosomes()
   Dim pArr() As Double, i As Long, n As Long, sMsg As String
   Dim pAvg As Double, pMin As Double, pMax As Double, pCount As Long
   sMsg = sMsg & "run" & vbTab & "min" & vbTab & "avg" & vbTab & "max" & vbCr
   Do
      For i = 0 To 100000
         ReDim Preserve pArr(i)
         pArr(i) = WorksheetFunction.Binom_Inv(23, 0.5, Rnd)
      Next i
      n = n + 1
      pAvg = FormatNumber(WorksheetFunction.Average(pArr), 2)
      pMin = WorksheetFunction.Min(pArr)
      pMax = WorksheetFunction.Max(pArr)
      pCount = UBound(pArr)
      sMsg = sMsg & n & vbTab & pMin & vbTab & pAvg & vbTab & pMax & vbCr
   Loop Until MsgBox(sMsg, vbOKCancel) = vbCancel
End Sub
```

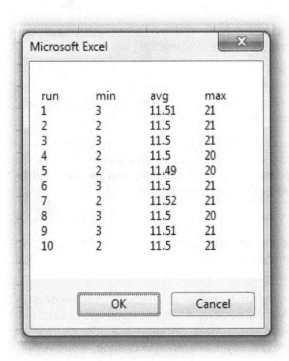

run	min	avg	max
1	3	11.51	21
2	2	11.5	21
3	3	11.5	21
4	2	11.5	20
5	2	11.49	20
6	3	11.5	21
7	2	11.52	21
8	3	11.5	20
9	3	11.51	21
10	2	11.5	21

Chapter 41: Sex Determination

What the simulation does

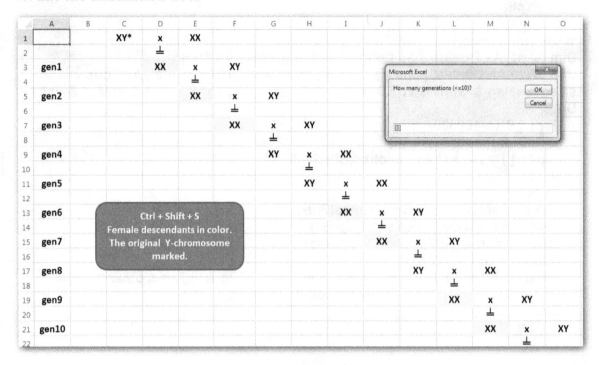

This sheet simulates what happens when a father (XY) and a mother (XX) have one descendant, who has in turn another descendant, and so forth. It is something like a family tree.

If the descendant is a female (XX), that cell gets marked with a color. If the descendant still has the original Y-chromosome (Y*) from the (great-great-grand-) father, that chromosome is marked with an asterix (*). In the figure above, there happen to be seven female descendants, and the ancestral Y-chromosome got already "lost" by mere chance in the first generation.

The macro asks the user first how many generations they want to simulate (the maximum is set to 10). The macro keeps asking that question by calling itself again, and it does so until the user hits the *Cancel* button of the *Inputbox*. It is possible, by mere change, that the paternal X-chromosome persists for six generations (see picture below)—or even longer.

What you need to know

One of the 23 pairs of chromosomes is called the sex-chromosome pair. It either holds two similar chromosomes (XX) or two unalike chromosomes (XY; Y is actually a very short chromosome). The presence of the Y-chromosome determines maleness.

The father (XY) produces sperm cells with either an X-chromosome (50% chance) or a Y-chromosome (50% chance). If the egg cell—which has always one X-chromosome—is fertilized by a sperm cell with a Y-chromosome, the descendant will be a male. So there is a 50% chance for either a male or a female descendant (in reality, there is a slight difference in chance, though).

What you need to do

```
Option Explicit

Sub Sex()
  Dim r As Integer, c As Integer, sGens As String, oCell As Range
  sGens = InputBox("How many generations (<=10)?", , 10, 10000, 2000)
  If sGens = "" Then Exit Sub
  If CInt(sGens) > 10 Then MsgBox "Not more than 10": Exit Sub
  For Each oCell In Range("D3:O22")
    If oCell = "XX" Or oCell = "XY" Or oCell = "XY*" Then
      oCell.ClearContents: oCell.Interior.ColorIndex = 0
    End If
  Next oCell
  c = 3
  For r = 3 To (2 * CInt(sGens) + 1) Step 2
    c = c + 1
    Cells(r, c) = IIf(Rnd > 0.5, "XX", IIf(Cells(r - 2, c - 1) = "XY*", "XY*", "XY"))
    Cells(r, c + 2) = IIf(Cells(r, c) = "XX", "XY", "XX")
    If Cells(r, c) = "XX" Then
      Cells(r, c).Interior.Color = vbYellow
    Else
      Cells(r, c).Interior.ColorIndex = 0
    End If
  Next r
  Call Sex 'the Sub calls itself again
End Sub
```

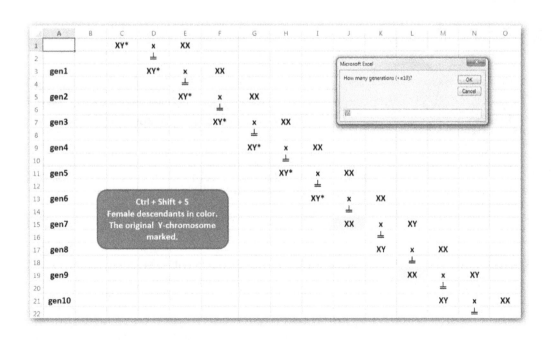

Chapter 42: Mendelian Laws

What the simulation does

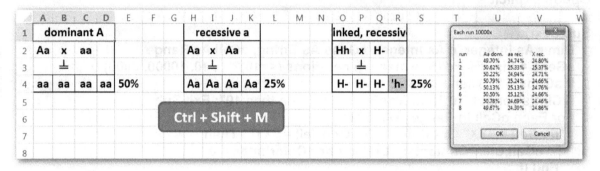

Certain diseases, such as a particular form of dwarfism, are based on a *dominant* allele (say, *A*). Anyone who carries such an allele (*Aa*) is called a heterozygote and has the disease.

Other diseases, such as cystic fibrosis, are based on a *recessive* allele (say, *a*). Only people with two of those alleles (*aa*) show the disease and is called a homozygote. So someone can be a carrier (*Aa*) of the disease without showing its symptoms.

Then there are also diseases, such as a known form of hemophilia, that are called sex-linked because they are based on a recessive allele (say, *h*) located on the X-chromosome; such alleles come always to expression in males (XY)—because there is no second chromosome to counteract it—but in females (XX) only when both X-chromosomes have that recessive allele.

The simulation applies Mendelian laws each time for 10,000 cases. Because of such a large sample, the results come very close to what we would expect. Besides, the user can repeat these 10,000 runs again and again. There will be differences, but they fluctuate within a very narrow margin (see below). All of this is based on simple Mendelian rules.

What you need to know

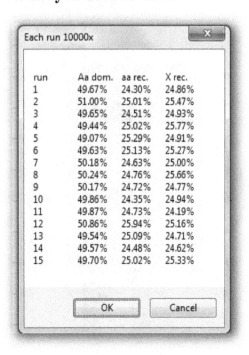

This sheet simulates the chances for passing on such an allele to the next generation. When the allele does come to expression, it is marked with conditional formatting. Because conditional formatting cannot distinguish between lowercase and uppercase characters—it's not case sensitive—we need to mark the capital with an apostrophe, or something like it.

The first case: Parents with *Aa* and *aa* have 50% *Aa* children and 50% *aa* children. The chance that a dominant allele (*A*) from such parents comes to expression in the next generation is 50%.

The second case: The offspring of parents who are both *Aa* is *AA* (25%), *Aa* (50%), and *aa* (25%). The chance that a recessive allele (*a*) comes to expression in the next generation is 25% (*aa*).

The third case: The offspring of a mother with *Hh* and a father with *H-* would be *HH* (25%), *Hh* (25%), *H-* (25%), and *h-* (25%). The chance that a recessive, X-linked allele (*h*) comes to expression in the next generation is therefore 25% (*h-*).

What you need to do

```
Option Explicit

Sub Mendel()
   Dim arrDom() As Variant, arrRec() As Variant, arrX() As Variant '3 arrays
   Dim iDom As Long, iRec As Long, iX As Long, i As Long, n As Long, sMsg As
String
   sMsg = "run" & vbTab & "Aa dom." & vbTab & "aa rec." & vbTab & "X rec." & vbCr
Again:
   n = n + 1
   sMsg = sMsg & n & vbTab
   For i = 0 To 10000
      ReDim Preserve arrDom(i)
      arrDom(i) = IIf(Rnd < 0.5, "'Aa", "aa")
      If arrDom(i) = "'Aa" Then iDom = iDom + 1
   Next i
   sMsg = sMsg & FormatPercent(iDom / 10000, 2) & vbTab
   For i = 0 To 10000
      ReDim Preserve arrRec(i)
      arrRec(i) = IIf(Rnd < 0.5, "'AA", IIf(Rnd < 0.5, "Aa", "'aa"))
      If arrRec(i) = "'aa" Then iRec = iRec + 1
   Next i
   sMsg = sMsg & FormatPercent(iRec / 10000, 2) & vbTab
   For i = 0 To 10000
      ReDim Preserve arrX(i)
      arrX(i) = IIf(Rnd < 0.25, "HH", IIf(Rnd < 0.33, "H'h", IIf(Rnd < 0.5, "H-", "'h-")))
      If arrX(i) = "'h-" Then iX = iX + 1
   Next i
   sMsg = sMsg & FormatPercent(iX / 10000, 2) & vbCr

   If MsgBox(sMsg, vbOKCancel, "Each run 10000x") = vbOK Then
      iDom = 0: iRec = 0: iX = 0
      GoTo Again
   End If
End Sub
```

Chapter 43: The Hardy-Weinberg Law

What the simulation does

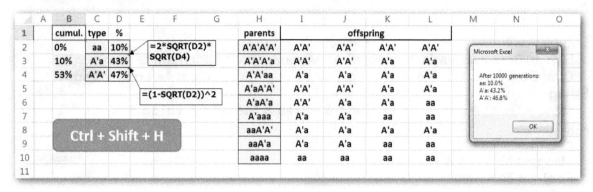

A gene can carry various alleles. Let us assume there are only two alleles, *A* and *a*. People who have two of the same alleles are homozygotes (*AA* or *aa*). Those who carry both alleles are heterozygotes (*Aa*). Let us take the example of an allele for albinism (*a*), which is recessive, so albinos must be *aa*, whereas individuals with the genotypes *AA* and *Aa* are not albinos. If we know the percentage (q^2) of albinos (*aa*), we can calculate the frequency q of allele *a*, as well as the frequency p of allele *A*—provided there are no other alleles—since $p=1-q$.

As a consequence, the frequency would be p^2 for the homozygotes *AA* (cell D4), q^2 for the homozygotes *aa* (cell D2), and *2pq* for the heterozygotes (in cell D3: *pq* for *Aa* and *qp* for *aA*). So if we know that *aa* has a frequency of 10%, we can deduce what the frequencies are for *Aa* and *AA* (see the comments in those cells shown in the figure above).

What you need to know

The Hardy-Weinberg law states that if these genotypes would *randomly* mate, the frequencies would stay the same in the next generations. We are going to simulate this with a macro. We know, based on Mendelian laws, what the offspring would be of certain pairs of parents (see H1:L10). The macro is going to randomly make these combinations and randomly determine what their offspring would be. The result, based on 10,000 runs, is displayed in a *MsgBox*. Notice how the frequencies in the next generation are extremely close to the frequencies of the parent generation—which is exactly what the Hardy-Weinberg law states.

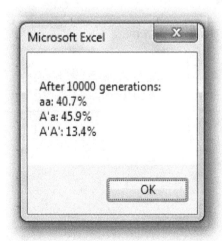

The VLOOKUP function plays an important role in this simulation. It finds randomly the genotype of each parent and then finds randomly (with a random number between 2 and 5) the child's genotype in one of the 2nd to 5th columns of range H:L.

If we change the frequency of *aa* to 40%, the next generation will more or less keep that frequency because of random mating. Obviously, the total of the frequencies should be 100%

What you need to do

```
Option Explicit

Sub HardyWeinberg()
    Dim arrMales() As String, arrFemales() As String, arrChildren() As String
    Dim iHomDom As Long, iHetero As Long, iHomRec As Long
    Dim i As Long, pRec As Double, iRnd As Integer, sMsg As String, iCount As Long
    pRec = InputBox("Frequency of aa", , 0.1)
    Range("D2") = pRec
    ReDim arrMales(0 To 10000)
    ReDim arrFemales(0 To 10000)
    ReDim arrChildren(0 To 10000)
    For i = 0 To 10000
        arrMales(i) = WorksheetFunction.VLookup(Rnd, Range("B2:C4"), 2, 1)
        arrFemales(i) = WorksheetFunction.VLookup(Rnd, Range("B2:C4"), 2, 1)
        iRnd = WorksheetFunction.RandBetween(2, 5)
        arrChildren(i) = WorksheetFunction.VLookup(arrMales(i) & arrFemales(i),
Range("H2:L10"), iRnd, False)
        If arrChildren(i) = "A'A'" Then iHomDom = iHomDom + 1
        If arrChildren(i) = "A'a" Then iHetero = iHetero + 1
        If arrChildren(i) = "aa" Then iHomRec = iHomRec + 1
    Next i
    iCount = UBound(arrChildren)
    sMsg = "After " & iCount & " generations:" & vbCr
    sMsg = sMsg & "aa: " & FormatPercent(iHomRec / iCount, 1) & vbCr
    sMsg = sMsg & "A'a: " & FormatPercent(iHetero / iCount, 1) & vbCr
    sMsg = sMsg & "A'A': " & FormatPercent(iHomDom / iCount, 1)
    MsgBox sMsg
End Sub
```

Chapter 44: Genetic Drift

What the simulation does

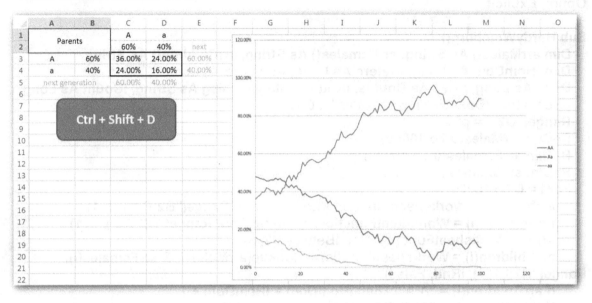

The Hardy-Weinberg law (see Chapter 44) states that allele frequencies remain the same over the next generations. Even in case of a recessive allele, it will not entirely disappear. However, by random chance, the percentage of alleles may, and usually does, change in the next generations. This is called "genetic drift." The effect increases when the population size decreases—the so-called "founder effect."

The macro simulates the effect of genetic drift during 50 generations assuming that the frequencies randomly fluctuate by a certain percentage. The macro asks the users which "drift factor" they want to apply (by default 2% for each generation). During this ongoing process, recessive homozygotes (*aa*) may eventually, by mere chance, disappear from stage, to the advantage of the dominant homozygotes (*AA*). This happened in the picture above.

The macro does part of its work by temporarily using the range D8:D108, which it deletes later. It is through this range that curves can be plotted in a chart. Because a chart cannot display anything after its source data are deleted, we change the chart into a picture before the macro deletes its source data.

What you need to know

If the frequency of allele *A* is 0.6 (=*p*), then the frequency of allele *a* must be 1-0.6 = 0.4 (=*q*)—assuming there are only two alleles for this gen. So the frequency of genotype *AA* would be p^2 and the frequency of genotype *aa* would be q^2. The frequency of *Aa* and *aA* would then be *2pq*.

The VBA code also uses some form of so-called Error Handling (see Appendix). The simplest version of Error Handling is the following VBA line: *On Error Resume Next*. When some error occurs, this line skips over the line that caused the error, and executes the next line in the VBA code. That can easily be troubling, though. That's why it is better to use a more robust kind of Error Handling: *On Error GoTo [label]*. The label is something you chose (in our case: *ErrTrap*). Place that label at the end after *Exit Sub* but before *End Sub*. Usually after the label, we place a line that is based on the *Err* object, which deals with the latest error. One option is: *MsgBox Err.Description*, which tells the user what the actual error was. It is always wise to have some kind of Error Handling in every macro you create. (I skipped this part for most macros in this book.)

What you need to do

```vba
Option Explicit

Sub Drifting()
    Dim pDrift As Double, i As Long, oRange As Range, oChart As Chart, oShape As Shape
    On Error GoTo ErrTrap
    pDrift = InputBox("Drift factor", , 0.02)
    Set oRange = Range("A8:A108")
    oRange.Formula = "=ROW(A1)-1"
    Range("B7") = "AA"
    Range("B8").Formula = "=C3"
    Range("C7") = "Aa"
    Range("C8").Formula = "=C4+D3"
    Range("D7") = "aa"
    Range("D8").Formula = "=D4"
    Set oRange = Range("B9:B108")
    oRange.Formula = "=NORMINV(RAND(),B8," & pDrift & ")"
    Set oRange = Range("C9", "C108")
    oRange.Formula = "=IFERROR(2*SQRT(B9)*(1-SQRT(B9)),NA())"
    Set oRange = Range("D9:D108")
    oRange.Formula = "=IFERROR((1-SQRT(B9))^2,NA())"
    Set oRange = Range("B7").CurrentRegion
    Set oChart = Charts.Add
    oChart.SetSourceData oRange
    oChart.ChartType = xlXYScatterLinesNoMarkers
    Sheets(1).Select
    ActiveChart.ChartArea.Copy
    Sheets(2).Select
    ActiveSheet.PasteSpecial Format:="Picture (JPEG)"
    Selection.ShapeRange.ScaleWidth 0.8, msoFalse
    Selection.ShapeRange.ScaleHeight 0.8, msoFalse
    Selection.ShapeRange.IncrementLeft 100
    Selection.ShapeRange.IncrementTop 100
    Application.DisplayAlerts = False
    Sheets(1).Delete
    oRange.Clear
    Application.DisplayAlerts = True
    Exit Sub
ErrTrap:
    Err.Clear
End Sub
```

Chapter 45: Two Selective Forces

What the simulation does

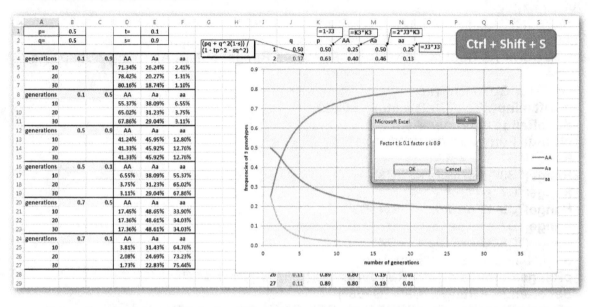

It is rather common that both alleles have a selection factor working against them; let's designate those two factors with the symbols *s* and *t*. The most well-known case is sickle-cell anemia. Because there is strong selection pressure (*s*) against the homozygote (*aa*), who suffers from anemia, we would expect allele *a* to disappear from the population. However, in malaria areas it has a rather stable frequency (*q*). The explanation is that there is also a selection pressure (*t*) against the other homozygote (*AA*), who is more vulnerable to malaria than the other individuals, especially the heterozygotes (*Aa*).

Our simulation loops through six different settings for the selective factors *s* and *t*, shown in range A4:F27. The first two settings come close to the situation for sickle-cell anemia; the first one is shown in the figure above, where we see the frequencies of the heterozygotes increase at the cost of both types of homozygotes.

What you need to know

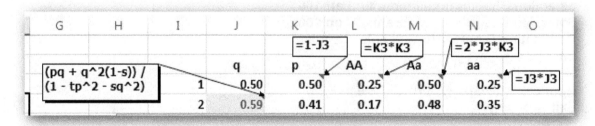

The columns J:N calculate frequencies for 33 generations (from row 2 to row 35). See the formulas here above. The columns D:F derive their information from the calculations in these columns (J:N).

What you need to do

```vba
Option Explicit

Sub Selecting()
   Dim i As Integer, n As Integer, oRange As Range, j As Integer
   Set oRange = Range("D4:F27")
   For i = 1 To 24
     If i Mod 4 <> 1 Then oRange.Range(Cells(i, 1), Cells(i, 4)).ClearContents
   Next i
   MsgBox "This starts looping through 6 settings for t and s."
   For i = 4 To 24 Step 4
      Range("E1") = Cells(i, 2)
      Range("E2") = Cells(i, 3)
      For n = 1 To 3
         Set oRange = Range(Cells(i + n, 4), Cells(i + n, 6))
         oRange.FormulaArray = "=INDEX(L2:N34," & Cells(i + n, 1) & ",0)"
         oRange.NumberFormat = "0.00%"
         oRange.Formula = oRange.Value
      Next n
      If MsgBox("Factor t is " & Range("E1") & " factor s is " & _
            Range("E2"), vbOKCancel) = vbCancel Then Exit Sub
   Next i
End Sub
```

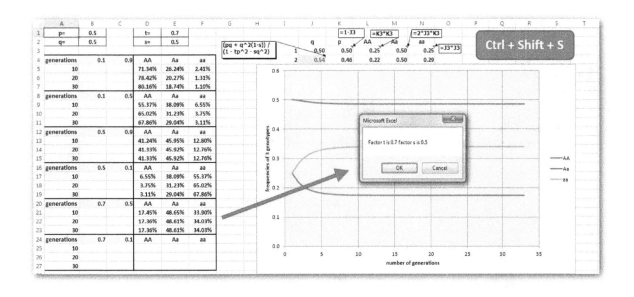

Chapter 46: Differential Fitness

What the simulation does

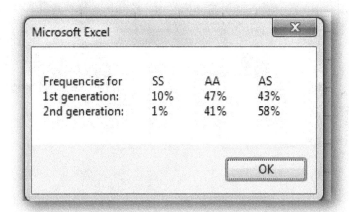

This simulation is similar to the previous one. Again, we assign relative fitness factors—for instance, genotype AS (fitness factor 1 in cell M4) is more "fit" than genotype SS (fitness factor 0.4 in cell). So gradually, up to a certain point, the frequency of AS will increase, while the frequency of genotype SS (sickle cell anemia, for instance) will decrease in future generations.

All the gray cells on the sheet have formulas in it. We assume that each combination of parents has up to 4 children each generation (columns F:I). Most formulas are identical to the ones used in Chapter 45. The main difference is that the range P2:S10 is based on the different fitness factors for each genotype. The offspring is not only determined by Mendel's laws but also by the fitness of that specific genotype. That's why certain cells remain empty in P2:S10.

This will obviously affect frequencies in the next generation. The simulation calculates the average frequencies of the three genotypes based on 10,000 couples with each couple having up to 4 children. The simulation calculates the results for the next generation and compares them with the original frequencies in the 1st generation of the parents. It is to be expected that there is a change of frequencies—but again, not always, for there is still randomness involved. Sometimes, the effect is quite dramatic (see the picture below).

Microsoft Excel				X
Frequencies for	SS	AA	AS	
1st generation:	10%	47%	43%	
2nd generation:	1%	41%	58%	
			OK	

What you need to know

Only the gray cells on the sheet have formulas in it; the rest is manual input. To mark the cells with formulas in them, conditional formatting can be a helpful tool. Select all the cells and then use conditional formatting with the following formula: =ISFORMULA(A1). The function ISFORMULA came available in more recent versions of Excel.

What you need to do

```
Option Explicit

Sub Fitness()
    Dim arrParents() As String, arrChild() As String, i As Long, sMsg As String
    Dim pFreqAA As Double, pFreqAS As Double, pFreqSS As Double
    Dim pAA As Double, pAS As Double, pSS As Double, iCount As Long, iBlank As
Long
    pFreqSS = Range("D2")
    pFreqAA = Range("D3")
    pFreqAS = Range("D4")
    sMsg = "Frequencies for" & vbTab & "SS" & vbTab & "AA" & vbTab & "AS" & vbCr
    sMsg = sMsg & "1st generation: " & vbTab & FormatPercent(pFreqSS, 0) & vbTab &
FormatPercent(pFreqAA, 0) & vbTab & FormatPercent(pFreqAS, 0) & vbCr
    Range("P2:S10") = ""
    Range("P2:S10").Formula = "=IF(RAND()<VLOOKUP(G2,$L$2:$M$4,2,0),G2,"""")"
    For i = 0 To 10000
        ReDim Preserve arrParents(i)
        ReDim Preserve arrChild(i)
        arrParents(i) = WorksheetFunction.VLookup(Rnd, Range("B2:C4"), 2, 1) &
WorksheetFunction.VLookup(Rnd, Range("B2:C4"), 2, 1)
        arrChild(i) = IIf(WorksheetFunction.RandBetween(0, 6) > 1,
WorksheetFunction.VLookup(arrParents(i), Range("O2:S10"),
WorksheetFunction.RandBetween(2, 5), False), "")
        If arrChild(i) = "AA" Then pAA = pAA + 1
        If arrChild(i) = "AS" Then pAS = pAS + 1
        If arrChild(i) = "SS" Then pSS = pSS + 1
        If arrChild(i) = "" Then iBlank = iBlank + 1
    Next i
    iCount = UBound(arrChild) - iBlank
    sMsg = sMsg & "2nd generation: " & vbTab & FormatPercent(pSS / iCount, 0) &
vbTab & FormatPercent(pAA / iCount, 0) & vbTab & FormatPercent(pAS / iCount, 0) &
vbCr
    'For more generations, Range("D2") needs to be reset to (pSS/iCount)
    MsgBox sMsg
End Sub
```

Chapter 47: Molecular Clock

What the simulation does

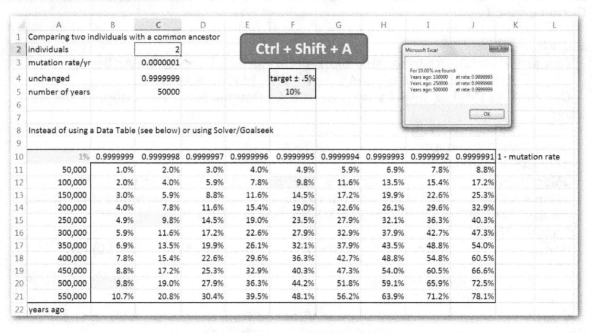

	A	B	C	D	E	F	G	H	I	J	K	L
1	Comparing two individuals with a common ancestor											
2	individuals		2									
3	mutation rate/yr		0.0000001									
4	unchanged		0.9999999			target ± .5%						
5	number of years		50000			10%						
6												
7												
8	Instead of using a Data Table (see below) or using Solver/Goalseek											
9												
10	1%	0.9999999	0.9999998	0.9999997	0.9999996	0.9999995	0.9999994	0.9999993	0.9999992	0.9999991	1 - mutation rate	
11	50,000	1.0%	2.0%	3.0%	4.0%	4.9%	5.9%	6.9%	7.8%	8.8%		
12	100,000	2.0%	4.0%	5.9%	7.8%	9.8%	11.6%	13.5%	15.4%	17.2%		
13	150,000	3.0%	5.9%	8.8%	11.6%	14.5%	17.2%	19.9%	22.6%	25.3%		
14	200,000	4.0%	7.8%	11.6%	15.4%	19.0%	22.6%	26.1%	29.6%	32.9%		
15	250,000	4.9%	9.8%	14.5%	19.0%	23.5%	27.9%	32.1%	36.3%	40.3%		
16	300,000	5.9%	11.6%	17.2%	22.6%	27.9%	32.9%	37.9%	42.7%	47.3%		
17	350,000	6.9%	13.5%	19.9%	26.1%	32.1%	37.9%	43.5%	48.8%	54.0%		
18	400,000	7.8%	15.4%	22.6%	29.6%	36.3%	42.7%	48.8%	54.8%	60.5%		
19	450,000	8.8%	17.2%	25.3%	32.9%	40.3%	47.3%	54.0%	60.5%	66.6%		
20	500,000	9.8%	19.0%	27.9%	36.3%	44.2%	51.8%	59.1%	65.9%	72.5%		
21	550,000	10.7%	20.8%	30.4%	39.5%	48.1%	56.2%	63.9%	71.2%	78.1%		
22	years ago											

Genes may undergo changes, called mutations. Mutations to non-essential portions of the DNA are useful for measuring time—the so-called molecular clock. It is assumed that such mutations occur with a uniform probability per unit of time in a particular portion of DNA, because they are not exposed to selection. If P is the percentage of *no*-mutations in a year, then P^N is the probability of *no*-mutations over N years.

On average, given two individuals who had a common ancestor many generations ago, you would expect—assuming that mutations are so rare that it is very unlikely that a mutation in the same segment has occurred in two individuals—that the percentage of segments that are mutated in one or the other is, on average, $2(1 - P^N)$. This is an estimate of the percentage of segments to be found different when comparing two individuals with a common ancestor N years ago.

This macro provides a simplified version of the technique that has been used to locate the first common ancestors of all human beings in evolution—the first female and the first male, so to speak. Non-essential DNA sections can be tested for single-nucleotide-polymorphisms (SNPs, pronounced "snips"), which are single base pair changes in DNA that occur throughout the genome, including its "silent" DNA sections.

What you need to know

Place in cell C6: =2*(1-C4^C5). This is the mutation percentage after a certain numbers of years this case 50,000 years as shown in cell C4).

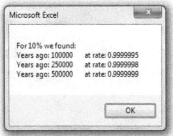

Notice the following: If two individuals have a 10% difference, their most recent common ancestor lived 100,000 years ago if the mutation rate for those DNA segments is 0.9999995, but 250,000 years ago based on a rate of 0.9999998, or even 50,000 years ago based on a rate of 0.9999999. So small differences in mutation rate can have an enormous impact. Apparently, the accuracy of the molecular clock depends heavily on the accuracy of the mutation rate.

What you need to do

```
Option Explicit

Sub Ancestry()
    Dim pTarget As Double, sTarget As String, pPerc As Double, iStepYrs As Long
    Dim iUnchanged As Long, iYrs As Double, iRate As Double, sMsg As String
    sTarget = InputBox("Percentage of DNA difference?", , "10%")
    If Right(sTarget, 1) <> "%" Then sTarget = sTarget & "%"
    pTarget = Left(sTarget, Len(sTarget) - 1) / 100
    Range("F5") = sTarget 'OR: FormatPercent(pTarget, 2)
    iStepYrs = Range("C5")
    iUnchanged = Range("C4") * 10000000
    sMsg = "For " & sTarget & " we found:" & vbCr
    For iYrs = iStepYrs To (iStepYrs + 10 * iStepYrs) Step iStepYrs
        For iRate = (iUnchanged - 8) To iUnchanged
            pPerc = 2 * (1 - (iRate / 10000000) ^ iYrs)
            If pPerc < (pTarget + 0.005) And pPerc > (pTarget - 0.005) Then
                sMsg = sMsg & "Years ago: " & iYrs & vbTab & "at rate: " & iRate / 10000000
& vbCr
            End If
        Next iRate
    Next iYrs
    If Len(sMsg) < 25 Then sMsg = sMsg & "No results"
    MsgBox sMsg
End Sub
```

	A	B	C	D	E	F	G
1	Comparing two individuals with a						
2	individuals		2			Ctrl + Shift + A	
3	mutation rate/yr		0.0000001				
4	unchanged		=1-C3			target ± .5%	
5	number of years		50000			0.95	
6							
7							
8	Either using a Data Table (see belo						
9		=2*(1-C4^C5)					
10	=2*(1-C4^C5)	0.9999999	0.9999998	0.9999997	0.9999996	0.9999995	0.9999994
11	50000	=TABLE(C4,C5)	=TABLE(C4,C5)	=TABLE(C4,C5)	=TABLE(C4,C5)	=TABLE(C4,C5)	=TABLE(C4,C
12	100000	=TABLE(C4,C5)	=TABLE(C4,C5)	=TABLE(C4,C5)	=TABLE(C4,C5)	=TABLE(C4,C5)	=TABLE(C4,C
13	150000	=TABLE(C4,C5)	=TABLE(C4,C5)	=TABLE(C4,C5)	=TABLE(C4,C5)	=TABLE(C4,C5)	=TABLE(C4,C
14	200000	=TABLE(C4,C5)	=TABLE(C4,C5)	=TABLE(C4,C5)	=TABLE(C4,C5)	=TABLE(C4,C5)	=TABLE(C4,C
15	250000	=TABLE(C4,C5)	=TABLE(C4,C5)	=TABLE(C4,C5)	=TABLE(C4,C5)	=TABLE(C4,C5)	=TABLE(C4,C
16	300000	=TABLE(C4,C5)	=TABLE(C4,C5)	=TABLE(C4,C5)	=TABLE(C4,C5)	=TABLE(C4,C5)	=TABLE(C4,C
17	350000	=TABLE(C4,C5)	=TABLE(C4,C5)	=TABLE(C4,C5)	=TABLE(C4,C5)	=TABLE(C4,C5)	=TABLE(C4,C
18	400000	=TABLE(C4,C5)	=TABLE(C4,C5)	=TABLE(C4,C5)	=TABLE(C4,C5)	=TABLE(C4,C5)	=TABLE(C4,C
19	450000	=TABLE(C4,C5)	=TABLE(C4,C5)	=TABLE(C4,C5)	=TABLE(C4,C5)	=TABLE(C4,C5)	=TABLE(C4,C
20	500000	=TABLE(C4,C5)	=TABLE(C4,C5)	=TABLE(C4,C5)	=TABLE(C4,C5)	=TABLE(C4,C5)	=TABLE(C4,C
21	550000	=TABLE(C4,C5)	=TABLE(C4,C5)	=TABLE(C4,C5)	=TABLE(C4,C5)	=TABLE(C4,C5)	=TABLE(C4,C
22	years ago						

Ancestry   (+)

Chapter 48: DNA Sequencing

What the simulation does

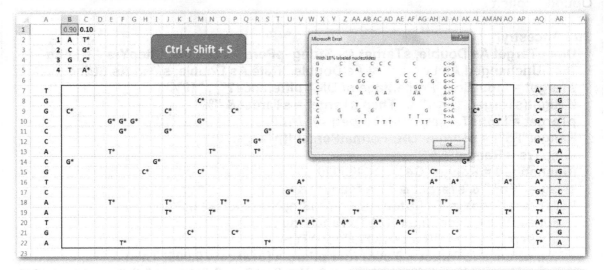

This is a very simple simulation of what was done in the Human Genome Project. Today, "dideoxy sequencing" is the method of choice to sequence very long strands of DNA. DNA is composed of 4 different nucleotides—A, C, G, and T. The composition of a DNA string is randomly generated in column A. It is clear that this composition is not known yet until we use a technique in the middle section that we are going to describe soon. The end result is shown in the columns AQ and AR by using formulas on the sheet, but the macro also does this work in the background and then displays the outcome in a *MsgBox*.

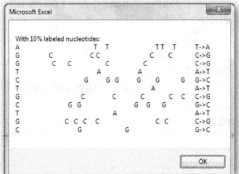

What you need to know

To determine the unknown sequence of nucleotides in a DNA section of interest, the double-stranded DNA is separated into single strands (denaturation). In the next step, a new DNA strand is made, complementary to the template strand, by using the bacterial enzyme DNA polymerase. During this step, A-nucleotides will be "paired" with T-nucleotides, and C-nucleotides with G-nucleotides—they are called complementary.

Then follows a key step. In addition to the four regular single nucleotides, the reaction mixture also contains small amounts of four dideoxy-nucleotides which lack a group necessary for chain extension. Once in a while—by low chance, because of its much lower concentration—a dideoxy-nucleotide will be incorporated into the growing DNA strand instead of the regular nucleotide. This will prevent the DNA chain from growing further. Since each of these four special nucleotides is labeled with a different fluorescent dye, a certain type of laser can later detect them. We marked them with an asterix (*) in our simulation.

So DNA chains end up being very short, very long, and of every possible length in between. The newly synthesized DNA strands are then passed through a laser beam that excites the fluorescent dye attached to the dideoxy-nucleotide at the end of each strand. This color is then detected by a photocell, which feeds the information to a computer. Finally, the computer does the rest of the work by piecing the short sequences together like a puzzle.

What you need to do

```
Option Explicit

Sub Sequencing()
    Dim pNoLabel As Double, i As Integer, j As Integer, sMsg As String
    Dim arrDNA() As String, arrStrand() As String, sNucl As String, bFound As Boolean
    pNoLabel = InputBox("Choose % unlabeled between 0.85 and 0.95", , 0.9)
    If pNoLabel > 0.95 Then Exit Sub
    Range("B1") = pNoLabel
    sMsg = "With " & FormatPercent(1 - pNoLabel, 0) & " labeled nucleotides:" & vbCr
    ReDim arrDNA(0 To 10)
    For i = 0 To 10
        arrDNA(i) = WorksheetFunction.VLookup(WorksheetFunction.RandBetween(1, 4),
Range("A2:B5"), 2, 0)
        sMsg = sMsg & arrDNA(i) & vbTab
        ReDim arrStrand(0 To 39)
        For j = 0 To 39
            arrStrand(j) = IIf(Rnd > Range("B1"),
Left(WorksheetFunction.VLookup(arrDNA(i), Range("B2:C5"), 2, 0), 1), " ")
            If arrStrand(j) <> " " Then sNucl = arrStrand(j): bFound = True
        Next j
        sMsg = sMsg & Join(arrStrand) & vbTab
        sMsg = sMsg & IIf(bFound, sNucl, "-") & "->" & arrDNA(i) & vbCr
        sNucl = "": bFound = False
    Next i
    MsgBox sMsg
End Sub
```

	A	B	C	D	E
1		0.9	=1-B1		
2	1	A	T*		
3	2	C	G*		
4	3	G	C*		
5	4	T	A*		
6					
7	=VLOOKUP(RANDBETWEEN(1,4),$A$2:$B$5,2,0)	=IF(RAND()>$B$1,VLOOKUP($A7,$B$2:$C$5,2,0),"")	=IF(RAND(=IF(RAI =IF(RAI		
8	=VLOOKUP(RANDBETWEEN(1,4),$A$2:$B$5,2,0)	=IF(RAND()>$B$1,VLOOKUP($A8,$B$2:$C$5,2,0),"")	=IF(RAND(=IF(RAI =IF(RAI		
9	=VLOOKUP(RANDBETWEEN(1,4),$A$2:$B$5,2,0)	=IF(RAND()>$B$1,VLOOKUP($A9,$B$2:$C$5,2,0),"")	=IF(RAND(=IF(RAI =IF(RAI		
10	=VLOOKUP(RANDBETWEEN(1,4),$A$2:$B$5,2,0)	=IF(RAND()>$B$1,VLOOKUP($A10,$B$2:$C$5,2,0),"")	=IF(RAND(=IF(RAI =IF(RAI		
11	=VLOOKUP(RANDBETWEEN(1,4),$A$2:$B$5,2,0)	=IF(RAND()>$B$1,VLOOKUP($A11,$B$2:$C$5,2,0),"")	=IF(RAND(=IF(RAI =IF(RAI		

V. SCIENCE

Chapter 49: Matrix Elimination

What the simulation does

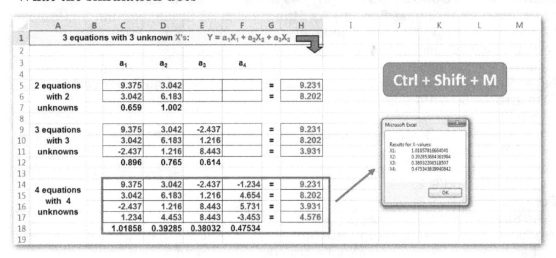

If you need to solve equations, it can be helpful to use *matrixes*. This file has a few examples of such equations. Let's focus on the last one: four equations with four unknown X-values. The equation uses four different coefficients for *a*, as shown in matrix *[A]* (C14:F17). These four equations should equate to the Y-values shown in matrix *[Y]* (H14:H17).

You need to determine what the four X-values must be to solve the equations. Here's what you do. 1. Invert matrix *[A]* by using the multi-cell array function MINVERSE. 2. Multiply the matrix *Inv[A]* with the matrix *[Y]* by using the array function MMULT. 3. You could have combined both steps by using a nested function instead: =MMULT(MINVERSE([A]),[Y]). 4. This creates vertical array results, so to plot them horizontally you need also the TRANSPOSE function.

So we end up with: =TRANSPOSE(MMULT(MINVERSE([A]),[Y]))). Thanks to this technique of matrix elimination, you can solve the equations and find the four X-values for a_1 through a_4 in the cells C18:F18. These four X-values make the four equations, based on the *a* values specified in the first matrix, equate to the Y-values specified in the second matrix. To test the outcome in a cell like J14, use this formula: =C14*$C$18+D14*$D$18+E14*$E$18+F14*$F$18.

14		9.375	3.042	-2.437	-1.234	=	9.230812
15	4 equations with 4	3.042	6.183	1.216	4.654	=	8.202251
16	unknowns	-2.437	1.216	8.443	5.731	=	3.93069
17		1.234	4.453	8.443	-3.453	=	4.576
18	4 X's	=TRANSPOSE(MMUI	=TRANSPOSE(MMUI	=TRANSPOSE(MMUI	=TRANSPOSE(MMUI		

What you need to know

The VBA code applies all these formulas in the background, without using formulas on the sheet, but be aware that they are array functions, so we need the VBA property *FormulaArray*.

In addition we used a different type of *InputBox*: *Application.InputBox*. This kind of *InputBox* lets the user select manually and directly a certain range of cells by using the mouse. If you want the *InputBox* to return a range—instead of a range address or so—you must set its last argument to the number 8. You can also include a default range address for what the user had selected already.

What you need to do

```
Option Explicit

Sub MatrixElimination()
   Dim oMatrixA As Range, oMatrixY As Range, oResults As Range, sMsg As String, i
As Integer
   On Error GoTo ErrTrap 'Set Tools|Options|General: Break on unhandled errors
   Set oMatrixA = Application.InputBox("Select range of A-coefficients", ,
Range("C14:F17").Address, , , , , 8)
   Set oMatrixY = Application.InputBox("Select corresponding range of Y's", ,
Range("H14:H17").Address, , , , , 8)
   Set oResults = oMatrixA.Rows(oMatrixA.Rows.Count + 1)
   oResults.FormulaArray = "=TRANSPOSE(MMULT(MINVERSE(" & oMatrixA.Address
& ")," & _
                          oMatrixY.Address & "))"
   sMsg = "Results for X-values:" & vbCr
   For i = 1 To oResults.Cells.Count
      sMsg = sMsg & "X" & i & ":" & vbTab & oResults.Cells(1, i) & vbCr
   Next i
   MsgBox sMsg
   Exit Sub
ErrTrap:
   MsgBox "There was an error: " & Err.Description
   Err.Number = 0
End Sub
```

Chapter 50: Integration with Simulation

What the simulation does

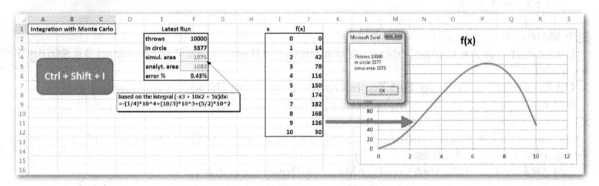

Instead of performing integration the mathematical way, you can also use a simulation. With a large number of runs, you can get very close to the analytic result found based on an integral. To do so, consider a circle inscribed within a square with sides of *s* units. The radius of the circle equates to *s*/2. Now, ten-thousand darts (F2) are randomly thrown at the diagram and then we count the number of darts that fall inside the circle (F3).

Although this is basically an integration problem that has an analytical solution, we can also simulate it with a Monte Carlo technique that gives us an approximation of the analytical integral. The advantage of using this example is that we can compare the simulation result (F4) with the analytical result (F5), telling us how close we came to the "real" solution.

What you need to know

I won't explain this part, but the integral would be $(-x^3 + 10x^2 + 5x)dx$. This formula is used in cell F5. The graph plots the analytic solution based on columns I and J. The curve is within a 10 by 200 rectangle.

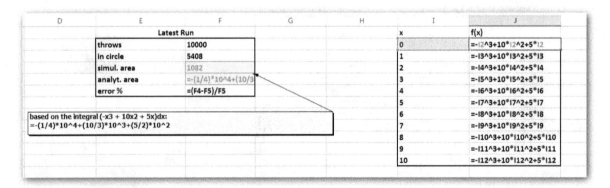

The VBA code creates an array of X's with a random number between 0 and 10, plus an array of Y's with a random number between 0 and 200 (so the curve is within a 10 by 200 rectangle). Then it checks in a 3rd array whether the "dart" is inside or outside the circle by using the integral formula: $IIf(pY(i) > -pX(i) ^ 3 + 10 * pX(i) ^ 2 + 5 * pX(i), 0, 1)$. So 1 is "in," 0 is "out."

The simulation does all of this 10,000 times—or whatever the user decides. After each trial, the macro shows the previous results and the new result in a *MsgBox*.

What you need to do

```
Option Explicit

Sub Integration()
    Dim i As Long, n As Long, pX() As Double, pY() As Double, pInOut() As Integer
    Dim iCount As Long, iSimulArea As Long, sMsg As String, iLoops As Integer
    n = InputBox("How many runs?", , 10000)
    Do
        For i = 0 To n - 1
            ReDim Preserve pX(i)
            pX(i) = Rnd * 10 '=RAND()*10
            ReDim Preserve pY(i)
            pY(i) = Rnd * 200
            ReDim Preserve pInOut(i)
            pInOut(i) = IIf(pY(i) > -pX(i) ^ 3 + 10 * pX(i) ^ 2 + 5 * pX(i), 0, 1)
        Next i
        Range("F2") = n
        iCount = WorksheetFunction.Sum(pInOut)
        Range("F3") = iCount
        iSimulArea = 2000 * iCount / n
        Range("F4") = iSimulArea
        MsgBox "Throws: " & n & vbCr & "in circle: " & iCount & vbCr & "simul.area: " &
iSimulArea
        iLoops = iLoops + 1
        sMsg = sMsg & "Loop " & iLoops & " area: " & vbTab & iSimulArea & vbCr
    Loop Until MsgBox(sMsg & vbCr & "Keep looping?", vbYesNo) = vbNo
End Sub
```

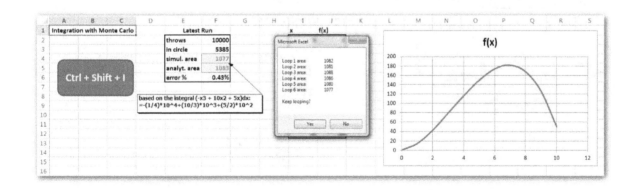

Chapter 51: Two Monte Carlo Integrations

What the simulation does

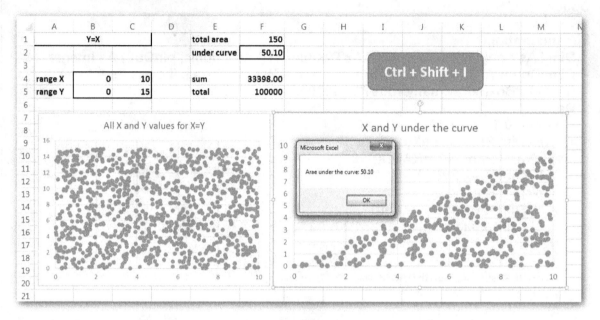

This time, we discuss only two equations as an example: Y=X (on the 1st sheet) and Y=X^2 (on the 2nd sheet), and we do so without using any integration formula.

What you need to know

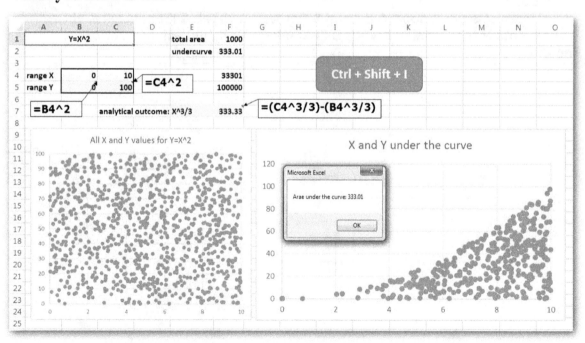

VBA generates two arrays of random X-values and random Y-values. They are plotted in the left graph. Then another set of two arrays, according to the formulas shown in VBA. Those two are plotted in the right graph. In a 5th array, we assign 1's when the two previous columns have X- and Y-values in it, so we can calculate the area under the curve. All of this is done 100,000 times.

What you need to do

```
Sub Integration()
   Dim pXmin As Double, pXmax As Double, pYmin As Double, pYmax As Double
   Dim oWS As Worksheet, pX() As Double, pY() As Double, i As Long, iCount As
Long
   Dim pXif() As Double, pYif() As Double, pInOut() As Double, pSum As Double
   If MsgBox("Do you want to be on Sheet1?", vbYesNo) = vbYes Then
      Sheet1.Select
   Else
      Sheet2.Select
   End If
   iCount = InputBox("How many runs?", , 100000)
   Set oWS = ActiveSheet
   pXmin = Range("B4"): pXmax = Range("C4")
   pYmin = Range("B5"): pYmax = Range("C5")
   For i = 0 To (iCount - 1)
      ReDim Preserve pX(i)
      pX(i) = pXmin + (pXmax - pXmin) * Rnd
      ReDim Preserve pY(i)
      pY(i) = pYmin + (pYmax - pYmin) * Rnd
      ReDim Preserve pXif(i)
      If oWS.Name = Sheet1.Name Then
         pXif(i) = IIf(pY(i) < pX(i), pX(i), 0) '=IF(C8<B8,B8,0)
      Else
         pXif(i) = IIf(pY(i) < (pX(i) ^ 2), pX(i), 0) '=IF(C8<B8,B8,0)
      End If
      ReDim Preserve pYif(i)
      pYif(i) = IIf(pXif(i) = 0, 0, pY(i))
      ReDim Preserve pInOut(i)
      pInOut(i) = IIf(pYif(i) = 0, 0, 1)
      pSum = pSum + pInOut(i)
   Next i
   Range("F4") = pSum
   Range("F5") = iCount
   Range("F1") = (pXmax - pXmin) * (pYmax - pYmin)
   Range("F2") = Range("F1") * Range("F4") / Range("F5")
   MsgBox "Arae under the curve: " & FormatNumber(Range("F2"), 2)
End Sub
```

The 2nd sheet (Y=X^2) has a few differences with the 1st sheet (Y=X):

	A	B	C	D	E	F
1		Y=X^2			total area	1000
2					undercurve	333.01
3						
4	range X	0	10		sum	33301
5	range Y	=B4^2	=C4^2		total	100000
6						
7			analytical outcome:		X^3/3	=(C4^3/3)-(B4^3/3)

Chapter 52: Monte Carlo Approach of Pi

What the simulation does

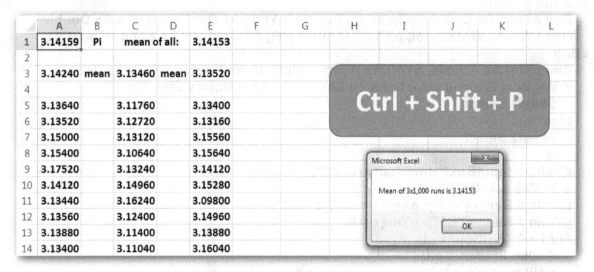

	A	B	C	D	E	F	G	H	I	J	K	L
1	3.14159	Pi	mean of all:		3.14153							
2												
3	3.14240	mean	3.13460	mean	3.13520							
4												
5	3.13640		3.11760		3.13400							
6	3.13520		3.12720		3.13160							
7	3.15000		3.13120		3.15560							
8	3.15400		3.10640		3.15640							
9	3.17520		3.13240		3.14120							
10	3.14120		3.14960		3.15280							
11	3.13440		3.16240		3.09800							
12	3.13560		3.12400		3.14960							
13	3.13880		3.11400		3.13880							
14	3.13400		3.11040		3.16040							

Ctrl + Shift + P

Microsoft Excel

Mean of 3x1,000 runs is 3.14153

OK

This simulation estimates what Pi is by using a custom (user-defined) function *PiEstimate*, which has one argument: the number of times you want to run this calculation. By default it runs two random numbers internally 10,000 times.

The function *PiEstimate* is used in a *Sub* called *PiSimulation* which places that function in three columns of 1,000 rows. And then it calculates the average of these 3,000 cells. Notice that the results in each of these cells can vary quite a bit, but their average in E1 is rather stable.

What you need to know

Because Excel has also a PI function, we can compare its value (cell A1) with the value we received through our simulation (E1). There are only very minor deviations, because of the large number of runs.

Notice that the custom function has *Application.Volatile* not enforced. What that line would do is recalculating the function each time something on the sheet changes. We don't want that here.

	A	B	C	D	E
1	=PI()	Pi	mean of all:		=AVERAGE(A5:E1004)
2					
3	3.1468	mean	3.1476	mean	3.14
4					
5	=PiEstimate(10000)		=PiEstimate(10000)		=PiEstimate(10000)
6	=PiEstimate(10000)		=PiEstimate(10000)		=PiEstimate(10000)
7	=PiEstimate(10000)		=PiEstimate(10000)		=PiEstimate(10000)
8	=PiEstimate(10000)		=PiEstimate(10000)		=PiEstimate(10000)
9	=PiEstimate(10000)		=PiEstimate(10000)		=PiEstimate(10000)
10	=PiEstimate(10000)		=PiEstimate(10000)		=PiEstimate(10000)

What you need to do

```
Option Explicit

Function PiEstimate(n As Long)
    Dim pRand As Double, pInside As Double, i As Integer, pApprox As Double
    Dim XRand As Double, YRand As Double, RRand As Double
    'Application.Volatile True 'recalculates whenever anything changes on the sheet
    pInside = 0
    For i = 1 To n
      XRand = Rnd
      YRand = Rnd
      RRand = XRand ^ 2 + YRand ^ 2
      If (RRand <= 1) Then
         pInside = pInside + 1
      End If
    Next i
    pApprox = 4 * pInside / n
    PiEstimate = pApprox
End Function

Sub PiSimulation()
    Dim i As Integer
    MsgBox "Be patient until the next MsgBox appears"
    Cells.EntireColumn.AutoFit
    Cells.EntireColumn.NumberFormat = "0.00000"
    Range("A1").Formula = "=Pi()"
    For i = 1 To 6 Step 2
       Range(Cells(5, i), Cells(1004, i)).Formula = "=PiEstimate(10000)"
       Cells(3, i) = WorksheetFunction.Average(Cells(5, i), Cells(1004, i))
    Next i
    Range("E1").Formula = "=AVERAGE(A5:E1004)"
    MsgBox "Mean of 3x1,000 runs is " & FormatNumber(Range("E1"), 5)
End Sub
```

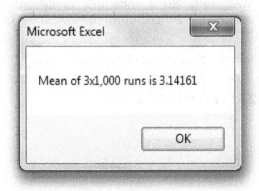

Chapter 53: A Population Pyramid

What the simulation does

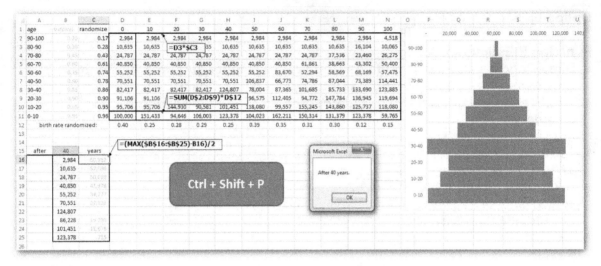

This simulation shows how a population pyramid may change over the course of 100 years. The simulation is based on several grossly oversimplified assumptions.

Assumption #1: The population starts at 100,000 (cell D11).

Assumption #2: The birth rate is partially randomized (row 12) and is based on participation by everyone over 20 years old.

Assumption #3: Every age group has a certain survival value (column B) which is subject to small fluctuations, determined by a randomize factor (*InputBox*, by default 2%).

With three InputBoxes you can determine your randomize factor (by default 0.02), the minimum birth rate (by default 0.1), and the maximum birth rate (by default 0.4). Then the macro loops through 100 years in steps of 10 and shows the situation after that number of years.

What you need to know

The cells B16:B25 use the function HLOOKUP, which searches for a value in the top row of a table or an array of values, and then returns a value in the same column from a row you specify in the table or array. It has the following syntax: HLOOKUP(value, table or array, row index number, exact match or not). So the formula in B16 is: =HLOOKUP([Years],$D$1:$N$11,ROW(A2),0)., where ROW(A2), copied down, becomes ROW(A3), etc. So it finds the number of years horizontally in the first row of D1:N11, and then returns the 2nd cell down, 3rd cell, etc. For 100 years, B16:B25 should be the same as N2:N11.

The cells C16:C25 calculate how far each bar in the chart should be offset to the right, which is done with the formula: =(MAX($B$16:$B$25)-B16)/2.

The chart is a stacked bar chart, and plots A2:A11 against B6:B25 and C6:C25.

What you need to do

```
Option Explicit

Sub Pyramid()
   Dim iYears As Integer, pSurvivalFluct As Double, pMinRate As Double, pMaxRate
As Double
   MsgBox "You can manually change survival rates in the cells B2:B11"
   pSurvivalFluct = InputBox("What is the randomize factor?", , 0.02)
   pMinRate = InputBox("Minimum birthrate", , 0.1)
   pMaxRate = InputBox("Maximum birthrate", , 0.4)
   'iYears = InputBox("The situation after how many years?", , 100)
   Do
      Range("C2:C11").Formula = "=NORMINV(RAND(),B2," & pSurvivalFluct & ")"
      Range("C2:C11").Formula = Range("C2:C11").Value
      Range("D12:N12").Formula = "=RANDBETWEEN(" & (pMinRate * 100) & "," &
(pMaxRate * 100) & ")/100"
      Range("D12:N12").Formula = Range("D12:N12").Value
      For iYears = 10 To 100 Step 10
         Range("B15") = iYears
         Range("B16:B25").Formula = "=HLOOKUP(" & iYears &
",$D$1:$N$11,ROW(A2),0)"
         MsgBox "After " & iYears & " years."
      Next iYears
      Range("B16:B25").Formula = Range("B16:B25").Value
   Loop Until MsgBox("Another run?", vbYesNo) = vbNo
End Sub
```

	A	B	C	D	E	F	G	H	I
1	age	survival	randomize	0	10	20	30	40	50
2	90-100	0.2	0.171980966799729	=D3*$C3	=D3*$C3	=E3*$C3	=F3*$C3	=G3*$C3	=H3*$C3
3	80-90	0.3	0.280546786281342	=D4*$C4	=D4*$C4	=D3*$C3		=G4*$C4	=H4*$C4
4	70-80	0.45	0.42903522784283	=D5*$C5	=D5*$C5	=E5*$C5	=F5*$C5	=G5*$C5	=H5*$C5
5	60-70	0.6	0.606789828050401	=D6*$C6	=D6*$C6	=E6*$C6	=F6*$C6	=G6*$C6	=H6*$C6
6	50-60	0.75	0.739340989717628	=D7*$C7	=D7*$C7	=E7*$C7	=F7*$C7	=G7*$C7	=H7*$C7
7	40-50	0.8	0.783153132476069	=D8*$C8	=D8*$C8	=E8*$C8	=F8*$C8	=G8*$C8	=H8*$C8
8	30-40	0.95	0.8560191527801	=D9*$C9	=D9*$C9	=E9*$C9	=F9*$C9	=G9*$C9	=H9*$C9
9	20-30	0.9	0.904631646496482	=D10*$C10	=D10*$C10	=SUM(D$2:D$9)*D$12			=10*$C10
10	10-20	0.95	0.95193645948201	=D11*$C11	=D11*$C11	=E11*$C11	=F11*$C11	=G11*$C11	=H11*$C11
11	0-10	0.95	0.957059937681503	100000	=SUM(D$2:D$9)*D$12	=SUM(E$2:E$9)*E$12	=SUM(F$2:F$9)*F$12	=SUM(G$2:G$9)*G$1	=SUM(H$2:H$9
12		birth rate randomized:		0.4	0.25	0.28	0.29	0.25	0.39
13									

Chapter 54: Predator-Prey Cycle

What the simulation does

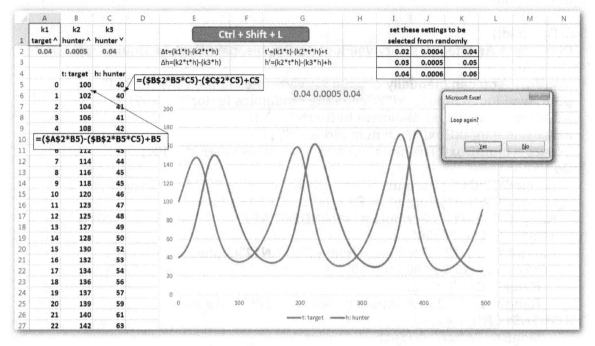

The so-called Lotka-Volterra model, dealing specifically with the relationship between predator and prey (or hunter and target) makes the following simplified assumptions: The change in the prey's numbers is given by its own growth minus the rate at which it is preyed upon (E2). On the other hand, the change in growth of the predator population is fueled by the food supply, minus natural death (E3). The equations that were used are explained on the sheet.

What you need to know

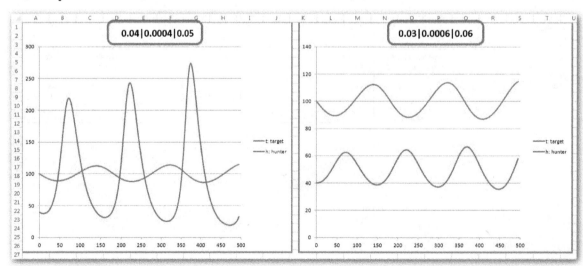

This simulation loops randomly through the values in I2:K4 to determine the three settings for A2:C2. Based on these settings, it plots the corresponding charts next to each other on a new sheet. The title of each chart specifies what the specific three values for A2:C2 were (see also Chapter 97).

What you need to do

```
Sub LotkaVolterra()
  Do
    Range("A2") = Cells(WorksheetFunction.RandBetween(2, 4), 9)
    Range("B2") = Cells(WorksheetFunction.RandBetween(2, 4), 10)
    Range("C2") = Cells(WorksheetFunction.RandBetween(2, 4), 11)
    CreateCharts 'see Sub below
  Loop Until MsgBox("Loop again?", vbYesNo) = vbNo
End Sub


Sub CreateCharts()
  Dim oRange As Range, i As Integer, oChart As Chart, sCaption As String
  Dim oWS As Worksheet, bWS As Boolean, oAS As Worksheet
  Set oAS = ActiveSheet
  For Each oWS In Worksheets
    If oWS.Name = "Chart" Then bWS = True
  Next oWS
  If bWS = False Then
    Set oWS = Worksheets.Add(, ActiveSheet):   oWS.Name = "Chart"
  Else
    Set oWS = Worksheets("Chart")
  End If
  oAS.Select
  Set oRange = Range("B5").CurrentRegion
  Set oChart = Charts.Add
  With oChart
    .SetSourceData oRange:   .ChartArea.Border.Weight = xlThick
    .ChartType = xlXYScatterSmoothNoMarkers
    .HasTitle = True:   .Axes(xlCategory).MaximumScale = 500
    .FullSeriesCollection(1).XValues = .FullSeriesCollection(1).XValues
    .FullSeriesCollection(2).Values = .FullSeriesCollection(2).Values
    sCaption = oAS.Range("A2") & "|" & oAS.Range("B2") & "|" & oAS.Range("C2")
    .ChartTitle.Caption = sCaption:   .Location xlLocationAsObject, oWS.Name
  End With
  oWS.Activate
  For i = 1 To oWS.ChartObjects.Count
    With oWS.ChartObjects(i)
      .Width = ActiveWindow.Width * 0.4:      .Height = ActiveWindow.Height * 0.6
      .Left = ((i - 1) Mod oWS.ChartObjects.Count) * ActiveWindow.Width * 0.41
      .Top = Int((i - 1) / oWS.ChartObjects.Count) * 150
    End With
  Next i
  MsgBox "Here is the Chart":   oAS.Activate
End Sub
```

Chapter 55: Taking Medication

What the simulation does

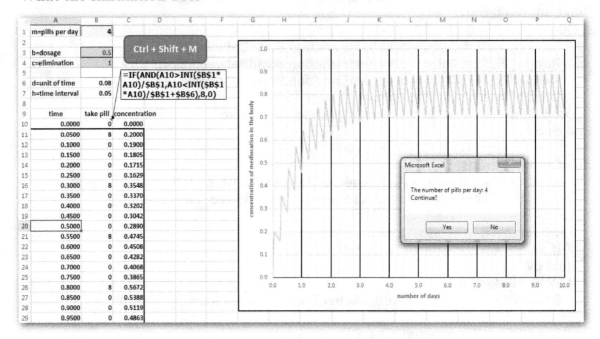

When taking medication, we want to reach a rather steady concentration of the medicine inside the body. The concentration rises each time we take a pill, but then it also declines because the body metabolizes and/or excretes it.

We simulate this process based on at least 5 parameters. The three important ones are the number of pills a day (B1), the strength of each pill (B3), and the elimination factor (B4). You may want to change these variables manually to find out what the best regimen is.

What you need to know

The simplest model would be as follows: If $u(t)$ is the concentration of the medication in the body, then $du = b\,f(t)\,dt - cu\,dt$. In words: the change in concentration equals (the amount of medication entering the body at time t during the period dt) minus (the amount of medication leaving the body during a small time interval dt). Instead of differentiating the equation, we use an Excel simulation.

The formula in cell B10 and down is complex and looks like this: =IF(AND(A10>INT($B$1*A10)/$B$1,A10<INT($B$1*A10)/$B$1+$B$6),8,0). In VBA, we build this formula up in two pieces to keep the line more manageable.

The formula in C11 and down determines the concentration at a specific point in time: =C10+$B$5*($B$2*B11-$B$3*C10).

The simulation loops through the number of pills, running from 1 to 5 pills, and another loop that builds up the cells 11 to 211 in columns A:C. Since the 2nd loop has a *Timer* interval in it, we see the data and the chart gradually building up.

What you need to do

```
Option Explicit

Sub Medication()
    Dim n As Integer, i As Integer, pTime As Double, sStr As String
    Dim pDosage As Double, pElim As Double, pUnit As Double, pInterv As Double
    pDosage = Range("B3"):    pElim = Range("B4"):    pUnit = Range("B6"):    pInterv =
Range("B7")
    For n = 1 To 5 'for number of pills
        Range("B1") = n
        Range(Cells(11, 1), Cells(211, 3)).ClearContents
        For i = 11 To 211
            Cells(i, 1) = Cells(i - 1, 1) + pInterv
            sStr = "INT(R1C2*RC[-1])/R1C2"
            Cells(i, 2).FormulaR1C1 = "=IF(AND(RC[-1]>" & sStr & ",RC[-1]<" & sStr &
"+R6C2),8,0)"
            Cells(i, 2).Formula = Cells(i, 2).Value
            Cells(i, 3) = Cells(i - 1, 3) + pInterv * (pDosage * Cells(i, 2) - pElim * Cells(i - 1,
3))
            pTime = Timer + 0.005
            Do While Timer < pTime
                DoEvents
            Loop
        Next i
        sStr = "This is for " & n & " pills per day."
        If n < 5 Then
            If MsgBox(sStr & vbCr & "Continue?", vbYesNo) = vbNo Then Exit Sub
        Else
            MsgBox sStr
        End If
    Next n
End Sub
```

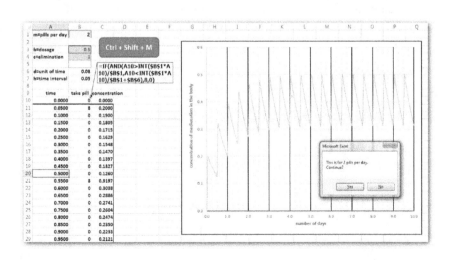

Chapter 56: The Course of an Epidemic

What the simulation does

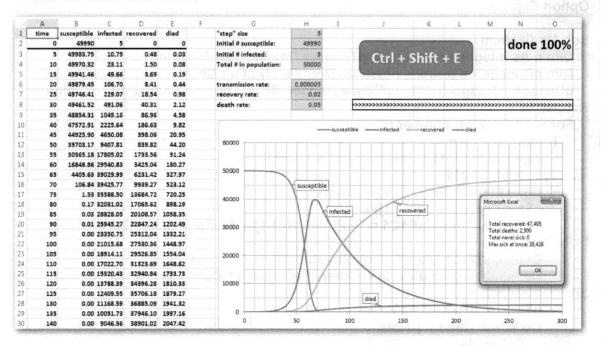

In this simple simulation, we follow the course of an epidemic (e.g. the flu) based on certain variables in column H. In general, epidemics follow a more or less fixed pattern. Initially only a few people get sick, but soon the number of sick cases rises exponentially until stabilization sets in, and more and more people have recovered.

We need some essential parameters, although they may not always be exactly known. We will only focus on transmission rate, recovery rate, and death rate—without going into issues such as mutation rate for the virus or bacterium.

The model that we apply is the standard *SIR* model, commonly used for many infectious diseases. The name of the model reflects the three groups of individuals that it models: *S*usceptible people, *I*nfected people, and *R*ecovered people. There are a number of important thresholds in this model. Reaching, or failing to reach, these thresholds is a crucial feature of managing the spread of infectious diseases. The system is sensitive to certain changes and not to others, so this may give us some insight as to when and where the problem should be attacked.

In order to make the appropriate calculations, we use the Euler's method, without explaining it any further. You can find it explained elsewhere.

What you need to know

The simulation gradually fills 300 cells in each of the columns A:E with the appropriate equations. It does this in steps, thanks to a *Timer* loop. To keep track of its progress, cell N1 is being updated during the process. This is also done with some kind of simple progress bar in cell J8 by using the function REPT. This function repeats a certain charcter as often as the 2nd argument indicates.

At the end of the simulation, a *MsgBox* reports how many people were susceptible, infected, recovered, or died during the course of the epidemic

What you need to do

```
Option Explicit

Sub Epidemic()
    Dim sMsg As String, pTime As Double, i As Long
    Range("A3:E302").ClearContents
    'If MsgBox("Are the values in column H as you want them?", vbYesNo) = vbNo
Then Exit Sub
    For i = 3 To 302
        Cells(i, 1).FormulaR1C1 = "=R[-1]C+R1C8" 'A2+$H$1"
        Cells(i, 2).FormulaR1C1 = "=R[-1]C-(R6C8*R[-1]C*R[-1]C[1])*R1C8"
        Cells(i, 3).FormulaR1C1 = "=R[-1]C+(R6C8*R[-1]C[-1]*R[-1]C-R7C8*R[-1]C)*R1C8"
        Cells(i, 4).FormulaR1C1 = "=R[-1]C+((1-R8C8)*R7C8*R[-1]C[-1])*R1C8"
        Cells(i, 5).FormulaR1C1 = "=R[-1]C+(R8C8*R7C8*R[-1]C[-2])*R1C8"
        Range("N1") = "done " & FormatPercent(i / 302, 0)
        Range("J8") = WorksheetFunction.Rept(">", i / 302 * 100)
            If i / 302 <= 0.25 Then
                If i Mod 5 = 0 Then
                    pTime = Timer
                    Do While Timer < pTime + 1.5
                        DoEvents
                    Loop
                End If
            End If
    Next i
    sMsg = "Total recovered: " & FormatNumber(Range("D302"), 0) & vbCr
    sMsg = sMsg & "Total deaths: " & FormatNumber(Range("E302"), 0) & vbCr
    sMsg = sMsg & "Total never sick: " & FormatNumber(Range("B302"), 0) & vbCr
    sMsg = sMsg & "Max sick at once: " &
FormatNumber(WorksheetFunction.Max(Columns(3)), 0)
    MsgBox sMsg
    If MsgBox("Do you want to keep the formulas on the sheet?", vbYesNo) = vbNo
Then
        Range("A3:E302").Formula = Range("A3:E302").Value
    End If
End Sub
```

	A	B	C	D	E
1	time	susceptible	infected	recovered	died
2	0	=H2	=H3	0	0
3	=A2+$H$1	=B2-($H$6*B2*C2)*$H$1	=C2+($H$6*B2*C2-$H$7*C2)*$H$1	=D2+((1-$H$8)*$H$7*C2)*$H$1	=E2+($H$8*$H$7*C2)*$H$1
4	=A3+$H$1	=B3-($H$6*B3*C3)*$H$1	=C3+($H$6*B3*C3-$H$7*C3)*$H$1	=D3+((1-$H$8)*$H$7*C3)*$H$1	=E3+($H$8*$H$7*C3)*$H$1
5	=A4+$H$1	=B4-($H$6*B4*C4)*$H$1	=C4+($H$6*B4*C4-$H$7*C4)*$H$1	=D4+((1-$H$8)*$H$7*C4)*$H$1	=E4+($H$8*$H$7*C4)*$H$1
6	=A5+$H$1	=B5-($H$6*B5*C5)*$H$1	=C5+($H$6*B5*C5-$H$7*C5)*$H$1	=D5+((1-$H$8)*$H$7*C5)*$H$1	=E5+($H$8*$H$7*C5)*$H$1
7	=A6+$H$1	=B6-($H$6*B6*C6)*$H$1	=C6+($H$6*B6*C6-$H$7*C6)*$H$1	=D6+((1-$H$8)*$H$7*C6)*$H$1	=E6+($H$8*$H$7*C6)*$H$1
8	=A7+$H$1	=B7-($H$6*B7*C7)*$H$1	=C7+($H$6*B7*C7-$H$7*C7)*$H$1	=D7+((1-$H$8)*$H$7*C7)*$H$1	=E7+($H$8*$H$7*C7)*$H$1
9	=A8+$H$1	=B8-($H$6*B8*C8)*$H$1	=C8+($H$6*B8*C8-$H$7*C8)*$H$1	=D8+((1-$H$8)*$H$7*C8)*$H$1	=E8+($H$8*$H$7*C8)*$H$1
10	=A9+$H$1	=B9-($H$6*B9*C9)*$H$1	=C9+($H$6*B9*C9-$H$7*C9)*$H$1	=D9+((1-$H$8)*$H$7*C9)*$H$1	=E9+($H$8*$H$7*C9)*$H$1

Chapter 57: Boltzmann Equation for Sigmoidal Curves

What the simulation does

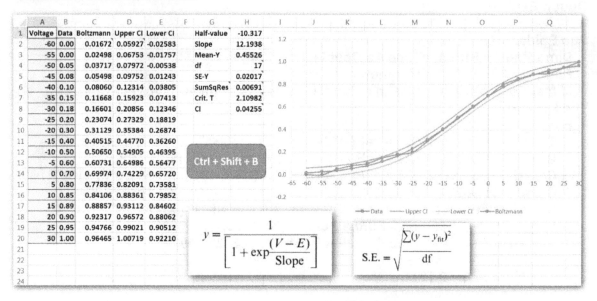

	A	B	C	D	E	F	G	H
1	Voltage	Data	Boltzmann	Upper CI	Lower CI		Half-value	-10.317
2	-60	0.00	0.01672	0.05927	-0.02583		Slope	12.1938
3	-55	0.00	0.02498	0.06753	-0.01757		Mean-Y	0.45526
4	-50	0.05	0.03717	0.07972	-0.00538		df	17
5	-45	0.08	0.05498	0.09752	0.01243		SE-Y	0.02017
6	-40	0.10	0.08060	0.12314	0.03805		SumSqRes	0.00691
7	-35	0.15	0.11668	0.15923	0.07413		Crit. T	2.10982
8	-30	0.18	0.16601	0.20856	0.12346		CI	0.04255
9	-25	0.20	0.23074	0.27329	0.18819			
10	-20	0.30	0.31129	0.35384	0.26874			
11	-15	0.40	0.40515	0.44770	0.36260			
12	-10	0.50	0.50650	0.54905	0.46395			
13	-5	0.60	0.60731	0.64986	0.56477			
14	0	0.70	0.69974	0.74229	0.65720			
15	5	0.80	0.77836	0.82091	0.73581			
16	10	0.85	0.84106	0.88361	0.79852			
17	15	0.89	0.88857	0.93112	0.84602			
18	20	0.90	0.92317	0.96572	0.88062			
19	25	0.95	0.94766	0.99021	0.90512			
20	30	1.00	0.96465	1.00719	0.92210			

Ctrl + Shift + B

$$y = \cfrac{1}{\left[1 + \exp\cfrac{(V - E)}{Slope}\right]}$$

$$S.E. = \sqrt{\cfrac{\sum(y - y_{fit})^2}{df}}$$

This simulation deals with curves that are of the logistic, s-shaped, or sigmoidal type, so we could use the Boltzmann equation as explained in the figure above (where E is the independent variable in column A, and V the half-way activity). The values in columns C:E and H are all calculated (see figure on the next page), except for the values in H1 and H2, which are based on an educated guess.

Something similar can be done for EC50 or IC50 determination. The term "half maximal effective concentraion" (EC50) refers to the concentration of a drug, antibody, or toxicant which induces a response halfway between the baseline and maximum after a specified exposure time. It is commonly used as a measure of a drug's *effective* potency. (IC50, on the other hand, is the "half maximal *inhibitory* response.")

The columns D and E calculate the confidence interval on both sides of the curve of observed values based on cell H8 (see Chapter 18).

What you need to know

In order to get a more accurate value for the half-way value and the slope, we need to set the *Sum of Squared Residuals* (H6) to a minimum, which means that the difference between what we observed and what we expected according to the equation is minimal.

We can do so by using Excel's *Solver* tool. Make sure *Solver* is active in VBA: Tools | References | Solver ON. Now the macro can call Solver. On the screen shot to the left, cell H6 is set to a minimum by changing the variable cells H1:H2 (the educated guesses). Since there can be several solutions to this problem, it is wise to add some constraints—for instance, that H1 should be between -5 and -15.

What you need to do

```
Option Explicit

Sub Boltzman()
  Dim pHalfX As Double, pSlope As Double
  Range("C2:E20").ClearContents:      Range("H1:H8").ClearContents
  pHalfX = InputBox("Guess half-X-value for half-Y at 0.5", , -10)
  pSlope = InputBox("Guess what the slope would be", , 10)
  Range("H1").Formula = pHalfX:      Range("H2").Formula = pSlope
  Range("H3").Formula = "=AVERAGE(B:B)" 'mean Y
  Range("H4").Formula = "=COUNT(B:B)-COUNT(H1:H2)" 'degrees of freedom
  Range("H5").FormulaArray = "=SQRT(SUM((B2:B20-C2:C20)^2)/H4)" 'Standard
Error Y
  Range("H6").FormulaArray = "=SUM((B2:B20-C2:C20)^2)" 'Sum Squared Residuals
  Range("H7").Formula = "=TINV(0.05,H4)" 'Critical t-value
  Range("H8").Formula = "=H7*H5" 'Confidence Interval
  Range("C2:C20").Formula = "=(1/(1+EXP(($H$1-A2)/$H$2)))"
  Range("D2:D20").Formula = "=C2+$H$8"
  Range("E2:E20").Formula = "=C2-$H$8"
  'Tools | References | Solver ON
  SolverOkDialog "H6", 2, 0, "H1:H2", 1, "GRG Nonlinear"
End Sub
```

	A	B	C	D	E	F	G	H
1	Voltage	Data	Boltzmann	Upper CI	Lower CI		Half-value	-15
2	-60	0	=(1/(1+EXP(($H$1-A2)/$H$2)))	=C2+$H$8	=C2-$H$8		Slope	5
3	-55	0	=(1/(1+EXP(($H$1-A3)/$H$2)))	=C3+$H$8	=C3-$H$8		Mean-Y	=AVERAGE(B:B)
4	-50	0.05	=(1/(1+EXP(($H$1-A4)/$H$2)))	=C4+$H$8	=C4-$H$8		df	=COUNT(B:B)-COUNT(H1:H2)
5	-45	0.08	=(1/(1+EXP(($H$1-A5)/$H$2)))	=C5+$H$8	=C5-$H$8		SE-Y	=SQRT(SUM((B2:B20-C2:C20)^2)/H4)
6	-40	0.1	=(1/(1+EXP(($H$1-A6)/$H$2)))	=C6+$H$8	=C6-$H$8		SumSqRes	=SUM((B2:B20-C2:C20)^2)
7	-35	0.15	=(1/(1+EXP(($H$1-A7)/$H$2)))	=C7+$H$8	=C7-$H$8		Crit. T	=TINV(0.05,H4)
8	-30	0.18	=(1/(1+EXP(($H$1-A8)/$H$2)))	=C8+$H$8	=C8-$H$8		CI	=H7*H5

Chapter 58: Interpolation

What the simulation does

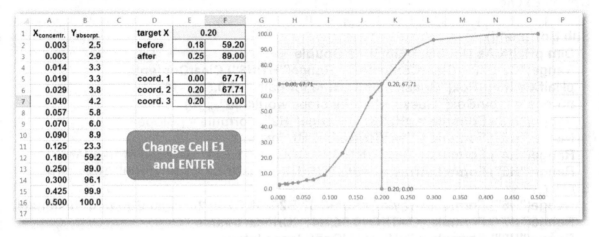

Interpolation is a process of estimating a missing value by using existing, observed values. For example, in a graph, you might want to mark a specific point on the curve that has not been measured; so it has to be interpolated. The graph must be of the *XY* type because interpolation works with values in between—and such values do not exist in charts carrying a *category* axis.

This time the simulation is not done with a macro script in a *Module*, but it is activated by the sheet itself when the user changes the number in cell E1. In the VBA editor, double-click the sheet in the panel to the left (see figure below). Then you select *Worksheet* from the dropdown in the left top corner followed by *Change* in the right top corner. This creates a *Sub Worksheet_Change* in your VBA code.

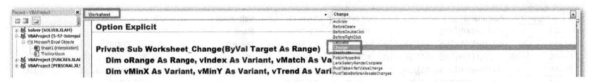

What you need to know

To plot an interpolation insert in your XY-graph you need three sets of coordinates (E5:F7) based on the observed value just before your target value and the one just after your target value. To find these coordinates you need three Excel functions: MATCH, INDEX, and TREND.

The function MATCH is needed to locate in which row the value of E1 was found. MATCH has 3 arguments: what to match (E1), in which range (column A), and with which match type 1 for an ascending list (0 for an exact match, and -1 for a descending list). This locates the target value (E1) in column A, by looking for the closest previous value in an ascending order (1).

Now INDEX can find the corresponding value in the same row and in one row farther down (+1)—that is, for column A: E2+E3; for column B: F2:F3.

To calculate the interpolated X-value between E2 and E3, and the interpolated Y-value between F2 and F3, we need the TREND function. It has this syntax: TREND(2 known Y's, two known X's, target X). This way, we are able to find E6:E7 and F5:F6. Cells E5 and F6 should be 0 if both axes start at 0.

What you need to do

```vba
Private Sub Worksheet_Change(ByVal Target As Range)
    Dim oRange As Range, vIndex As Variant, vMatch As Variant
    Dim vMinX As Variant, vMinY As Variant, vTrend As Variant
    If Target.Address <> "$E$1" Then Exit Sub
    Set oRange = Range(Cells(2, 1), Cells(Range("A1").CurrentRegion.Rows.Count, 2))
    If Range("E1") >= WorksheetFunction.Max(oRange.Columns(1)) Then Exit Sub
    Range("E1:F1").Merge
    vMatch = WorksheetFunction.Match(Range("E1"), oRange.Columns(1), 1)
    vIndex = WorksheetFunction.Index(oRange, vMatch, 1):    Range("E2") = vIndex
    vIndex = WorksheetFunction.Index(oRange, vMatch, 2):    Range("F2") = vIndex
    vIndex = WorksheetFunction.Index(oRange, vMatch + 1, 1):    Range("E3") = vIndex
    vIndex = WorksheetFunction.Index(oRange, vMatch + 1, 2):    Range("F3") = vIndex
    vMinX = WorksheetFunction.Min(oRange.Columns(1)):    Range("E5") = vMinX
    Range("E6") = Range("E1"):    Range("E7") = Range("E1")
    vTrend = WorksheetFunction.Trend(Range("F2:F3"), Range("E2:E3"), Range("E1"))
    Range("F5") = vTrend:    Range("F6") = vTrend
    vMinY = WorksheetFunction.Min(oRange.Columns(2)):    Range("F7") = vMinY
    If MsgBox("A separate graph?", vbYesNo) = vbYes Then Charting
End Sub


Sub Charting()
    Dim r As Long, pMin1 As Double, pMin2 As Double, sX As String, sY As String
    Dim oChart As Chart, oRange As Range
    Set oRange = Range("A1").CurrentRegion:        r = oRange.Rows.Count
    sX = Range(Cells(2, 1), Cells(r, 1)).Address:    sY = Range(Cells(2, 2), Cells(r, 2)).Address
    Set oRange = Union(Range(sX), Range(sY)): Set oChart = Charts.Add(, ActiveSheet)
    With oChart
        .ChartType = xlXYScatterSmooth:            .SetSourceData oRange
        .HasTitle = True: .HasLegend = True:.Axes(xlCategory).HasMajorGridlines = True
        .Axes(xlCategory).HasMinorGridlines = True:
        pMin1 = WorksheetFunction.Min(Columns(1)):    pMin2 = WorksheetFunction.Min(Columns(2))
        .Axes(xlValue).MinimumScale = IIf(pMin1 < pMin2, Int(pMin1), Int(pMin2))
        .Axes(xlValue).HasMinorGridlines = True
        .ChartTitle.Caption = "Graph based on columns " & _
                vbCr & Cells(1, 1) & " and " & Cells(1, 2) & " for X=" & Range("E1")
        .SeriesCollection(1).Name = Cells(1, 1):    .SeriesCollection(2).Name = Cells(1, 2)
    End With
    With oChart.SeriesCollection.NewSeries
        .XValues = Range("E5:E7"):    .Values = Range("F5:F7")
        .Name = "insert":    .ChartType = xlXYScatterLines
        .HasDataLabels = True:    .DataLabels.Select
        Selection.ShowCategoryName = True:    Selection.ShowValue = True
    End With
    oChart.SizeWithWindow = True
End Sub
```

Chapter 59: A Rigid Pendulum

What the simulation does

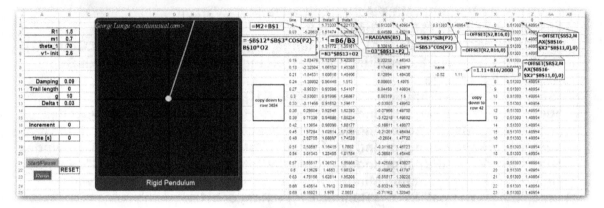

Sheet5 has two *Commandbuttons* which run VBA code on Sheet5 when you click on the buttons. This way the pendulum can start swinging, can pause swinging, or can be reset. The calculations in the background (columns M through Z) are based on the values that can be manually set in column B. The VBA code only regulates when the calculations are being updated.

What you need to know

This simulation is partly borrowed from George Lungu. The major factor involved in the equations for calculating the frequency of a pendulum is the length of the rod or wire, provided the initial angle or amplitude of the swing is small. The mass or weight of the bob is not a factor in the frequency of the simple pendulum, but the acceleration of gravity is in the equation. Knowing the length of the pendulum, you can determine its frequency. Or, if you want a specific frequency, you can determine the necessary length.

The period of the motion for a pendulum is how long it takes to swing back-and-forth, measured in seconds. Period is designated as *T*. The frequency of a pendulum is how many back-and-forth swings there are in a second, measured in hertz. Frequency is usually designated as *f*. The period *T* is the reciprocal of the frequency: *T=1/f* and *f=1/T*.

The equation for the period of a simple pendulum starting at a small angle (*a*) is: *T=2pi*SQRT(L/g)* or *T = 2π√(L/g)*.

Notice how columns Y and Z change dramatically and quickly while the macro runs.

K	L	M	N	O	P	Q	R	S	T	U	V	W	X	Y	Z	AA	AB
		time	theta1°	theta1'	theta1		X	Y						0	0		
	=M2+B$1		1.73333	1.22173			0.51303	1.40954		0.51303	1.40954		0	0.51303	1.40954		=OFFSET($S$2,M
		0.03	-5.2863	1.57474	1.26897		0.44589	1.43219		0	0	=OFFSET(S2,B16,0)		0.51303	1.4095		AX($B$16-
=-$B$12*$B$3*COS(P2)-		1.4	=B6/B3	1.31772	1.35161		=RADIANS(B5)			=$B$3*SIN(P2)				0.51303	1.4095		$X2*$B$11,0),0)
B$10*O2							0.32616	1.46411		=$B$3*COS(P2)		=OFFSET(R2,B16,0)		0.51303	1.4095		
			=N3*$B$13+O2				=O3*$B$13+P2							0.51303	1.4095		
		0.15	-2.83476	1.13127	1.42203		0.22232	1.48343					5	0.51303			=OFFSET($R$2,M
		0.18	-2.32504	1.06152	1.45388		0.17498	1.48976		name							AX($B$16-
		0.21	-1.84531	1.00616	1.48406		0.12994	1.49436		-0.52	1.11	=1.11+B16/2000					$X2*$B$11,0),0)
		0.24	-1.38992	0.96446	1.513		0.08665	1.4975					8	0.51303	1.40954		
		0.27	-0.95331	0.93586	1.54107		0.04458	1.49934					9	0.51303	1.40954		
		0.3	-0.53001	0.91996	1.56867		0.00319	1.5				copy	10	0.51303	1.40954		
	copy down to	0.33	-0.11466	0.91652	1.59617		-0.03805	1.49952				down to	11	0.51303	1.40954		
	row 3024	0.36	0.29804	0.92546	1.62393		-0.07966	1.49788				row 42	12	0.51303	1.40954		
		0.39	0.71336	0.94686	1.65234		-0.12218	1.49502					13	0.51303	1.40954		

What you need to do

```
'This code is on Sheet5

Private Sub Reset__Click()
   Range("B22") = "RESET"
   Range("B16") = 0
End Sub

Private Sub Release__Click()
  i = Range("B16")
  If Not (Range("B22") = "ON") Then
    Range("B22") = "ON"
  Else
    Range("B22") = "PAUSE"
    Exit Sub
  End If
  Do
    If i < 3000 And Range("B22") = "ON" Then
      DoEvents
      i = i + 1
      Range("B16") = i
      If Range("B22") = "PAUSE" Then Exit Sub
      If Range("B22") = "RESET" Then Range("B16") = 0:  Exit Sub
    Else
      i = 0
      Range("B16") = 0
    End If
  Loop
End Sub
```

Chapter 60: A Piston Sinusoid

What the simulation does

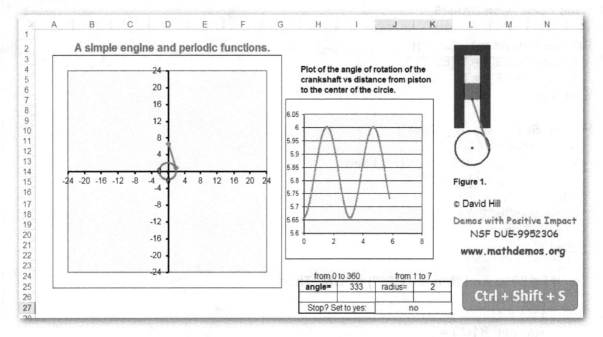

The periodic rotation of the piston-crankshaft assembly in an engine generates a sinusoid when we plot the angle of rotation of the crankshaft versus the distance from the piston to the center of the circle. If the radius of the circle is changed, then the sinusoid also changes.

This file simulates the engine and the resulting sinusoid. The VBA code runs *a* (the minimum distance from the piston to the top of the circle) from 1 to 7, and the radius from 0 to 360. During each loop, the accompanying graph nicely builds up in a timed fashion.

What you need to know

Sheet1 uses equations implemented on Sheet2. The simulation is partly borrowed from David Hill. It plots the angle of rotation of the crankshaft versus the distance from piston to the center of the circle. Here are the needed equations on Sheet2.

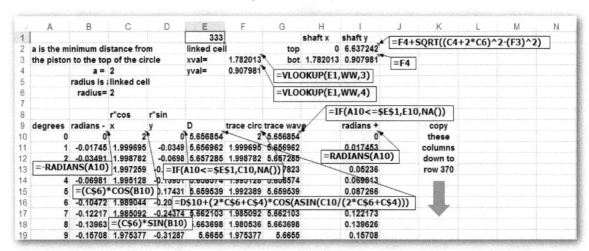

What you need to do

```
Option Explicit

Sub Sinusoid()
   Dim i As Integer, j As Integer, pTime As Double
   Range("J27") = "no": Range("J27").Select
   For i = 1 To 7
      Sheet2.Range("C6") = i
      For j = 0 To 360
         Sheet2.Range("E1") = j
         pTime = Timer + 0.005 'Timer: secs since midnight; pause by .005 seconds
         Do While Timer < pTime
            DoEvents
            Calculate
            If Range("J27") = "yes" Then Exit Sub
         Loop
      Next j
   Next i
End Sub
```

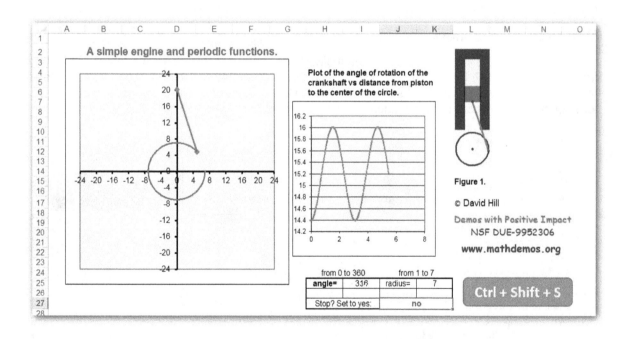

Chapter 61: The Brusselator Model

What the simulation does

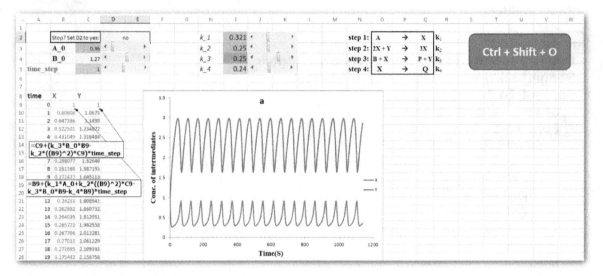

The Brusselator model was proposed by Prigogine and his coworkers in 1967 at Free University of Brussels. This model was created for the explanation of the mechanism of a Bray-Liebhafsky reaction proposed by Bray and Liebhafsky at University of California, Berkeley. This model is one of the oscillating reactions which can be seen in real cases.

What you need to know

The sheet has sliders that you can manually move. If you run the VBA code instead, it loops from 35 to 100 for cell D3 (behind the control) and from 100 to 240 for cell D4. If you want to stop the loops, type "yes" in cell D2 (and Enter). The cells C3:C5 do not have values in them but a formula that is connected to cells hidden behind the sliders.

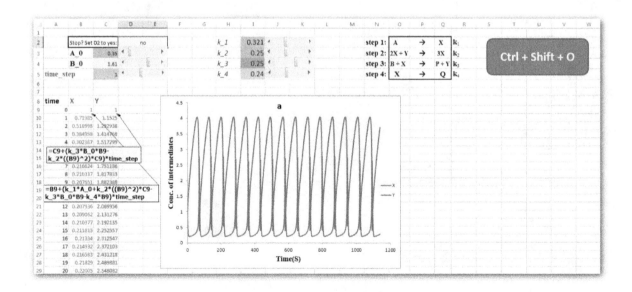

What you need to do

```
Option Explicit

Sub Oscillation()
   Dim i As Integer, j As Integer, pTime As Double
   Range("D2") = "no": Range("D2").Select
   For i = 35 To 100
      Range("D3") = i
      For j = 100 To 240
         Range("D4") = j
         pTime = Timer + 0.005 'Timer: secs since midnight; pause by .005 seconds
         Do While Timer < pTime
            DoEvents
            Calculate
            If Range("D2") = "yes" Then Exit Sub
         Loop
      Next j
   Next i
End Sub
```

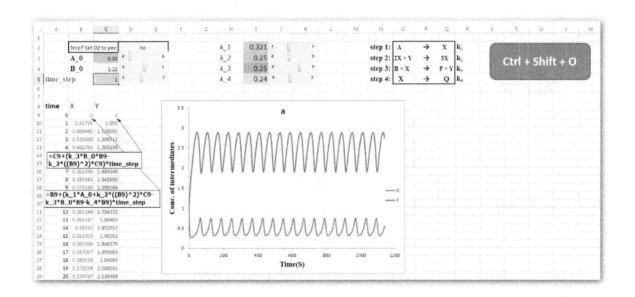

Chapter 62: A Hawk-Dove Game

What the simulation does

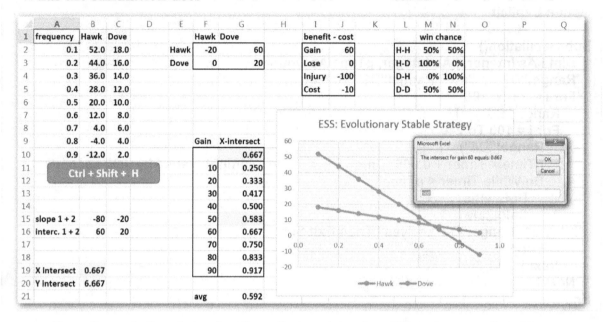

Game theory is the study of mathematical models of conflict and cooperation. The name "Hawk-Dove" refers to a situation in which there is a competition for a shared resource and the contestants can choose either conciliation or conflict; this terminology is most commonly used in biology and economics.

The traditional payoff matrix for the Hawk-Dove game includes the value of the contested resource, and the cost of an escalated fight. It is assumed that the value of the resource is less than the cost of a fight. Sometimes the players are supposed to split the payoff equally, other times the payoff is assumed to be zero. These values can be found in columns J, M, and N.

A "mixed" evolutionary strategy (ESS) is where two strategies permanently coexist. For a given set of payoffs, there will be one set of frequencies where this mix is stable. A mixed ESS can be achieved if individuals either play one strategy all of the time in a population where the two strategies are at the equilibrium frequencies (for example, 60% of the individuals always call and 40% always act as satellites), or all individuals play a mixed strategy where each behavior in the mix is performed at the equilibrium frequency.

What you need to know

The VBA code loops for the "gain" setting (cell J2) from 10 to 90 by increments of 10, and displays each time an *InputBox*, which can be cancelled to stop the loop.

Unlike a *MsgBox*, an *InputBox* can be positioned on the screen (through the 4th and 5th argument). When an *Inputbox* is cancelled, it returns an empty string (""). So we can check for an empty string and then exit the *For*-loop.

What you need to do

```
Option Explicit

Sub HawkDove()
   Dim iGain As Integer, sMsg As String, iTrick As String
   Range("B2:B10").Formula = "=A2*$F$2+(1-A2)*$G$2"
   Range("C2:C10").Formula = "=A2*$F$3+(1-A2)*$G$3"
   For iGain = 10 To 90 Step 10
      Range("J2") = iGain
      Sheet1.Calculate
      sMsg = "The intersect for gain " & iGain & " equals: " & _
            FormatNumber(Range("B19"), 3)
      'to position the MsgBox use an InputBox instead
      iTrick = InputBox(sMsg, , "next", 1000, 2500)
      If iTrick = "" Then Exit Sub
   Next iGain
   Range("J2") = 50
End Sub
```

	A	B	C	D	E	F	G
1	frequency	Hawk	Dove			Hawk	Dove
2	0.1	=A2*$F$2+(1-A2)*$G$2	=A2*$F$3+(1-A2)*$G$3		Hawk	=($M$2*$J$2)+(($N$2*$J$4))	=$M$3*$J$2-0
3	0.2	=A3*$F$2+(1-A3)*$G$2	=A3*$F$3+(1-A3)*$G$3		Dove	=$M$4*$J$2+$N$4*$J$3	=$M$5*($J$2+$J$5)-N
4	0.3	=A4*$F$2+(1-A4)*$G$2	=A4*$F$3+(1-A4)*$G$3				
5	0.4	=A5*$F$2+(1-A5)*$G$2	=A5*$F$3+(1-A5)*$G$3				
6	0.5	=A6*$F$2+(1-A6)*$G$2	=A6*$F$3+(1-A6)*$G$3				
7	0.6	=A7*$F$2+(1-A7)*$G$2	=A7*$F$3+(1-A7)*$G$3				
8	0.7	=A8*$F$2+(1-A8)*$G$2	=A8*$F$3+(1-A8)*$G$3				
9	0.8	=A9*$F$2+(1-A9)*$G$2	=A9*$F$3+(1-A9)*$G$3			Gain	X-intersect
10	0.9	=A10*$F$2+(1-A10)*$G$2	=A10*$F$3+(1-A10)*$G$3				=B19
11						10	=TABLE(,J2)
12						20	=TABLE(,J2)
13						30	=TABLE(,J2)
14						40	=TABLE(,J2)
15	slope 1 + 2	=SLOPE(B2:B10,$A$2:$A$10)	=SLOPE(C2:C10,$A$2:$A$10)			50	=TABLE(,J2)
16	interc. 1 + 2	=INTERCEPT(B2:B10,$A$2:$A$10)	=INTERCEPT(C2:C10,$A$2:$A$10)			60	=TABLE(,J2)
17						70	=TABLE(,J2)
18						80	=TABLE(,J2)
19	X intersect	=(inter2-inter1)/(slope1-slope2)				90	=TABLE(,J2)
20	Y intersect	=slope1*B19+inter1					
21						avg	=AVERAGE(G10:G19)
22							

VI. BUSINESS

Chapter 63: Prognosis of Sales

What the simulation does

	Year	Product1	Product2	Product3	Product4	Product5	Product6	Product7	Product8	Product9	Product10					
2	2000	$14,002.00	$15,957.00	$16,685.00	$19,420.00	$15,479.00	$29,271.00	$23,168.00	$31,295.00	$32,394.00	$15,212.00					
3	2001	$31,000.00	$26,988.00	$48,901.00	$27,771.00	$11,660.00	$20,209.00	$41,797.00	$41,202.00	$16,421.00	$38,746.00					
4	2002	$34,577.00	$35,689.00	$49,594.00	$17,490.00	$31,206.00	$33,148.00	$46,040.00	$43,106.00	$26,141.00	$26,752.00					
5	2003	$41,732.00	$11,770.00	$31,441.00	$15,257.00	$41,343.00	$11,542.00	$22,185.00	$34,362.00	$30,811.00	$40,623.00					
6	2004	$45,602.00	$20,850.00	$45,404.00	$18,480.00	$28,507.00	$16,507.00	$35,370.00	$40,080.00	$15,620.00	$42,291.00					
7	2005	$38,828.00	$48,262.00	$29,163.00	$11,122.00	$36,491.00	$37,172.00	$33,524.00	$26,674.00	$36,485.00	$37,180.00					
8	2006	$25,774.00	$37,809.00	$22,168.00	$43,452.00	$20,707.00	$25,296.00	$44,391.00	$37,048.00	$43,386.00	$43,883.00					
9	2007	$20,440.00	$37,916.00	$31,121.00	$43,401.00	$10,117.00	$37,649.00	$35,478.00	$28,096.00	$46,507.00	$49,406.00					
10	2008	$46,297.00	$24,274.00	$17,033.00	$31,454.00	$20,617.00	$27,858.00	$38,808.00	$14,678.00	$12,286.00	$31,479.00					
11	2009	$20,560.00	$48,689.00	$24,128.00	$13,225.00	$46,012.00	$30,691.00	$23,124.00	$35,450.00	$13,630.00	$12,388.00					
12	2010	$48,490.00	$34,912.00	$14,208.00	$36,686.00	$29,818.00	$49,833.00	$32,385.00	$30,419.00	$22,260.00	$35,335.00					
13	2011	$22,823.00	$10,164.00	$41,990.00	$46,173.00	$23,896.00	$13,460.00	$27,417.00	$26,683.00	$43,961.00	$29,795.00					
14	2012	$27,220.00	$27,754.00	$16,649.00	$26,923.00	$27,866.00	$23,673.00	$27,912.00	$16,311.00	$25,199.00	$23,089.00					
15	2013	$34,886.00	$12,634.00	$47,870.00	$46,031.00	$12,205.00	$35,214.00	$49,974.00	$36,648.00	$32,127.00	$36,492.00					
16	2014	$36,852.00	$24,378.00	$40,371.00	$15,392.00	$12,361.00	$23,062.00	$16,617.00	$47,308.00	$25,746.00	$16,377.00					
17	2015	$41,098.00	$10,298.00	$25,981.00	$31,890.00	$19,148.00	$37,841.00	$38,198.00	$31,135.00	$29,924.00	$44,980.00					
18	2016	$12,013.00	$16,547.00	$24,217.00	$21,912.00	$15,999.00	$17,816.00	$11,841.00	$19,619.00	$20,651.00	$45,518.00					
19	2017	$41,356.00	$26,986.00	$38,402.00	$47,741.00	$26,932.00	$42,590.00	$37,884.00	$27,937.00	$15,563.00	$14,516.00					
20																
21	25%	$24,804.43	$17,937.39	$23,224.88	$19,851.12	$16,883.30	$21,457.04	$25,663.00	$25,617.91	$20,042.18	$24,466.46					
22	mean	$32,270.89	$26,180.97	$31,551.57	$28,423.55	$23,802.16	$28,387.14	$32,540.40	$31,681.51	$27,058.42	$32,399.94					
23	75%	$39,839.83	$34,564.34	$39,708.22	$36,980.10	$30,706.55	$35,362.23	$39,524.83	$37,751.10	$34,141.17	$40,255.74					

Ctrl + Shift + P

This is basically a simple simulation. It gives a prognosis for each product based on its previous performance. It assumes that each product will sell next year according to a random distribution based on the average of pervious years' sales and the standard deviation of those sales. It does so with the Excel function NORMINV. The simulation also plots the 25th and 75th percentile. Obviously, results will vary, but using a high number of loops (10,000) limits fluctuations.

What you need to know

The simulation loops slowly through each product, from B through K, thanks to a *Timer* interval. It shows progress by assigning a color to each finished cell of averages in row 22.

20											
21	25%	$24,821.32	$17,682.12	$23,073.07	$20,051.31	$16,766.18	$21,402.10	$25,435.22	$25,350.75	$19,897.24	$24,369.36
22	mean	$32,404.11	$26,173.45	$31,415.04	$28,646.42	$23,746.73	$28,469.50	$32,521.78	$31,602.60	$27,187.55	$32,374.05
23	75%	$39,957.69	$34,632.37	$39,676.89	$37,365.56	$30,803.74	$35,471.94	$39,509.88	$37,779.70	$34,394.44	$40,410.39

20											
21	25%	$24,823.07	$18,111.55	$23,437.53	$19,919.97	$16,712.92	$21,402.10	$25,435.22	$25,350.75	$19,897.24	$24,369.36
22	mean	$32,404.24	$26,310.68	$31,462.79	$28,388.94	$23,753.22	$28,469.50	$32,521.78	$31,602.60	$27,187.55	$32,374.05
23	75%	$39,947.12	$34,462.31	$39,774.35	$37,116.02	$30,726.30	$35,471.94	$39,509.88	$37,779.70	$34,394.44	$40,410.39

20											
21	25%	$24,885.11	$17,718.25	$23,160.19	$19,948.62	$16,786.12	$21,284.68	$25,688.11	$25,546.42	$20,069.43	$24,348.39
22	mean	$32,383.64	$26,151.29	$31,443.97	$28,541.91	$23,847.46	$28,478.00	$32,742.33	$31,723.80	$27,309.27	$32,558.15
23	75%	$39,871.83	$34,379.76	$39,629.97	$37,208.23	$31,050.86	$35,612.20	$39,759.64	$37,952.44	$34,623.29	$40,686.92

What you need to do

```
Option Explicit

Sub Prognosis()
   Dim r As Long, c As Integer, oRange As Range, i As Long, iTime As Long
   Dim pAvg As Double, pSD As Double, arrRuns() As Double
   MsgBox "Prognosis per column based on 10,000 iterations."
   With Range("A1").CurrentRegion
      .Rows(.Rows.Count + 3).Interior.Color = vbWhite
      r = .Rows.Count
      For c = 2 To .Columns.Count
         pAvg = WorksheetFunction.Average(.Columns(c))
         pSD = WorksheetFunction.StDev(.Columns(c))
         ReDim arrRuns(0 To 9999)
         For i = 0 To 9999
            arrRuns(i) = WorksheetFunction.Norm_Inv(Rnd, pAvg, pSD)
         Next i
         iTime = Timer + 1
         Do Until Timer > iTime
            DoEvents
         Loop
         .Cells(r + 2, c) = WorksheetFunction.Percentile(arrRuns, 0.25)
         .Cells(r + 3, c) = WorksheetFunction.Average(arrRuns)
         .Cells(r + 4, c) = WorksheetFunction.Percentile(arrRuns, 0.75)
         With .Cells(r + 3, c).Interior
            If .Color = vbYellow Then .Color = vbWhite Else .Color = vbYellow
         End With
      Next c
   End With
End Sub
```

Chapter 64: Cycle Percentiles

What the simulation does

	A	B	C	D	E	F	G	H	I	J	K	L	M
1		Sunday	Monday	Tuesday	Wednesday	Thursday	Friday	Saturday					
2	Jan	$21,156.00					$17,779.00	$16,921.00					
3	Feb			$18,562.00		$24,043.00	$24,310.00	$20,154.00					
4	Mar			$16,676.00			$21,121.00						
5	Apr	$18,451.00											
6	May	$17,756.00	$18,157.00		$20,094.00		$24,807.00	$23,797.00					
7	Jun	$24,290.00	$24,505.00	$22,918.00				$23,007.00					
8	Jul			$22,584.00		$24,846.00							
9	Aug	$18,010.00						$21,737.00					
10	Sep		$18,495.00	$18,978.00									
11	Oct				$16,808.00	$17,393.00							
12	Nov				$17,420.00			$23,347.00					
13	Dec	$20,898.00	$24,152.00	$19,505.00	$23,232.00			$16,429.00					
14													

Ctrl + Shift + P

Microsoft Excel

Above the 60th percentile: $16,429.00
Next?

OK   Cancel

This is a simple macro to show the user during a nice cycle of views what the best or worst sales were—in which months and on which days.

The macro does so by cycling through percentile views in steps of 10. It allows the user to specify whether to go up from the 10th to 90th percentile, or down from the 90th percentile to the 10th percentile. It also calculates the total amount of sales for each percentile view.

What you need to know

There is nothing really new in this VBA code. Based on a *Boolean* variable, set through a *MsgBox*, the cycle goes either up or down.

For the percentile scores, we used the Excel function PERCENTILE. This function works in all Excel versions. In version 2010 and later, it can be replaced with PERCENTILE.EXC or PERCENTILE. INC. The former function does not include k=1, whereas the latter one does. So the latter one is equivalent to the older function PERCENTILE.

Depending on the percentile step, certain numbers are "hidden" by assigning a white font. This is done by adding to the collection of *FormatConditions*. To prevent that these pile up, we delete all *FormatConditions* in the range of sales figures at the end.

To make everything work properly, the macro also needs to "play" with *ScreenUpdating* settings.

	A	B	C	D	E	F	G	H	I	J	K	L
1		Sunday	Monday	Tuesday	Wednesday	Thursday	Friday	Saturday				
2	Jan	$21,156.00	$ 8,310.00	$13,602.00	$14,363.00	$13,573.00	$17,779.00	$16,921.00				
3	Feb	$12,750.00	$14,798.00	$18,562.00	$10,273.00	$24,043.00	$24,310.00	$20,154.00				
4	Mar	$13,695.00	$ 8,005.00	$16,676.00	$14,154.00	$ 6,036.00	$21,121.00	$ 5,724.00				
5	Apr	$18,451.00	$ 6,964.00	$ 6,513.00	$ 6,445.00	$10,611.00	$12,655.00	$15,348.00				
6	May	$17,756.00	$18,157.00	$ 9,004.00	$20,094.00	$13,731.00	$24,807.00	$23,797.00				
7	Jun	$24,290.00	$24,505.00	$22,918.00	$13,960.00	$ 5,575.00	$12,111.00	$23,007.00				
8	Jul	$10,515.00	$ 5,017.00	$22,584.00	$10,133.00	$24,846.00	$15,429.00	$ 9,445.00				
9	Aug	$18,010.00	$12,663.00	$15,648.00	$ 7,464.00	$12,420.00	$12,619.00	$21,737.00				
10	Sep	$ 9,615.00	$18,495.00	$18,978.00	$14,235.00	$15,345.00	$16,216.00	$11,548.00				
11	Oct	$ 6,217.00	$ 5,125.00	$ 5,168.00	$16,808.00	$17,393.00	$14,806.00	$ 9,839.00				
12	Nov	$12,394.00	$15,879.00	$11,605.00	$17,420.00	$ 7,623.00	$11,010.00	$23,347.00				
13	Dec	$20,898.00	$24,152.00	$19,505.00	$23,232.00	$ 8,414.00	$ 9,733.00	$16,429.00				
14												

Ctrl + Shift + P

What you need to do

```
Option Explicit

Sub PercentileUpOrDown()
   Dim oRange As Range, oFormat As FormatCondition
   Dim bDown As Boolean, i As Integer, iPerc As Integer, pPerc As Double, sMsg As
String
   If ActiveSheet.Name <> Sheet1.Name Then Exit Sub
   Set oRange = Range("A1").CurrentRegion
   Set oRange = oRange.Offset(1, 1).Resize(oRange.Rows.Count - 1,
oRange.Columns.Count - 1)
   If MsgBox("Go Down? (No = Go Up)", vbYesNo) = vbYes Then bDown = True: iPerc
= 100
   For i = 1 To 9
      Application.ScreenUpdating = False
      If bDown Then iPerc = iPerc - 10 Else iPerc = iPerc + 10
      pPerc = WorksheetFunction.Percentile_Exc(oRange, iPerc / 100)
      Set oFormat = oRange.FormatConditions.Add(xlExpression, xlFormula, "=B2<" &
pPerc)      'not A1
      Application.ScreenUpdating = True
      oFormat.Font.Color = vbWhite    '.Interior.Color = RGB(0, 0, 0) with max of 255
      sMsg = "Above the " & iPerc & "th percentile: " & FormatCurrency(pPerc) & vbCr
& "Next?"
      If MsgBox(sMsg, vbOKCancel) = vbCancel Then i = 9
      Application.ScreenUpdating = False
      oRange.FormatConditions.Delete
      Application.ScreenUpdating = True
   Next i
End Sub
```

Chapter 65: Cost Estimates

What the simulation does

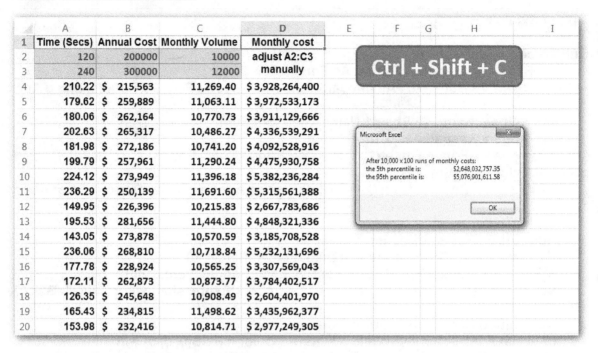

The cells A2:C3 are based on manual input, with the low estimates in row 2 and the high estimates in row 3.

For each of the columns A, B, and C, we simulate normally distributed values with a mean between low (row 2) and high (row 3) as well as a standard deviation of 2 units on either side. On the sheet, we use only 100 repeats up to row 103—which is rather risky. Column D calculates the monthly costs for each case.

To reduce the risk of estimating costs, the macro repeats these 100 steps some 10,000 times by storing the results for each run in arrays. Arrays work very swiftly and make our estimates less subject to random fluctuations.

At the end of the macro, a *MsgBox* displays the 5th and 95th percentile for these 1,000,000 projections. A new run of the macro will yield different results, but they differ only slightly.

What you need to know

	Time (Secs)	Annual Cost	Monthly Volume	Monthly cost
1	Time (Secs)	Annual Cost	Monthly Volume	Monthly cost
2	120	200000	10000	adjust A2:C3 manually
3	240	300000	12000	
4	=NORMINV(RAND(),SUM(A$2:A$3)/2,(MAX(A$2:A$3)-MIN(A$2:A$3))/4)	=NORMINV(RAND(),SUM(B$2:B:	=NORMINV(RAND(),SUM(C$2	=A4/130*B4*C4
5	=NORMINV(RAND(),SUM(A$2:A$3)/2,(MAX(A$2:A$3)-MIN(A$2:A$3))/4)	=NORMINV(RAND(),SUM(B$2:B:	=NORMINV(RAND(),SUM(C$2	=A5/130*B5*C5
6	=NORMINV(RAND(),SUM(A$2:A$3)/2,(MAX(A$2:A$3)-MIN(A$2:A$3))/4)	=NORMINV(RAND(),SUM(B$2:B:	=NORMINV(RAND(),SUM(C$2	=A6/130*B6*C6
7	=NORMINV(RAND(),SUM(A$2:A$3)/2,(MAX(A$2:A$3)-MIN(A$2:A$3))/4)	=NORMINV(RAND(),SUM(B$2:B:	=NORMINV(RAND(),SUM(C$2	=A7/130*B7*C7
8	=NORMINV(RAND(),SUM(A$2:A$3)/2,(MAX(A$2:A$3)-MIN(A$2:A$3))/4)	=NORMINV(RAND(),SUM(B$2:B:	=NORMINV(RAND(),SUM(C$2	=A8/130*B8*C8
9	=NORMINV(RAND(),SUM(A$2:A$3)/2,(MAX(A$2:A$3)-MIN(A$2:A$3))/4)	=NORMINV(RAND(),SUM(B$2:B:	=NORMINV(RAND(),SUM(C$2	=A9/130*B9*C9

What you need to do

```
Option Explicit

Sub Costs()
   Dim i As Long, d5Perc As Double, d95Perc As Double, sMsg As String
   Dim arr5Perc() As Double, arr95Perc() As Double
   With Range("A4:D103")
      .ClearContents
      MsgBox "First normally distributed random calculations:"
      Application.Calculation = xlCalculationManual
      .Columns(1).Formula = "=NORMINV(RAND(),SUM(A$2:A$3)/2,(MAX(A$2:A$3)-
MIN(A$2:A$3))/4)"
      .Columns(2).Formula = "=NORMINV(RAND(),SUM(B$2:B$3)/2,(MAX(B$2:B$3)-
MIN(B$2:B$3))/4)"
      .Columns(3).Formula = "=NORMINV(RAND(),SUM(C$2:C$3)/2,(MAX(C$2:C$3)-
MIN(C$2:C$3))/4)"
      .Columns(4).Formula = "=A4/130*B4*C4"
      MsgBox "Now follow 10,000 runs with arrays:"
      ReDim arr5Perc(0 To 9999): ReDim arr95Perc(0 To 9999)
      For i = 0 To 9999
         .Calculate
         arr5Perc(i) = WorksheetFunction.Percentile(.Columns(4), 0.05)
         arr95Perc(i) = WorksheetFunction.Percentile(.Columns(4), 0.95)
      Next i
   End With
   d5Perc = WorksheetFunction.Average(arr5Perc)
   d95Perc = WorksheetFunction.Average(arr95Perc)
   sMsg = "After 10,000 x 100 runs of monthly costs:" & vbCr
   sMsg = sMsg & "the 5th percentile is:" & vbTab & vbTab
   sMsg = sMsg & FormatCurrency(d5Perc, 2) & vbCr & "the 95th percentile is:"
   sMsg = sMsg & vbTab & FormatCurrency(d95Perc, 2)
   MsgBox sMsg
End Sub
```

	A	B	C	D	E	F	G	H	I
1	Time (Secs)	Annual Cost	Monthly Volume	Monthly cost					
2	120	200000	10000	adjust A2:C3					
3	240	300000	12000	manually					
4	140.10	$ 262,519	11,286.60	$ 3,193,069,216					
5	210.57	$ 236,562	12,311.95	$ 4,717,623,339					
6	165.30	$ 252,137	10,663.90	$ 3,418,857,122					
7	178.65	$ 226,212	11,669.60	$ 3,627,607,932					
8	161.43	$ 240,053	11,106.80	$ 3,310,862,276					
9	203.06	$ 220,358	10,668.50	$ 3,672,153,381					
10	203.69	$ 237,088	9,811.33	$ 3,644,801,749					
11	136.52	$ 251,841	12,033.68	$ 3,182,497,973					
12	191.49	$ 263,496	10,951.46	$ 4,250,613,908					
13	199.14	$ 224,615	9,969.40	$ 3,430,290,437					

Ctrl + Shift + C

Microsoft Excel

After 10,000 x 100 runs of monthly costs:
the 5th percentile is: $2,647,268,435.09
the 95th percentile is: $5,076,008,497.58

OK

Chapter 66: A Filtering Table

What the simulation does

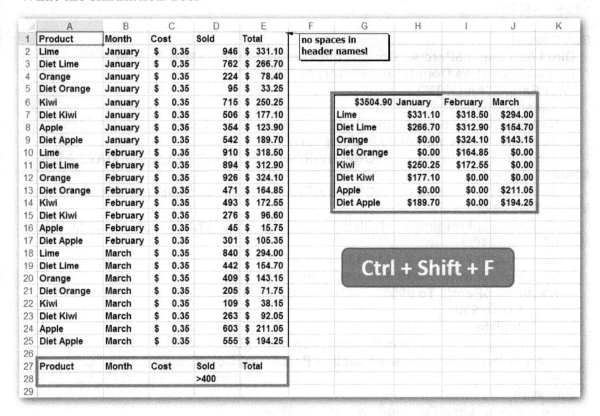

Range G6:J14 contains a 2-dimensional table with information that the macro has extracted from the database A1:E25. The macro also creates a filter in A27:E28 which regulates what the table G6:J14 displays (in this case, whatever was sold with quantities over 400.

The filter works through the labels, or headers, of the database. The filter sums the totals by using the function DSUM at the origin of the table (G6).

27	Product	Month	Cost	Sold	Total
28				>400	>300

What you need to know

To create a list of unique entries in row1 and column1 of the table (G6:J14), we can use *AdvancedFilter*. It has four arguments: Action (e.g. xlFilterCopy), CriteriaRange (optional), CopyToRange, Unique (True).

Since *AdvancedFilter* returns a vertical list of unique entries, we need to manipulate the two lists. This can be done by storing the two lists in a *Variant* array that is 2-dimensional. The array helps us to place the lists in a 2-dimensional table by using a loop for the 1st dimension inside a loop for the 2nd dimension. The function *UBound*(array, 1) returns the index number of the last element in the 1st dimension; *UBound*(array,2) does that for the 2nd dimension.

In cell G5, the macro implements DSUM. Unlike SUM, it accepts also certain criteria as to what to sum. It has 3 arguments: the database, the field label, and the criteria range (A27:E28).

What you need to do

```
Option Explicit

Sub Filtering()
    Dim vArr As Variant, i As Integer, j As Integer, sFilter As String
    Dim oFilter As Range, oRange As Range
    Range("G6").CurrentRegion.Delete xlShiftToLeft
    With Range("A1").CurrentRegion
        i = .Rows.Count
        .Range(Cells(i + 2, 1), Cells(i + 3, 5)).Delete xlShiftUp
        MsgBox "Prepare the matrix and the filter"
        .Columns(1).AdvancedFilter xlFilterCopy, , Range("G6"), True
        .Columns(2).AdvancedFilter xlFilterCopy, , Range("H6"), True
        Set oFilter = .Range(Cells(i + 2, 1), Cells(i + 3, 5))
        oFilter.Rows(1) = .Rows(1).Value
    End With
    With Range("G6")
        vArr = .CurrentRegion
        .CurrentRegion.ClearContents
        MsgBox "Fix the matrix"
        For i = 2 To UBound(vArr, 1) '1 is label | UBound(x,1) is 1st dimension
            For j = 2 To UBound(vArr, 2) '1 is label | UBound(x,2) is 2nd dimension
                .Offset(i - 1, 0) = vArr(i, 1)
                .Offset(0, i - 1) = vArr(i, 2)
            Next j
        Next i
        MsgBox "Implement the filter"
        Set oRange = Range("A1").CurrentRegion
        .Cells(1, 1).Formula = "=DSUM(" & oRange.Address & ",E1," & oFilter.Address & _
")" 'E1 is the Totals label
        .Cells(1, 1).CurrentRegion.Table Range("B28"), Range("A28")
        .Cells(1, 1).CurrentRegion.NumberFormat = "$##0.00"
        .Cells(1, 1).CurrentRegion.EntireColumn.AutoFit
    End With
    oFilter.Cells(2, 4) = InputBox("Sold filter (or Cancel)", , ">400")
    oFilter.Cells(2, 5) = InputBox("Total filter (or Cancel)", , ">300")
End Sub
```

$1286.60	January	February	March
Lime	$331.10	$318.50	$0.00
Diet Lime	$0.00	$312.90	$0.00
Orange	$0.00	$324.10	$0.00
Diet Orange	$0.00	$0.00	$0.00
Kiwi	$0.00	$0.00	$0.00
Diet Kiwi	$0.00	$0.00	$0.00
Apple	$0.00	$0.00	$0.00
Diet Apple	$0.00	$0.00	$0.00

Chapter 67: Profit Changes

What the simulation does

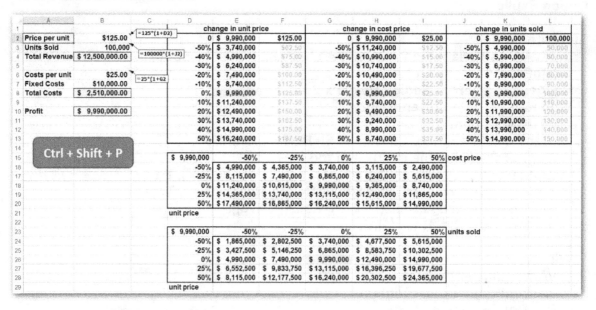

This simulation creates and populates five different *Data Table* ranges. The first three have a column input of D2, which holds the price per unit. However, we have a powerful "trick" here: there is no value in cell D2 but a formula that multiplies its value with (1+D2), so the *Data Table* can use price changes in percentages in its 1st column, and the corresponding price in the 3rd column.

What you need to know

Since cells such as B2 and B3 don't contain a value but a formula, the macro locks and protects all cells, so no formulas can be overwritten. The *Protect* method of VBA can do so; it has many arguments; the 5th one is *UserInterfaceOnly*; when set to True, macro's can still change cells, but users cannot.

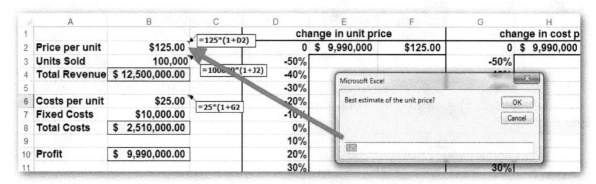

A *Variant* type of variable can hold an array, even an array that comes from the VBA function *Array*. In our simulation, the *Array* function holds the addresses of 5 cell ranges, and returns a 1-dimensional array. (You can always check this in your code by placing a *BreakPoint* after the array line and then opening the *Locals Window*.) Based on this list, the corresponding ranges can be cleared.

A combination of *Offset* and *Resize* allows VBA to change ranges. For example. *Range("A1:D4").Offset(1,1).Resize(4,4).Address* would change the range from A1:D4 to B2:E5.

What you need to do

```
Option Explicit

Sub Profits()
  Dim oUnitPrice As Range, oCostPrice As Range, oUnitsSold As Range
  Dim oUnitAndCost As Range, oUnitAndSold As Range
  Dim pUnitPrice As Double, pCostprice As Double, iSold As Long, vArr As Variant, i
As Integer
  vArr = Array("E3:F13", "H3:I13", "K3:L13", "E16:I20", "E24:I28")
  For i = 0 To UBound(vArr)
     Range(vArr(i)).ClearContents
  Next i
  Sheet1.Protect , , , , True 'no changes on sheet except throug macro (=true)
  pUnitPrice = InputBox("Best estimate of the unit price?", , 125)
  Range("B2").Formula = "=(1+D2)*" & pUnitPrice
  pCostprice = InputBox("Best estimate of the cost price?", , 25)
  Range("B6").Formula = "=(1+G2)*" & pCostprice
  iSold = InputBox("Best estimate of items sold?", , 100000)
  Range("B3").Formula = "=(1+J2)*" & iSold
  Set oUnitPrice = Range(vArr(0)).Offset(-1, -1).Resize(Range(vArr(0)).Rows.Count +
1, Range(vArr(0)).Columns.Count + 1)
  Set oCostPrice = Range(vArr(1)).Offset(-1, -1).Resize(Range(vArr(1)).Rows.Count +
1, Range(vArr(1)).Columns.Count + 1)
  Set oUnitsSold = Range(vArr(2)).Offset(-1, -1).Resize(Range(vArr(2)).Rows.Count +
1, Range(vArr(2)).Columns.Count + 1)
  Set oUnitAndCost = Range(vArr(3)).Offset(-1, -1).Resize(Range(vArr(3)).Rows.Count
+ 1, Range(vArr(3)).Columns.Count + 1)
  Set oUnitAndSold = Range(vArr(4)).Offset(-1, -1).Resize(Range(vArr(4)).Rows.Count
+ 1, Range(vArr(4)).Columns.Count + 1)
  oUnitPrice.Table , Range("D2")
  oCostPrice.Table , Range("G2")
  oUnitsSold.Table , Range("J2")
  oUnitAndCost.Table Range("G2"), Range("D2")
  oUnitAndSold.Table Range("J2"), Range("D2")
End Sub
```

	A	B	C	D	E	F
1					change in unit price	
2	Price per unit	=(1+D2)*125		0	=B10	=B2
3	Units Sold	=(1+J2)*100000		-0.5	=TABLE(,D2)	=TABLE(,D2)
4	Total Revenue	=B2*B3		-0.4	=TABLE(,D2)	=TABLE(,D2)
5				-0.3	=TABLE(,D2)	=TABLE(,D2)
6	Costs per unit	=(1+G2)*25		-0.2	=TABLE(,D2)	=TABLE(,D2)
7	Fixed Costs	10000		-0.1	=TABLE(,D2)	=TABLE(,D2)
8	Total Costs	=B3*B6+B7		0	=TABLE(,D2)	=TABLE(,D2)
9				0.1	=TABLE(,D2)	=TABLE(,D2)
10	Profit	=B4-B8		0.2	=TABLE(,D2)	=TABLE(,D2)
11				0.3	=TABLE(,D2)	=TABLE(,D2)
12				0.4	=TABLE(,D2)	=TABLE(,D2)
13				0.5	=TABLE(,D2)	=TABLE(,D2)

Chapter 68: Risk Analysis

What the simulation does

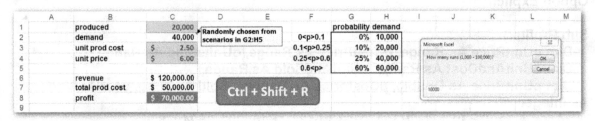

If the demand for some product is regulated by a range of probabilities (G2:H4), then you can determine your optimal production by simulating demand within that range of probabilities and calculating profit for each level of demand.

The top left section (B:C) calculates the profit for one trial production quantity. Cell C1 has a trial production quantity. Cell C2 has a random number. In cell C3, we simulate demand for this product with the function VLOOKUP: =VLOOKUP(RAND(),G2:H5,2,1).

The macro creates a *Data Table* which simulates each possible production quantity (10,000, 20,000, 40,000 or 60,000) some 1,000 to 100,000 times and calculates profits for each trial number (1 to 1,000) and each production quantity (10,000, etc.). At the origin of the *Data Table* (A13) is a reference to the profit calculation in C8. The *Data Table* uses cell C1 (a specific production quantity) for the row input, and an empty cell (say, G14) for the column input.

Finally, row 10 calculates the mean profit for the four different production quantities. In the example shown at the end, the results indicate that production of 40,000 units results in maximum profits. Row 11 does something similar, but now for the standard deviation. Notice that the SD increases when the quantities increase.

What you need to know

The VLOOKUP function in C3 matches the value in C1 with the closest match in the first column of table F2:G5. The corresponding value from the second column in table F2:G5 is then entered into C3.

How does the *Data Table* work? Consider cell D14: the column input cell value of 1 is placed in a blank cell (G14) and the random number in cell C2 recalculates. The corresponding profit is then recorded in cell D14. Next the column cell input value of 2 is placed in the blank cell G14, and the random number in cell C2 again recalculates. The corresponding profit is entered in cell D15. And so on. A *Data Table* has an amazing power!

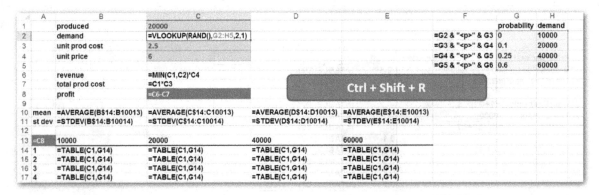

What you need to do

```
Option Explicit

Sub Risks()
  Dim oRange As Range, oTable As Range, i As Long
  Range("B10:E11").ClearContents
  Range("C2").Formula = "=VLOOKUP(RAND(),G2:H5,2,1)"
  Set oRange = Range("B14").CurrentRegion
  With oRange
    Set oTable = .Offset(1, 1).Resize(.Rows.Count - 1, .Columns.Count - 1)
  End With
  oTable.ClearContents
  i = InputBox("How many runs (1,000 - 100,000)?", , 10000)
  Set oRange = Range(Cells(13, 1), Cells(13 + i, 5))
  oRange.Table Range("C1"), Range("G14")
  i = i + 3
  Range("B10:E10").FormulaR1C1 = "=AVERAGE(R14C:R[" & i & "]C)"
  Range("B11:E11").FormulaR1C1 = "=STDEV(R14C:R[" & i-1 & "]C)"
  MsgBox "Results based on 1,000 x " & Format(i - 3, "#,##0") & " runs."
End Sub
```

	A	B	C	D	E	F	G	H	I
1		produced	20,000	Randomly chosen from scenarios in G2:H5			probability	demand	
2		demand	40,000			0<p>0.1	0%	10,000	
3		unit prod cost	$ 2.50			0.1<p>0.25	10%	20,000	
4		unit price	$ 6.00			0.25<p>0.6	25%	40,000	
5						0.6<p>	60%	60,000	
6		revenue	$ 120,000.00						
7		total prod cost	$ 50,000.00		Ctrl + Shift + R				
8		profit	$ 70,000.00						
9									
10	mean	$35,000.00	$63,808.00	$104,096.00	$101,670.00				
11	st dev	$ -	$ 18,254.11	$ 63,894.53	$104,980.73				
12									
13	$70,000.00		10,000	20,000	40,000	60,000			
14		1	$35,000.00	$70,000.00	$20,000.00	$90,000.00			
15		2	$35,000.00	$10,000.00	$140,000.00	$210,000.00			
16		3	$35,000.00	$70,000.00	$140,000.00	($30,000.00)			

Microsoft Excel

Results based on 1,000 x 10,000 runs.

OK

Chapter 69: Scenarios

What the simulation does

	A	B	C	D	E	F	G	H	I	J	K	L
1	scenarios	most likely		worst case		best case		uncertainty			scenario combinations	
2		2		4		6					2-4-6	246
3	Volume	2,000		1,400		2,200		1,823.09				
4	Cost/unit	$ 3.00		$ 2.75		$ 3.25		$3.11 copy down			Min	$ 78,647.88
5	Profit/unit	$ 60.00		$ 55.00		$ 65.00		$61.18			25%	$ 91,421.49
6	Overhead	$ 800.00		$ 800.00		$ 800.00					Median	$ 104,218.20
7											75%	$ 113,433.54
8	Revenues	$120,000.00		$77,000.00		$143,000.00		$111,529.71			Max	$ 135,190.35
9	Expenses	$6,800.00		$4,650.00		$7,950.00		$6,463.80				
10											Ctrl + Shift + S	
11	Profit	$113,200.00		$72,350.00		$135,050.00		$105,065.92				
12									Volume	Revenues	Expenses	Profit
13		most likely		worst case		best case		$105,065.92	1,823	$111,529.71	$6,463.80	$105,065.92
14	1	2	3	4	5	6			1,546	$ 90,114.07	$5,633.30	$ 84,480.77
15	1,500	2,000	1,200	1,400	2,100	2,200			1,861	$118,149.32	$6,377.54	$111,771.79
16	$ 2.50	$ 3.00	$ 2.30	$ 2.75	$ 2.70	$ 3.25			1,702	$106,405.08	$6,250.67	$100,154.41
17	$ 50.00	$ 60.00	$ 47.00	$ 55.00	$ 53.00	$ 65.00			2,070	$133,586.41	$7,240.55	$126,345.86
18									2,153	$137,444.17	$7,727.87	$129,716.30
19		scenarios	worst result	median result	best result				1,899	$112,172.54	$6,845.46	$105,327.08
20		135	$53,679.49	$ 80,235.72	$101,809.60				2,139	$137,306.38	$7,209.29	$130,097.09
21		136	$52,991.25	$ 88,922.14	$132,287.74				1,786	$115,746.69	$6,207.92	$109,538.77
22		145	$70,350.33	$ 91,422.90	$106,585.64				1,577	$ 88,508.86	$5,623.68	$ 82,885.18
23		146	$74,985.02	$101,073.85	$129,847.77				1,887	$106,425.61	$6,348.95	$100,076.66
24		235	$53,884.04	$ 77,927.30	$102,036.31				2,026	$114,446.66	$7,293.51	$107,153.15
25		236	$56,480.43	$ 90,218.55	$123,985.45				1,933	$120,040.42	$6,288.04	$113,752.38
26		245	$70,286.60	$ 85,682.25	$107,989.57				1,899	$113,247.55	$6,381.40	$106,866.14
27		246	$78,647.88	$ 104,218.20	$135,190.35	=INDEX($B$20:$B$27,MATCH(E29,E20:E27,0))			1,908	$123,883.16	$6,764.24	$117,118.92
28									1,634	$ 91,756.05	$5,375.80	$ 86,380.26
29	worst/median/best results:	$52,991.25	$ 87,926.10	$132,287.74					1,846	$108,314.55	$6,549.54	$101,765.01
30	scenario:	136		136					1,463	$ 86,261.06	$5,307.40	$ 80,953.66

Predictions of expenses and revenues are subject to lots of uncertainty. Nevertheless, let's say we want to predict these under a few defined scenarios, such as the most likely, the best case, and the worst case scenario, in order to project a range of possible profit levels.

We use several tables to set up this calculation. The top left table shows the 3 scenarios that were actually chosen. There are actually six scenarios—two for each case—with settings as displayed in the 2nd table (A13:F17).

The main calculations occur in the *Data Table* in the lower-right corner. It is two-dimensional, but has a "hidden" third dimension: the 3 scenarios that were actually chosen in the top left table. All values in column H depend on these 3 scenarios.

The user has a choice of six different scenarios—1 and 2 for the most likely scenario, 3 and 4 for the worst-case scenario, and 5 and 6 for the best-case scenario. So there are actually 8 possible combinations as is shown in B20:B27 (135, 136, etc.). The macro loops through these comnbinations and shows the results for each combination in the table B19:E27.

What you need to know

The cells B3:F5 use the function HLOOKUP, which stands for Horizontal lookup. It is similar to VLOOKUP, only it searches horizontal data rather than columnar data. HLOOKUP is used in the top left table to locate the correct input in the scenario table A14:F17. Because the scenario numbers are in a row (row 14), we need a *horizontal* lookup—HLOOKUP, not VLOOKUP.

What you need to do

```
Option Explicit

Sub Scenarios()
   Dim vArr As Variant, i As Integer, sCombo As String, iRow As Integer, oTable As
Range
   Range("C20:E27").ClearContents
   Range("I14:L1013").ClearContents
   i = InputBox("How many runs (100-1000)?", , 100)
   Set oTable = Range(Cells(13, 8), Cells(13 + i, 12)) 'Starts at $H$13
   oTable.Table , Range("F11")
   vArr = Array(135, 136, 145, 146, 235, 236, 245, 246)
   For i = 0 To 7
      sCombo = vArr(i)
      Cells(2, 2) = Left(sCombo, 1): Cells(2, 4) = Mid(sCombo, 2, 1): Cells(2, 6) =
Right(sCombo, 1)
      Application.Calculate
      iRow = WorksheetFunction.Match(CInt(sCombo), Range("B20:B27"))
      Range("C20:E27").Cells(iRow, 1) = Range("L4")
      Range("C20:E27").Cells(iRow, 2) = Range("L6")
      Range("C20:E27").Cells(iRow, 3) = Range("L8")
      Cells.EntireColumn.AutoFit
      MsgBox "Results for scenarios " & Range("K2")
   Next i
End Sub
```

Chapter 70: Market Growth

What the simulation does

	A	B	C	D	E	F	G	H	I	J	K	L	M	N	O
1			Market	4,000,000	Share	40%									
2															
3	mean		2	1.5			0.02				Ctrl + Shift + M				
4	SD		1	5			0.02								
5															
6			GDP Growth	Multiple	Market Growth	New Market Size	Market Share Growth	New Market Share	Sales Volume		Results of 100 x 100 runs.				
7			2.2824	0.7543	1.7217	10,886,947	0.041	0.441	4,800,971	6,167,707.35	6,167,707		MIN	2,037,142	
8			2.1862	-7.2040	-15.7493	-58,997,103	0.017	0.417	-24,611,715	2	12,370,481		MED	6,908,599	
9			1.8600	-5.5180	-10.2632	-37,052,777	0.053	0.453	-16,792,157	3	7,474,165		MAX	12,370,481	
10			1.4857	3.0110	4.4733	21,893,099	0.033	0.433	9,486,544	4	6,558,327				
11			2.7025	1.8462	4.9894	23,957,454	0.049	0.449	10,762,229	5	5,686,042				
12			4.4483	-5.0618	-22.5160	-86,064,048	0.042	0.442	-38,015,715	6	4,011,503				
13			1.2670	5.4104	6.8547	31,418,811	0.049	0.449	14,112,779	7	5,166,721				
14			1.5527	-4.9283	-7.6523	-26,609,040	0.023	0.423	-11,253,996	8	6,930,279				
15			3.0346	6.7943	20.6180	86,472,133	-0.001	0.399	34,500,103	9	4,281,658				
16			1.2134	-2.1361	-2.5919	-6,367,436	0.043	0.443	-2,822,337	10	7,106,865				
17			1.3390	-5.4670	-7.3206	-25,282,452	0.027	0.427	-10,805,069	11	6,866,835				
18			2.7460	-2.5434	-6.9844	-23,937,634	-0.009	0.391	-9,350,376	12	8,832,158				
19			0.8930	-5.9625	-5.3247	-17,298,641	0.002	0.402	-6,951,062	13	7,047,569				
20			1.3192	9.3452	12.3279	53,311,793	0.013	0.413	22,041,483	14	5,099,442				

Microsoft Excel

Results of 100 x 100 runs.

OK

When talking about GDP growth (*Gross Domestic Product*) and the relationship between GDP growth and market growth, or the increase in market share, we are dealing with three uncertain inputs. The obvious approach is to use the best estimate for each of these inputs.

A better approach might be using a probability distribution, rather than using the single best estimate. Monte-Carlo modelling would use the probability distributions of the inputs. Rather than using the distributions themselves as inputs, we use the distributions to generate random inputs.

Based on a certain market volume (cell D1) and a certain market share (cell F1), the simulation calculates possible sales volumes (column G). It uses random distributions in 100 to 1,000 runs to estimate GDP growth (column A), the relationship between GDP and market size (column B), and the market share growth (column E).

Then it repeats this set of runs another 100 to 1,000 times, in columns J:K. After at least 10,000 runs, we get an rather good estimate of the minimum and maximum sales volumes in column N. Needless to say that these figures can still vary quite a bit, because Monte Carlo simulations become more reliable when based on at least 1,000,000 runs.

What you need to know

The model we use is basically very simple:

- C3: market growth = GDP growth × multiple
- D3: market size = current size × (market growth + 1)
- F3: market share = current market share + gain
- G3: sales volumes = market size × market share

What you need to do

```
Option Explicit

Sub Market()
  Dim i As Long, n As Long, oRange As Range, oTable As Range
  Set oRange = Range("B6").CurrentRegion
  With oRange
    Set oRange = .Offset(1, 0).Resize(.Rows.Count - 1, .Columns.Count)
  End With
  oRange.ClearContents
  Set oTable = Range("J7").CurrentRegion
  With oTable
    Set oTable = .Offset(1, 1).Resize(.Rows.Count - 1, .Columns.Count - 4)
  End With
  oTable.ClearContents
  i = InputBox("How many row calculations (100-1000)?", , 100)
  n = InputBox("How many table runs (100-1000)?", , 100)
  Range("J6") = i & "x" & n & " = " & i * n & " calculations"
  Set oRange = Range(Cells(7, 2), Cells(6 + i, 8))
  oRange.Columns(1).Formula = "=NORMINV(RAND(),$B$3,$B$4)"
  oRange.Columns(2).Formula = "=NORMINV(RAND(),$C$3,$C$4)"
  oRange.Columns(3).Formula = "=B7*C7"
  oRange.Columns(4).Formula = "=$D$1*(D7+1)"
  oRange.Columns(5).Formula = "=NORMINV(RAND(),$F$3,$F$4)"
  oRange.Columns(6).Formula = "=$F$1+F7"
  oRange.Columns(7).Formula = "=E7*G7"
  Set oTable = Range(Cells(7, 10), Cells(6 + n, 11))
  oTable.Cells(1, 1).Formula = "=AVERAGE(" & oRange.Columns(7).Address & ")"
  oTable.Cells(1, 2).Formula = "=AVERAGE(" & oRange.Columns(7).Address & ")"
  oTable.Table , Range("I6")
  Range("N7").Formula = "=MIN(" & oTable.Columns(2).Address & ")"
  Range("N8").Formula = "=MEDIAN(" & oTable.Columns(2).Address & ")"
  Range("N9").Formula = "=MAX(" & oTable.Columns(2).Address & ")"
  Range("J6") = "Results of " & i & " x " & n & " runs."
  MsgBox Range("J6")
End Sub
```

Chapter 71: A Traffic Situation

What the simulation does

	A	B	C	D	E	F	G	H	I	J	K	L	M	N
1	1st stretch	Traffic light	2nd stretch	seconds	minutes			cumul.	secs					
2	111	65.96	240	416.96	6.95			0	240					
3	111	0.00	240	351.00	5.85			70	360					
4	111	0.00	240	351.00	5.85			80	180					
5	111	0.00	240	351.00	5.85			90	1800					
6	111	0.05	240	351.05	5.85									
7	111	37.16	240	388.16	6.47									
8	111	0.00	240	351.00	5.85				6.45	6.81				
9	111	57.83	240	408.83	6.81				6.52	6.87				
10	111	25.34	240	376.34	6.27				6.51	6.85				
11	111	53.50	240	404.50	6.74				6.45	6.80				
12	111	35.19	240	386.19	6.44				6.47	6.88				
13	360	17.74	240	617.74	10.30				6.53	6.88				
14	111	0.00	240	351.00	5.85				6.45	6.84				
15	111	32.10	240	383.10	6.39				6.46	6.81				
16	360	76.91	240	676.91	11.28				6.45	6.83				
17	111	47.36	240	398.36	6.64				6.51	6.84				
18	111	51.34	240	402.34	6.71				6.44	6.80				
19	360	55.25	240	655.25	10.92				6.44	6.78				
20	111	44.39	240	395.39	6.59									

Ctrl + Shift + T

Microsoft Excel

For 1000 x 12 runs:
Median: 6.459 mins.
Average: 6.831 mins.

OK

A Monte Carlo simulation really illustrates how we can tame the uncertainty of the future with ranges and probabilities, but it also shows how impossible it is to be extremely precise.

Column A: We simulate driving 2 miles on a highway, with 90% probability we will average 65 MPH, but with a 10% probability that a traffic jam will result in an average speed of 20 MPH (column A).

Column B: Then there is a traffic light that goes through a 120 second cycle with 90 seconds for "red" and 30 seconds for "green." If we hit it on green then there is no delay, but if we hit it on red we must wait for green.

Column C: Finally, we have 2 more miles to go: 70% of the time at 30 MPH, 10% at 20 MPH, 10% at 40 MPH, and 10% of the time it takes us 30 minutes. This can be calculated with a VLOOKUP function based on H2:I5.

Instead of using a fixed value for input variables, we can model an input variable with a probability distribution and then run the model a large number of times and see what impact the random variation has on the output.

Again, it is wise to run at least 1,000 iterations in the columns A:E. This is to ensure that we have a statistical chance of getting sufficient outliers (extreme values) to make the variance analysis meaningful. This is important because as the number of iterations increases, the variance of the average output decreases.

What you need to know

The simulation also adds a *Data Table* that shows how the median and the average can slightly vary when repeated some 12 times (see screen shot on the next page).

Much more could have been done to this simulation—such as using arrays, more looping, and higher numbers of runs—but I leave that up to you.

What you need to do

```
Option Explicit

Sub TrafficCommute()
   Dim oRange As Range, oTable As Range
   Dim sMsg As String, pMedian As Double, pAvg As Double
   Set oRange = Range("A1").CurrentRegion
   With oRange
      Set oRange = .Offset(1, 0).Resize(.Rows.Count - 1, .Columns.Count)
   End With
   oRange.ClearContents:     Range("I9:J19").ClearContents
   MsgBox "New calculations"
   oRange.Columns(1).Formula = "=IF(RAND() < 0.9, 111, 360)"
   oRange.Columns(2).Formula = "=MAX(0, (RAND() * 120) - 30)"
   oRange.Columns(3).Formula = "=VLOOKUP(RAND(),$H$2:$I$5, 2)"
   oRange.Columns(4).Formula = "=SUM(A2:C2)"
   oRange.Columns(5).Formula = "=D2/60"
   Range("I8").Formula = "=MEDIAN(E:E)": Range("J8").Formula = "=AVERAGE(E:E)"
   Set oTable = Range("H8:J19")
   oTable.Table , Range("G7")
   With oTable
      sMsg = "For 1000 x 12 runs:" & vbCr
      pMedian = FormatNumber(WorksheetFunction.Median(.Columns(2)), 3)
      sMsg = sMsg & "Median: " & vbTab & pMedian & " mins." & vbCr
      pAvg = FormatNumber(WorksheetFunction.Average(.Columns(3)), 3)
      sMsg = sMsg & "Average: " & vbTab & pAvg & " mins." & vbCr
   End With
   MsgBox sMsg
End Sub
```

E	F	G	H	I	J
minutes			cumul.	secs	
=D2/60			0	240	
=D3/60			70	360	
=D4/60			80	180	
=D5/60			90	1800	
=D6/60					
=D7/60					
=D8/60				=MEDIAN(E:E)	=AVERAGE(E:E)
=D9/60				=TABLE(,G7)	=TABLE(,G7)
=D10/60				=TABLE(,G7)	=TABLE(,G7)
=D11/60				=TABLE(,G7)	=TABLE(,G7)
=D12/60				=TABLE(,G7)	=TABLE(,G7)
=D13/60				=TABLE(,G7)	=TABLE(,G7)
=D14/60				=TABLE(,G7)	=TABLE(,G7)
=D15/60				=TABLE(,G7)	=TABLE(,G7)
=D16/60				=TABLE(,G7)	=TABLE(,G7)
=D17/60				=TABLE(,G7)	=TABLE(,G7)
=D18/60				=TABLE(,G7)	=TABLE(,G7)
=D19/60				=TABLE(,G7)	=TABLE(,G7)
=D20/60					

Chapter 72: Quality Control

What the simulation does

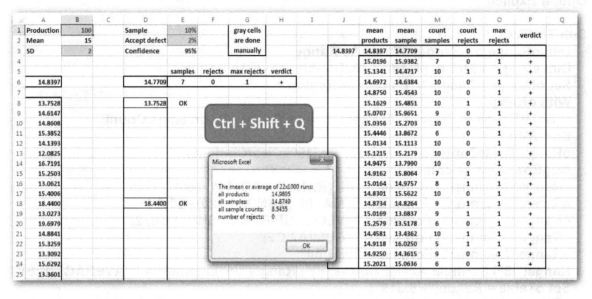

Here we are dealing with an assembly line that creates between 100 and 1,000 products (B1) per period of time. One particular variable of this product is supposed to be close to a value of 15 (B2) but is allowed to vary with a SD of 2 (B3), as shown some 1,000 times in column A.

To ensure quality, we take a certain percentage of samples (E1) in which we accept 2% defects (E2, or whatever is in there). Based on such a sample we decide, with 95% confidence (E3), to accept or reject the entire production lot.

Since this process is far from certain but depends heavily on probabilities, we repeat this process a number of times in the *Data Table* far to the right.

At the end of the simulation, the macro reports several averages in a *MsgBox*.

What you need to know

In cell D8, the VBA code inserts the following formula (copied down to E1007):
=IF(AND(ROW(D7)+1<=($B$1+7),COUNT($D$7:D7)<($B$1*$E$1)),IF(RAND()<=$E$1,A8,""),"")

In cell E8: =IF(D8<>"",IF((ABS($B$2-D8)/$B$3)>1.96,"reject","OK"),"")

The function used in G6 is CRITBINOM. It determines the greatest number of defective parts that are allowed to come off an assembly line sample without rejecting the entire lot. It has 3 arguments: The number of trials, the probability of a success on each trial, and the criterion value (alpha). Recently, this function has been replaced with BINOM.INV.

What you need to do

```vba
Option Explicit

Sub QualityControl()
    Dim oRange As Range, oTable As Range, sFormula As String, sMsg As String
    Dim pAvgProd As Double, pAvgSampl As Double, pAvgCount As Double, iReject As Integer
    Set oRange = Range("D8:E1007")
    With oRange
        .ClearContents
        sFormula = _
"=IF(AND(ROW(D7)+1<=($B$1+7),COUNT($D$7:D7)<($B$1*$E$1)),IF(RAND()<=$E$1,A8,""""),"""")"   'double quotes inside double quotes
        .Columns(1).Formula = sFormula
        sFormula = "=IF(D8<>"""",IF((ABS($B$2-D8)/$B$3)>1.96,""reject"",""OK""),"""")"
        .Columns(2).Formula = sFormula
    End With
    Set oTable = Range("J3").CurrentRegion
    With oTable
        Set oTable = .Offset(3, 1).Resize(.Rows.Count - 3, .Columns.Count - 1)
    End With
    With oTable
        .ClearContents
        Set oTable = .Offset(-1, -1).Resize(.Rows.Count + 1, .Columns.Count + 1)
        oTable.Table , Range("I1")
    End With
    With oTable
        pAvgProd = WorksheetFunction.Average(.Columns(2))
        pAvgSampl = WorksheetFunction.Average(.Columns(3))
        pAvgCount = WorksheetFunction.Average(.Columns(4))
        iReject = WorksheetFunction.CountIf(.Columns(7), "reject")
    End With
    sMsg = "The mean or average of 22x1000 runs:" & vbCr
    sMsg = sMsg & "all products: " & vbTab & FormatNumber(pAvgProd, 4) & vbCr
    sMsg = sMsg & "all samples: " & vbTab & FormatNumber(pAvgSampl, 4) & vbCr
    sMsg = sMsg & "all sample counts: " & vbTab & FormatNumber(pAvgCount, 4) & vbCr
    sMsg = sMsg & "number of rejects: " & vbTab & iReject
    MsgBox sMsg
End Sub
```

Chapter 73: Waiting Time Simulation

What the simulation does

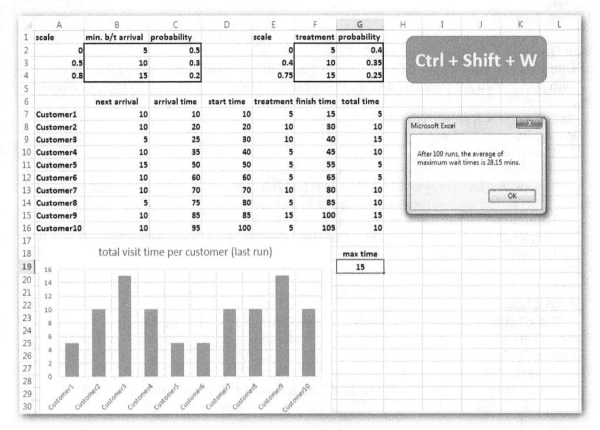

We simulate here the flow of patients in something like a walk-in clinic. Based on experience, we know the probabilities of patients coming in with 5, 10, or 15 minutes between arrivals (B2:C4). We also know the probabilities that the treatment takes 5, 10, or 15 minutes (F2:G4). Let's assume there are usually 10 patients in the morning (which we won't simulate, though). And there is only one nurse or doctor in the clinic.

Now we can simulate the flow of patients through the system (A7:G16). The chart shows how visit times can vary randomly. Since there is much volatility involved, we repeat this process some 100 to 1,000 times through the help of a VBA array in the background, so we can calculate what the average maximum visit time is, based on waiting time and treatment time. The simulation reports its results in a *MsgBox*.

What you need to know

To randomly assign arrival times and treatment times, we need an extra column in front of the two probability tables shown on top of the sheet. These two columns must start at 0 and then cumulatively increase, so we can use VLOOKUP to assign these times in a random manner.

Other formulas on the sheet are shown in the screen shot on the next page.

What you need to do

```
Option Explicit

Sub WaitingTime()
  Dim oRange As Range, iMaxVisitTime As Integer, arrVisTime() As Integer, i As
Integer, n As Long
  Set oRange = Range("B7:G16")
  With oRange
    .ClearContents
    .Columns(1).Formula = "=VLOOKUP(RAND(),$A$2:$B$4,2,TRUE)"
    .Columns(2).Formula = "=SUM($B$7:B7)"
    .Columns(3).Cells(1, 1).Formula = "=C7"
    Range("D8:D16").Formula = "=IF(C8<F7,F7,F7+(C8-F7))"
    .Columns(4).Formula = "=VLOOKUP(RAND(),$E$2:$F$4,2,TRUE)"
    .Columns(5).Formula = "=D7+E7"
    .Columns(6).Formula = "=F7-C7"
    .Calculate
  End With
  n = InputBox("How many runs (100-1000)?", , 100)
  ReDim arrVisTime(0 To n - 1)
  For i = 0 To n - 1
    Range("B7:G19").Calculate
    iMaxVisitTime = Range("G19")
    arrVisTime(i) = iMaxVisitTime
  Next i
  MsgBox "After " & n & " runs, the average of " & vbCr & _
    "maximum wait times is " & WorksheetFunction.Average(arrVisTime) & " mins."
End Sub
```

	A	B	C	D	E	F	G
1	scale	min. b/t arrival	probability		scale	treatment	probability
2	0	5	0.5		0	5	0.4
3	=SUM($C$2:C2)	10	0.3		=SUM($G$2:G2)	10	0.35
4	=SUM($C$2:C3)	15	0.2		=SUM($G$2:G3)	15	0.25
5							
6		next arrival	arrival time	start time	treatment	finish time	total time
7	Customer1	=VLOOKUP(RAND(),$A$2:$B$4,2,TRUE)	=SUM($B$7:B7)	=C7	=VLOOKUP(RAND(),$E$2:$F$4,2,TRUE)	=D7+E7	=F7-C7
8	Customer2	=VLOOKUP(RAND(),$A$2:$B$4,2,TRUE)	=SUM($B$7:B8)	=IF(C8<F7,F7,F7+(C8-F7))	=VLOOKUP(RAND(),$E$2:$F$4,2,TRUE)	=D8+E8	=F8-C8
9	Customer3	=VLOOKUP(RAND(),$A$2:$B$4,2,TRUE)	=SUM($B$7:B9)	=IF(C9<F8,F8,F8+(C9-F8))	=VLOOKUP(RAND(),$E$2:$F$4,2,TRUE)	=D9+E9	=F9-C9
10	Customer4	=VLOOKUP(RAND(),$A$2:$B$4,2,TRUE)	=SUM($B$7:B10)	=IF(C10<F9,F9,F9+(C10-F9))	=VLOOKUP(RAND(),$E$2:$F$4,2,TRUE)	=D10+E10	=F10-C10
11	Customer5	=VLOOKUP(RAND(),$A$2:$B$4,2,TRUE)	=SUM($B$7:B11)	=IF(C11<F10,F10,F10+(C11-F10))	=VLOOKUP(RAND(),$E$2:$F$4,2,TRUE)	=D11+E11	=F11-C11
12	Customer6	=VLOOKUP(RAND(),$A$2:$B$4,2,TRUE)	=SUM($B$7:B12)	=IF(C12<F11,F11,F11+(C12-F11))	=VLOOKUP(RAND(),$E$2:$F$4,2,TRUE)	=D12+E12	=F12-C12
13	Customer7	=VLOOKUP(RAND(),$A$2:$B$4,2,TRUE)	=SUM($B$7:B13)	=IF(C13<F12,F12,F12+(C13-F12))	=VLOOKUP(RAND(),$E$2:$F$4,2,TRUE)	=D13+E13	=F13-C13
14	Customer8	=VLOOKUP(RAND(),$A$2:$B$4,2,TRUE)	=SUM($B$7:B14)	=IF(C14<F13,F13,F13+(C14-F13))	=VLOOKUP(RAND(),$E$2:$F$4,2,TRUE)	=D14+E14	=F14-C14
15	Customer9	=VLOOKUP(RAND(),$A$2:$B$4,2,TRUE)	=SUM($B$7:B15)	=IF(C15<F14,F14,F14+(C15-F14))	=VLOOKUP(RAND(),$E$2:$F$4,2,TRUE)	=D15+E15	=F15-C15
16	Customer10	=VLOOKUP(RAND(),$A$2:$B$4,2,TRUE)	=SUM($B$7:B16)	=IF(C16<F15,F15,F15+(C16-F15))	=VLOOKUP(RAND(),$E$2:$F$4,2,TRUE)	=D16+E16	=F16-C16
17							
18							max time
19							=MAX(G7:G16)
20							

Chapter 74: Project Delays

What the simulation does

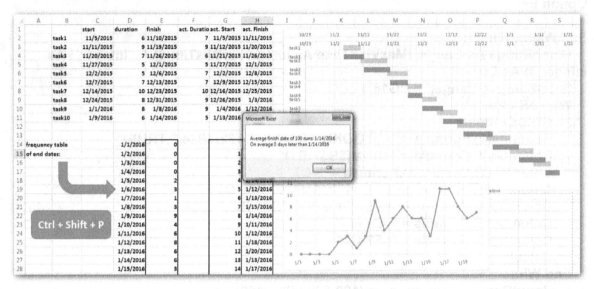

Here we have a sequence of tasks that start at a certain day, have a certain duration, and then end, to be followed by the next task. So the entire project is supposed to be finished on the date shown in cell E11.

Usually, however, there are random changes in the duration (column F)—say, up to 2 days shorter or longer than anticipated. Such random changes would obviously affect the end date of the total project. In cell H11, we calculate what the actual end date of the project would be.

We run this project some 100 times in a *Data Table* (G14:H151), so we can calculate what on average the "real" end date of the project would be after random changes in duration per task. We then calculate how the final end dates for each run are distributed in a frequency chart (in the right lower corner of the sheet).

What you need to know

There are some fomulas on this sheet (see screen shot on the next page). The only new function used in the VBA code is Excel's DAYS function. It returns the number of days between two dates, where the first argument indicates the end date, and the 2nd argument the start date. If the number of days is negative, then the end date is earlier than the start date.

The way Excel handles dates may need some explanation. Excel stores dates as sequential serial numbers so that they can be used in calculations. By default, Jan 1, 1900 is serial number 1, and January 1, 2008 is serial number 39448 because it is 39447 days after January 1, 1900. This number can also have decimals to indicate the time of the day. So basically 39447 is January 1, 2008 at 12 AM, and 39447.5 is 12 PM on that day.

The chart in the upper right of the sheet is a so-called Gantt chart. In Excel, it is a *stacked* bar chart with two series of values, of which the first series, or stack, has no fill color or line color, so it is actually invisible. We have actually 2 charts here. They both use B2:B11 as categories. One is based on series G2:G11 (invisible) and series F2:F11. The other one is plotted from series C2:C11 (invisible) and series D2:D11. The second chart has a plot area with no fill, so you can lay it over the first one with a slight offset down.

What you need to do

```vba
Option Explicit

Sub ProjectDelays()
   Dim oTable As Range, i As Integer, sMsg As String, dAvgDate As Date, iOff As Long
   With Range("E2:H11")
     .ClearContents
     .Columns(1).Formula = "=C2+D2-1"
     .Columns(2).Formula = "=D2+RANDBETWEEN(-2,2)"
     .Columns(3).Formula = "=IF(ROW()=2,C2, H1+1)"
     .Columns(4).Formula = "=G2+F2-1"
   End With
   Set oTable = Range("G14").CurrentRegion
   Range("H15:H115").ClearContents
   oTable.Table , Range("F13")
   Range("E14:E33") = WorksheetFunction.Frequency(oTable.Columns(2), Range("D14:D33"))
   'OR: Range("E14:E33").FormulaArray = "=FREQUENCY(R14C8:R115C8,R14C4:R33C4)"
   dAvgDate = Round(WorksheetFunction.Average(oTable.Columns(2)), 0)
   iOff = WorksheetFunction.Days(dAvgDate, Range("E11")) '+ IIf(iOff >= 0, 1, -1)
   If dAvgDate = Range("E11") Then iOff = 0
   sMsg = "Average finish date of 100 runs: " & FormatDateTime(dAvgDate, vbShortDate) & vbCr
   sMsg = sMsg & "On average " & Abs(iOff) & " days " & IIf(iOff >= 0, "later", "earlier")
   sMsg = sMsg & " than " & Range("E11")
   MsgBox sMsg
End Sub
```

	A	B	C	D	E	F	G	H
1			start		duration		finish	act. Duration	act. Start	act. Finish
2		task1	42313		6		=C2+D2-1	=D2+RANDBETWEEN(-2,	=IF(ROW()=2,C2, H1+1)	=G2+F2-1
3		task2	=E2+1		9		=C3+D3-1	=D3+RANDBETWEEN(-2,	=IF(ROW()=2,C3, H2+1)	=G3+F3-1
4		task3	=E3+1		7		=C4+D4-1	=D4+RANDBETWEEN(-2,	=IF(ROW()=2,C4, H3+1)	=G4+F4-1
5		task4	=E4+1		5		=C5+D5-1	=D5+RANDBETWEEN(-2,	=IF(ROW()=2,C5, H4+1)	=G5+F5-1
6		task5	=E5+1		5		=C6+D6-1	=D6+RANDBETWEEN(-2,	=IF(ROW()=2,C6, H5+1)	=G6+F6-1
7		task6	=E6+1		7		=C7+D7-1	=D7+RANDBETWEEN(-2,	=IF(ROW()=2,C7, H6+1)	=G7+F7-1
8		task7	=E7+1		10		=C8+D8-1	=D8+RANDBETWEEN(-2,	=IF(ROW()=2,C8, H7+1)	=G8+F8-1
9		task8	=E8+1		8		=C9+D9-1	=D9+RANDBETWEEN(-2,	=IF(ROW()=2,C9, H8+1)	=G9+F9-1
10		task9	=E9+1		8		=C10+D10-1	=D10+RANDBETWEEN(-:	=IF(ROW()=2,C10, H9+1)	=G10+F10-1
11		task10	=E10+1		6		=C11+D11-1	=D11+RANDBETWEEN(-:	=IF(ROW()=2,C11, H10+1)	=G11+F11-1
12									
13									
14	frequency table			42370	0				=H11
15	of end dates:			42371	0			=ROW(A1)	=TABLE(,F13)
16				42372	2			=ROW(A2)	=TABLE(,F13)
17				42373	0			=ROW(A3)	=TABLE(,F13)
18				42374	4			=ROW(A4)	=TABLE(,F13)
19				42375	2			=ROW(A5)	=TABLE(,F13)
20				42376	2			=ROW(A6)	=TABLE(,F13)

VII. FINANCE

Chapter 75: Buy or Sell Stock?

What the simulation does

	A	B	C	D	E	F	G	H
1	Date	Value						
2	1/6/2016	10.0000						
3	1/7/2016	10.1191						
4	1/8/2016	9.8428						
5	1/9/2016	9.7680			Ctrl + Shift + B			
6	1/12/2016	9.7327						
7	1/13/2016	9.5452						
8	1/14/2016	9.8715						
9	1/15/2016	9.7237						
10	1/16/2016	9.5760						

Based on the performance of a certain stock, we want to anticipate its value the next day, so we can decide whether to buy or to sell.

Since there is much uncertainty involved, we need to consider the mean and standard deviation of its past history, and based on this information, the macro projects some 10,000 normally distributed values in order to somewhat harnass volatility.

Part of the decision is determined by how far we want to go back in history. So the macro goes back in the entire history shown in column A by steps of 5 days, and then makes a provisional decision as to either buy or sell for each step. This decision is obviously debatable. The macro uses the following rule: if the average of 10,000 runs is greater than 0.01 times the SD, go for "buy"; if it is less than 0.01 times the SD, go for "sell." This rule can be adjusted at any time, of course.

Finally, the macro displays the verdict of all periods and lets the user determine which decision to make based on this information.

Latest 31	9.82539275763635	sell
Latest 26	9.81026893087344	sell
Latest 21	9.83749947555262	buy
Latest 16	9.85812976186832	buy
Latest 11	9.97397342731563	buy
Latest 6	10.0005335521494	buy

What you need to know

The background calculations are stored in an array with 10,000 elements. The average and standard deviation are based on those 10,000 values. There will always be volatility (and unexpected events!), but they can be better harnassed by using huge amounts of numbers.

What you need to do

```vba
Option Explicit

Sub BuySell()
    Dim i As Long, oCurReg As Range, oRange As Range, iOffset As Long, n As Long
    Dim pAvg As Double, pSD As Double, arrVal() As Double, sMsg As String, sVerdict As String
    Dim pAvgAvg As Double, pLatestVal As Double
    Set oCurReg = Range("A1").CurrentRegion
    With oCurReg
        iOffset = oCurReg.Rows.Count
        pLatestVal = .Cells(iOffset, 2)
        For i = iOffset To 2 Step -5
            Set oRange = .Range(Cells(iOffset - i + 1, 2), Cells(iOffset, 2))
            pAvg = WorksheetFunction.Average(oRange)
            pSD = WorksheetFunction.StDev(oRange)
            ReDim arrVal(0 To 9999)
            For n = 0 To 9999
                arrVal(n) = WorksheetFunction.Norm_Inv(Rnd, pAvg, pSD)
            Next n
            pAvgAvg = WorksheetFunction.Average(arrVal)
            sVerdict = IIf(pAvgAvg > (pLatestVal + pSD * 0.01), "buy", IIf(pAvgAvg < (pLatestVal - pSD * 0.01), "sell", "-"))
            sMsg = sMsg & "Latest " & i & vbTab & pAvgAvg & vbTab & sVerdict & vbCr
        Next i
        MsgBox sMsg
    End With
End Sub
```

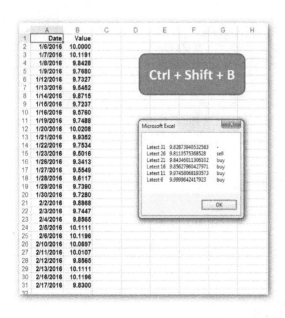

Chapter 76: Moving Averages

What the simulation does

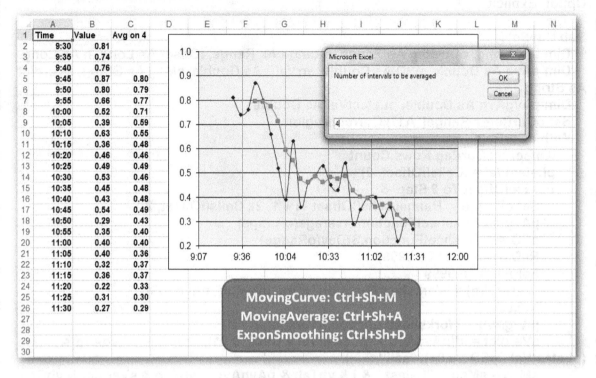

This file has 3 sheets and 3 similar macros for "moving averages" and "exponential smoothing." It simulates what happens when we reduce the amount of "noise" with a certain factor.

What you need to know

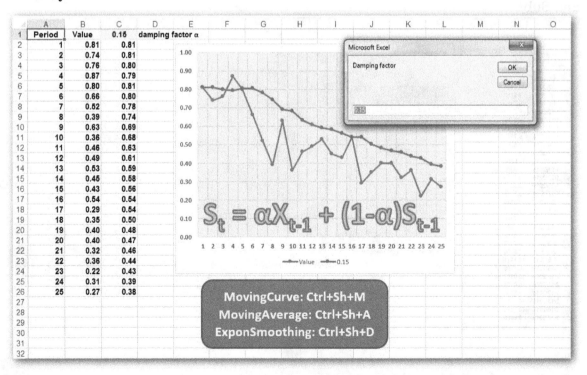

$$S_t = \alpha X_{t-1} + (1-\alpha) S_{t-1}$$

What you need to do

```
Sub MovingAverage()
  Dim oChart As Chart, oSelect As Range, oSeries As Series
  Dim oTrendCol As Trendlines, oTrend As Trendline
  Sheet12.Activate:    Range("A1").Select
  Set oSelect = ActiveCell.CurrentRegion :    Set oChart = Charts.Add
  oChart.SetSourceData oSelect
  oChart.ChartType = xlXYScatterLines
  oChart.HasLegend = False:    oChart.HasTitle = False
  oChart.Axes(xlCategory).HasMajorGridlines = True
  oChart.Location xlLocationAsNewSheet
  Set oSeries = oChart.SeriesCollection(1)
  Set oTrendCol = oSeries.Trendlines
  Set oTrend = oTrendCol.Add(xlMovingAvg, , InputBox("Period", , 3))
  oTrend.Border.LineStyle = xlDot :    Application.DisplayAlerts = False
  If MsgBox("Delete?", vbYesNo) = vbYes Then oChart.Delete
  Application.DisplayAlerts = True
End Sub


Sub AvgSmoothed()
  Dim i As Integer, oRange As Range
  Sheet10.Activate:    Range("A1").Select
  i = InputBox("Number of intervals to be averaged", , 2)
  With Range("C1")
    .Value = "Avg on " & i
    Set oRange = .Range(Cells(2, 1), Cells(.CurrentRegion.Rows.Count, 1))
    oRange.Clear
    Set oRange = .Range(Cells(i + 1, 1), Cells(.CurrentRegion.Rows.Count, 1))
    oRange.FormulaR1C1 = "=AVERAGE(RC[-1] : R[-" & i - 1 & "]C[-1])"
    oRange.NumberFormat = "0.00"
  End With
End Sub


Sub Damping()
  Dim pDamp As Double, oRange As Range
  Sheet11.Activate:    Range("A1").Select
  pDamp = InputBox("Damping factor", , 0.15)
  With Range("C1")
    .Value = pDamp :    .Offset(1, 0).Formula = "=B2"
    Set oRange = .Range(Cells(3, 1), Cells(.CurrentRegion.Rows.Count, 1))
    oRange.Clear
    Set oRange = .Range(Cells(3, 1), Cells(.CurrentRegion.Rows.Count, 1))
    oRange.Formula = "=$C$1*B2+(1-$C$1)*C2"
    oRange.NumberFormat = "0.00": oRange.Font.Bold = True
  End With
End Sub
```

Chapter 77: Automatic Totals and Subtotals

What the simulation does

	A	B	C	D	E	F	G	H	I
1		North	East	South	West	SUM	AVERAGE		
2	January	$7,379.99	$1,029.86	$6,381.49	$4,746.99	$19,538.33	$7,815.33		
3	February	$2,257.77	$5,642.29	$5,066.77	$2,838.23	$15,805.06	$6,322.02		
4	March	$6,362.84	$1,602.33	$8,578.92	$5,720.38	$22,264.47	$8,905.79		
5	April	$1,934.61	$1,956.97	$1,561.74	$9,946.94	$15,400.26	$6,160.10		
6	May	$994.72	$1,266.83	$3,662.34	$9,954.95	$15,878.84	$6,351.54		
7	June	$9,668.29	$4,438.05	$8,155.34	$5,717.85	$27,979.53	$11,191.81		
8	July	$7,110.15	$898.97	$851.53	$4,957.52	$13,818.17	$5,527.27		
9	August	$9,933.38	$7,873.05	$3,308.09	$898.18	$22,012.70	$8,805.08		
10	September	$3,136.02	$982.83	$4,453.91	$4,007.09	$12,579.85	$5,031.94		
11	October	$5,789.66	$2,322.59	$2,300.23	$2,698.55	$13,111.03	$5,244.41		
12	November	$4,595.87	$8,132.12	$7,699.10	$5,018.93	$25,446.02	$10,178.41		
13	December	$2,981.89	$7,243.42	$9,700.10	$6,795.27	$26,720.68	$10,688.27		
14	SUM	$62,145.19	$43,389.31	$61,719.56	$63,300.88	$230,554.94	$92,221.98		
15	AVERAGE	$5,178.77	$3,615.78	$5,143.30	$5,275.07	$19,212.91	$7,685.16		
16									

For totals:
Ctrl + Shift + T
For subtotals:
Ctrl + Shift + S

At the bounds of the database A1:E13, the first macro, *Totals*, adds summaries of your choosing—SUM, STDEV, MEDIAN, and so on. The second macro, *SubTotals*, creates subtotals and lets the users determine which columns they like to use for sorting and summing. Then it offers the option to copy this summary of subtotals to a new sheet.

What you need to know

The macro assumes that your database does not have formulas in it, so it can use the VBA property *HasFormula* to determine where the database ends.

What you need to do

```
Sub Subtotals()
    Dim oSelect As Range, oSort As Range, oTotal As Range, oWS As Worksheet
    Sheet1.Activate: Range("A1").Select
    With ActiveCell.CurrentRegion
        Set oSort = Application.InputBox("Sort by Label", , "G1", , , , , 8)
        .Sort oSort, xlAscending, , , , , , xlYes
        Set oTotal = Application.InputBox("SUM by Label", , "D1", , , , , 8)
        .Subtotal oSort.Column, xlSum, Array(oTotal.Column)
        Set oWS = ActiveSheet
        ActiveSheet.Outline.ShowLevels 2 '[row-levels],[col-levels]
        Set oSelect = Application.InputBox("Which range to copy", ,
Range("D1:D24,G1:G24").Address, , , , , 8)
        Set oSelect = oSelect.SpecialCells(xlCellTypeVisible)
        Set oWS = Worksheets.Add(, ActiveSheet)
        oSelect.Copy Cells(1, 1) :    oSelect.Font.Color = vbRed
        oSelect.Rows(1).Font.Color = vbBlack
        .EntireColumn.AutoFit:    Cells().EntireColumn.AutoFit
        Application.CutCopyMode = False ;     .Range("A1").RemoveSubtotal
    End With
End Sub
```

```
Sub Totals()
  Dim r As Long, c As Long, sOper As String, oRange As Range, oCurReg As Range,
n As Integer
  Sheet2.Select:    Range("A1").Select
  With ActiveCell.CurrentRegion
    r = .Rows.Count:    c = .Columns.Count
    If .Cells(r, c).HasFormula = False Then .BorderAround , xlThick
    sOper = InputBox("SUM/AVERAGE/MAX/STDEV/MODE/MEDIAN/COUNT", ,
"SUM")
    sOper = UCase(sOper)
    Do Until .Cells(r, c).HasFormula = False
      r = r - 1: c = c - 1: n = n + 1
    Loop
    If n > 0 Then
      If MsgBox("Add " & sOper & " (instead of replace)?", vbYesNo) = vbYes Then
        r = r + n: c = c + n
      End If
    End If
    .Cells(1, c + 1) = sOper:   .Cells(r + 1, 1) = sOper
    Set oRange = .Range(.Cells(r + 1, 2), .Cells(r + 1, c))
    oRange.FormulaR1C1 = "=" & sOper & "(R2C:R[-" & n + 1 & "]C)"
    oRange.NumberFormat = .Cells(r, c).NumberFormat
    Set oRange = .Range(.Cells(2, c + 1), .Cells(r + 1, c + 1))
    oRange.FormulaR1C1 = "=" & sOper & "(RC2:RC[-1])"
    oRange.NumberFormat = .Cells(r, c).NumberFormat
    If MsgBox("Delete summary?", vbYesNo) = vbYes Then
      With Range("B2").CurrentRegion
        For r = .Rows.Count To 1 Step -1
          If .Cells(r, 2).HasFormula Then .Rows(r).ClearContents
        Next r
        For c = .Columns.Count To 1 Step -1
          If .Cells(2, c).HasFormula Then .Columns(c).ClearContents
        Next c
      End With
    End If
  End With
End Sub
```

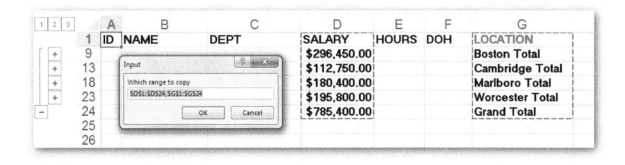

Chapter 78: Fluctuations of APR

What the simulation does

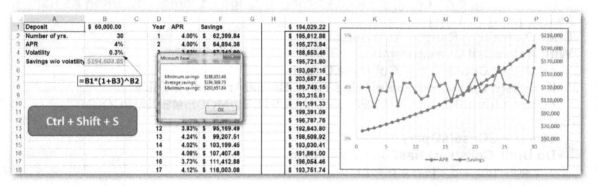

Let's pretend we are trying to predict what the total return would be over a period of years if the initial deposit is fixed and the annual percentage rate (APR) is fluctuating. So this sheet calculates how a fixed deposit compounds over a specific number of years with a fluctuating APR.

We use three tables to set up this calculation. In the left table, we set up our parameters and use a simple calculation of return without considering any volatility. In the middle table, we simulate how APR could fluctuate during the time period—in this case 30 years—if the volatility is 0.3% (cell B4). Since this middle table represents only one of the many possible outcomes, we need to run additional scenarios to model fluctuations in return. In the *Data Table* to the right, we run these additional scenarios of the middle table some 25 times.

The macro summarizes the results of 25 runs for what your savings would be after 30 years—minimum, average, and maximum.

What you need to know

Compounding a certain amount of money is based on a very simple formula: the starting amount multiplied by (1+APR) raised to the power of the number of years—or: X*(1+APR)^yrs. This is the formula used in the left table.

The middle table uses the function NORMINV to simulate fluctuations in the annual percentage rate each year.

The *Data Table* to the right runs the end result of the middle table at least 25 times by using the array formula {=TABLE(,G1)}—pointing to any empty cell outside the table (e.g., cell G1). The more runs, the more reliable the outcome is.

The chart is linked to columns D:F. One curve, the upward one, is for the compounding savings amount; the other curve shows APR fluctuations.

What you need to do

```
Option Explicit

Sub Savings()
   Dim oRange As Range, oTable As Range, oFormulas As Range, n As Integer
   Dim sMsg As String, sMin As String, sMax As String, sAvg As String
   Set oRange = Range("D1").CurrentRegion
   oRange.ClearContents
   Set oTable = Range("H1").CurrentRegion
   oTable.ClearContents
   n = InputBox("For how many years (max of 30)?", , 30)
   If n > 30 Then Exit Sub Else Range("B2") = n
   Set oRange = Range("D1").Range(Cells(1, 1), Cells(n + 1, 3))
   oRange.Cells(1, 1) = "Year": oRange.Cells(1, 2) = "APR": oRange.Cells(1, 3) =
"Savings"
   Set oFormulas = oRange.Range(Cells(2, 1), Cells(n + 1, 3))
   With oFormulas
      .Columns(1).Formula = "=ROW(A1)"
      .Columns(2).Formula = "=NORMINV(RAND(),$B$3,$B$4)"
      .Columns(3).Cells(1, 1).Formula = "=$B$1*(1+E2)^D2"
      .Columns(3).Range(Cells(2, 1), Cells(n, 1)).Formula = "=F2*(1+E3)"
      oTable.Cells(1, 2).Formula = "=" & .Columns(3).Cells(n, 1).Address
   End With
   Set oTable = Range("H1").Range(Cells(1, 1), Cells(26, 2))
   oTable.Table , Range("G1")
   With oTable
      sMin = FormatCurrency(WorksheetFunction.Min(.Columns(2)), 2)
      sAvg = FormatCurrency(WorksheetFunction.Average(.Columns(2)), 2)
      sMax = FormatCurrency(WorksheetFunction.Max(.Columns(2)), 2)
   End With
   sMsg = "Minimum savings: " & vbTab & sMin & vbCr
   sMsg = sMsg & "Average savings: " & vbTab & sAvg & vbCr
   sMsg = sMsg & "Maximum savings: " & vbTab & sMax & vbCr
   MsgBox sMsg
End Sub
```

	A	B	C	D	E	F	G	H	I
1	Deposit	60000		Year	APR	Savings			=$F$31
2	Number of yrs.	30		=ROW(A1)	=NORMINV(RAND(),$B$3,$B$4)	=$B$1*(1+E2)^D2			=TABLE(,G1)
3	APR	0.04		=ROW(A2)	=NORMINV(RAND(),$B$3,$B$4)	=F2*(1+E3)			=TABLE(,G1)
4	Volatility	0.003		=ROW(A3)	=NORMINV(RAND(),$B$3,$B$4)	=F3*(1+E4)			=TABLE(,G1)
5	Savings w/o volatility	=B1*(1+B3)^B2		=ROW(A4)	=NORMINV(RAND(),$B$3,$B$4)	=F4*(1+E5)			=TABLE(,G1)
6				=ROW(A5)	=NORMINV(RAND(),$B$3,$B$4)	=F5*(1+E6)			=TABLE(,G1)
7				=ROW(A6)	=NORMINV(RAND(),$B$3,$B$4)	=F6*(1+E7)			=TABLE(,G1)
8				=ROW(A7)	=NORMINV(RAND(),$B$3,$B$4)	=F7*(1+E8)			=TABLE(,G1)

Chapter 79: Net Present Value

What the simulation does

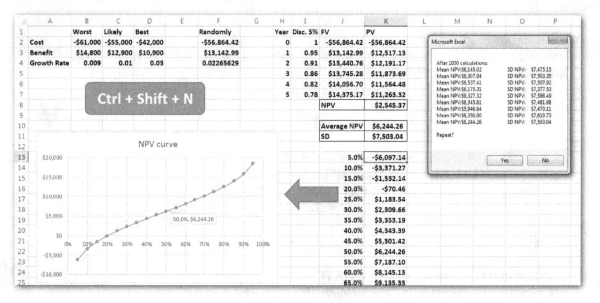

When you have three scenarios (likely, best, worst) for your costs, benefits, and growth rate (in A1:D4), you probably want a random outcome between the extremes of best and worst. Then ultimately you want to calculate the net present value (NPV) of your cash flows (in cell K10).

Here is some terminology. Having projected a company's free cash flow for the next five years, you want to figure out what these cash flows are worth today. That means coming up with an appropriate discount rate which you can use to calculate the net present value (NPV) of the cash flows. A discount rate of 5% is used in column I (see screen shot below).

The most widely used method of discounting is exponential discounting, which values future cash flows as "how much money would have to be invested currently, at a given rate of return, to yield the cash flow in the future."

After running your 5 year projection (H1:K8), the simulation repeats this with some 10,000 runs ithrough a VBA array. The simulation calculates the average NPV and its standard deviation in cell K10 and K11 for the latest run. The *MsgBox* keeps track of the results for previous runs.

Based on this information, you may want to find out what the distribution of NPV values would be given the average of K10 and the standard deviation of K11. This is done below them in cells J17:K51, ranging from 2.5% to 97.5%. The graph shows the results, with the "average" featuring at 50% (see screen shot on the next page).

What you need to know

F	G	H	I	J	K
Randomly		Year	Disc. 5%	FV	PV
=RAND()*(B2-D2)+D2		0	=1/1.05^H2	=F2	=I2*J2
=RAND()*(B3-D3)+D3		1	=1/1.05^H3	=F3	=I3*J3
=RAND()*(B4-D4)+D4		2	=1/1.05^H4	=J3*(1+$F$4)	=I4*J4
		3	=1/1.05^H5	=J4*(1+$F$4)	=I5*J5
		4	=1/1.05^H6	=J5*(1+$F$4)	=I6*J6
		5	=1/1.05^H7	=J6*(1+$F$4)	=I7*J7
				NPV	=SUM(K2:K7)

What you need to do

```
Option Explicit

Sub NPV()
  Dim i As Long, n As Long, pNPV As Double, arrNPV() As Double, sMsg As String
  Dim pSum As Double, pAvg As Double, pSD As Double, sAvg As String, sSD As String
  n = InputBox("How many iterations (1000 to 10,000)?", , 1000)
  sMsg = "After " & n & " calculations:" & vbCr
  Do
    ReDim arrNPV(0 To n - 1)
    For i = 0 To n - 1
      Range("A1:K8").Calculate
      arrNPV(i) = Range("K8")
      pSum = pSum + arrNPV(i)
    Next i
    pAvg = pSum / n:    sAvg = FormatCurrency(pAvg, 2): pSum = 0
    pSD = WorksheetFunction.StDev_S(arrNPV): sSD = FormatCurrency(pSD, 2)
    Range("K10") = sAvg: Range("K11") = sSD
    sMsg = sMsg & "Mean NPV:" & sAvg & vbTab & vbTab & "SD NPV:" & vbTab & sSD & vbCr
  Loop Until MsgBox(sMsg & vbCr & "Repeat?", vbYesNo) = vbNo
End Sub
```

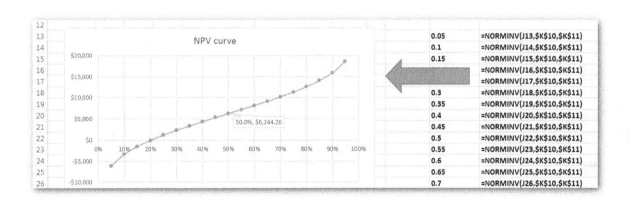

Chapter 80: A Loan with Balance and Principal

What the simulation does

	A	B	C	D	E	F	G	H	I	J	K	L	M
1			Loan	APR fixed	Years	Monthly							
2			65,000.00	5.60%	30	($373.15)							
3													
4	Period	Date	Balance	Payment	Interest	Principal	Cum.Interest	Cum.Principal			Ctrl + Shift + L		
5	1	Dec-16	65,000.00	($373.15)	($303.33)	($69.82)	($303.33)	($69.82)					
6	2	Jan-17	64,930.18	($373.15)	($303.01)	($70.14)	($606.34)	($139.96)					
7	3	Feb-17	64,860.04	($373.15)	($302.68)	($70.47)	($909.02)	($210.43)					
8	4	Mar-17	64,789.57	($373.15)	($302.35)	($70.80)	($1,211.37)	($281.23)					
9	5	Apr-17	64,718.77	($373.15)	($302.02)	($71.13)	($1,513.39)	($352.36)					
10	6	May-17	64,647.64	($373.15)	($301.69)	($71.46)	($1,815.08)	($423.83)					
11	7	Jun-17	64,576.17	($373.15)	($301.36)	($71.80)	($2,116.44)	($495.62)					
12	8	Jul-17	64,504.38	($373.15)	($301.02)	($72.13)	($2,417.46)	($567.75)					
13	9	Aug-17	64,432.25	($373.15)	($300.68)	($72.47)	($2,718.14)	($640.22)					
14	10	Sep-17	64,359.78	($373.15)	($300.35)	($72.81)	($3,018.49)	($713.03)					

This is basically a simple macro. We enter estimates for loan amount, term of the loan, and annual percentage rate through an *InputBox* three times. Then the macro calculates, on a new sheet, the monthly payments, the total of payments, and the total of interest.

Since there is not much "uncertainty" involved—all variables are fixed—don't expect any volatility here.

What you need to know

We need the Excel function PMT. Its syntax is: PMT(rate, nper, pv, [fv], [type]). It calculates the payment for a loan (*pv* or present value) based on constant monthly payments and a constant interest rate (*rate* per month) for a certain period of time (*nper* in months). The last two other arguments we can ignore here. Since we are dealing here with months, make sure to divide rate (APR) by 12, and multiply the number of years by 12. Be aware PMT returns a negative value (a value that is owed), unless you enter the present value as a negative amount.

In addition, we need the Excel functions IPMT to calculate the interest, and PPMT to calculate the principal. They have basically the same syntax. All formulas are shown here below.

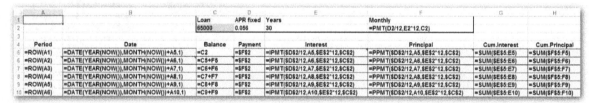

Here is the new sheet for $50,000 and an APR of 4.5%:

	A	B	C	D	E	F	G	H	I	J
1	Period	Month	Balance	Monthly	Interest	Principal	Cum. Interest	Cum. Principal		
2	1	Dec-16	$50,000.00	($18,750.00)	($18,750.00)	($0.00)	($18,750.00)	($0.00)		
3	2	Jan-17	$50,000.00	($18,750.00)	($18,750.00)	($0.00)	($37,500.00)	($0.00)		
4	3	Feb-17	$50,000.00	($18,750.00)	($18,750.00)	($0.00)	($56,250.00)	($0.00)		
5	4	Mar-17	$50,000.00	($18,750.00)	($18,750.00)	($0.00)	($75,000.00)	($0.00)		
6	5	Apr-17	$50,000.00	($18,750.00)	($18,750.00)	($0.00)	($93,750.00)	($0.00)		

Principal   50000-37.50%-360

What you need to do

```vba
Sub Loan()
    Dim cLoan As Currency, pAPR As Double, iDuration As Integer, i As Integer
    Dim oWS As Worksheet
    cLoan = InputBox("Loan amount", , 65000)
    pAPR = InputBox("Fixed APR", , 0.056) / 12
    iDuration = InputBox("Number of years", , 30) * 12
    Set oWS = Worksheets.Add(, ActiveSheet)
    oWS.Name = cLoan & "-" & FormatPercent(pAPR, 2) & "-" & iDuration
    Cells(1, 1) = "Period"
    Cells(1, 2) = "Month"
    Cells(1, 3) = "Balance"
    Cells(1, 4) = "Monthly"
    Cells(1, 5) = "Interest"
    Cells(1, 6) = "Principal"
    Cells(1, 7) = "Cum. Interest"
    Cells(1, 8) = "Cum. Principal"
    Application.Cursor = xlWait
    With Range("A1")
        For i = 1 To iDuration
            .Offset(i, 0).Formula = "=ROW()-1"
            '=DATE(YEAR(B5),MONTH(B5)+1,1)
            .Offset(i, 1).Formula = "=DATE(YEAR(TODAY()), MONTH(TODAY())+" & i & ",1)"
            .Offset(i, 1).NumberFormat = "mmm-yy"
            '=Loan and then =C3+F3
            .Offset(i, 2).FormulaR1C1 = IIf(i = 1, cLoan, "=R[-1]C3+R[-1]C6")
            '=PMT(pAPR,iDuration,cLoan)
            .Offset(i, 3).Formula = "=PMT(" & pAPR & "," & iDuration & "," & cLoan & ")"
            '=IPMT(pAPR,period,iDuration,cLoan)
            .Offset(i, 4).FormulaR1C1 = "=IPMT(" & pAPR & ",RC1," & iDuration & "," & cLoan & ")"
            '=PPMT(pAPR,period,iDuration,cLoan)
            .Offset(i, 5).FormulaR1C1 = "=PPMT(" & pAPR & ",RC1," & iDuration & "," & cLoan & ")"
            '=SUM($E$2:E2)
            .Offset(i, 6).FormulaR1C1 = "=SUM(R2C5:RC5)"
            '=SUM($F$2:F2)
            .Offset(i, 7).FormulaR1C1 = "=SUM(R2C6:RC6)"
        Next i
    End With
    Cells.EntireColumn.AutoFit
    Application.Cursor = xlDefault
End Sub
```

Chapter 81: S&P500 Performance

What the simulation does

	A	B	C	D	E	F	G	H	I
1	S&P 500				Daily	Cumulative			
2	Avg. Daily Return	0.03%		Monday	1.30%	1.30%			
3	Daily St. Dev.	0.98%		Tuesday	-0.46%	0.84%			
4				Wednesday	1.41%	2.26%			
5	from 3 January 1950 through 31 July 2012			Thursday	0.10%	2.36%			
6				Friday	1.07%	3.45%			
7	Ctrl + Shift + P								
8									

Microsoft Excel

6 x 10,000 runs:
Average: 0.136%   SD: 2.207%
Average: 0.188%   SD: 2.187%
Average: 0.205%   SD: 2.189%
Average: 0.128%   SD: 2.196%
Average: 0.148%   SD: 2.205%
Average: 0.169%   SD: 2.182%

OK

Based on data from 1950 to 2012, we have an average daily return value (in cell B2) and a daily standard deviation value (in cell B3) for S&P500 performance. This information we use to calculate what the percentage would be at the end of a week (in cell F6).

Then we repeat this volatile calculation some 10,000 times with a VBA array of 10,000 elements. There is going to be quite some volatility, but because we have a reasonable sample size now, we can find a more reliable average and SD through the array of 10,000 values. We can repeat this several times, while the *MsgBox* keeps track of the results. That may give is a bit more certainty in the midst of uncertainties.

What you need to know

	A	B	C	D	E	F
1	S&P 500				Daily	Cumulative
2	Avg. Daily Return	0.0003		Monday	=NORMINV(RAND(),$B$2,$B$3)	=E2
3	Daily St. Dev.	0.0098		Tuesday	=NORMINV(RAND(),$B$2,$B$3)	=(E3+1)*(F2+1)-1
4				Wednesday	=NORMINV(RAND(),$B$2,$B$3)	=(E4+1)*(F3+1)-1
5	from 3 January 1950 through 31 July 2012			Thursday	=NORMINV(RAND(),$B$2,$B$3)	=(E5+1)*(F4+1)-1
6				Friday	=NORMINV(RAND(),$B$2,$B$3)	=(E6+1)*(F5+1)-1
7						

The historical values in column B are used in column E with a NORMINV Excel function.

In column F, we calculate the cumulative end-of-week result: (daily % +1) * (previous cumulative % + 1) – 1.

What you need to do

```
Option Explicit

Sub Performance()
   Dim oRange As Range, arrVals() As Double, i As Long, n As Integer
   Dim pAvg As Double, pSD As Double, sMsg As String
   Do
      ReDim arrVals(0 To 9999)
      n = n + 1
      For i = 0 To 9999
         Range("E2:F6").Calculate
         arrVals(i) = (Cells(6, 5) + 1) * (Cells(5, 6) + 1) - 1
      Next i
      pAvg = WorksheetFunction.Average(arrVals)
      pSD = WorksheetFunction.StDev(arrVals)
      sMsg = sMsg & "Average: " & FormatPercent(pAvg, 3) & vbTab & _
             "SD: " & FormatPercent(pSD, 3) & vbCr
      MsgBox n & " x 10,000 runs:" & vbCr & sMsg
   Loop Until MsgBox("Another run?", vbYesNo) = vbNo
End Sub
```

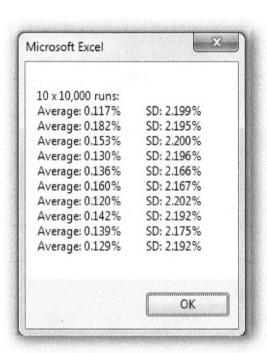

Microsoft Excel

```
10 x 10,000 runs:
Average: 0.117%    SD: 2.199%
Average: 0.182%    SD: 2.195%
Average: 0.153%    SD: 2.200%
Average: 0.130%    SD: 2.196%
Average: 0.136%    SD: 2.166%
Average: 0.160%    SD: 2.167%
Average: 0.120%    SD: 2.202%
Average: 0.142%    SD: 2.192%
Average: 0.139%    SD: 2.175%
Average: 0.129%    SD: 2.192%
```

OK

Chapter 82: Stock Market

What the simulation does

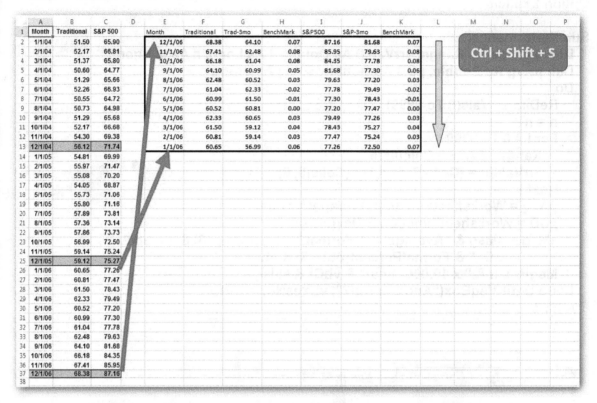

The left section of this sheet contains hard-coded data, comparing past S&P 500 values (C) with the past values of a traditional portfolio (B).

The right section analyses this information from the most recent month (12/1/06) down to the previous month (11/1/06) and much further back in time, if needed. The overview "grows" back in time if you copy its first row down as far as you want to go back in history.

In addition, when new records are added at the bottom of the left section, the first row in the right section will automatically update the history from the most recent data down.

The macro does all of this automatically, once you decide on the number of rows "back in history."

What you need to know

The only new function is COUNTA. The COUNTA function works like COUNT, but it also counts cells with text in them, such as the headers above each column.

As said before, the function INDEX is a more sophisticated version of VLOOKUP. It looks in a table at a certain row position and a certain column position. It uses this syntax: *INDEX(table, row#, col#)*. Whereas VLOOKUP works only with column numbers, INDEX also uses row numbers, which is very important when we want to look at a record that is located, for instance, 3 or 12 rows above another record (like in columns G and J).

This time we use the function ROW again, but for a different reason—to make the month go down: *row# – ROW(A1)+1*. Each time we copy that formula one row down, the formula subtracts one more row: – ROW(A2), then – ROW(A3), and so forth.

What you need to do

```
Option Explicit

Sub Stock()
  Dim oRange As Range, oTable As Range
  Dim vArr As Variant, i As Long, n As Long
  vArr = Array("Month", "Traditional", "Trad-3mo", "BenchMark", "S&P500", "S&P-
3mo", "BenchMark")
  Set oRange = Range("A1").CurrentRegion
  Set oTable = Range("E1").CurrentRegion
  oTable.Clear
  Range("E1:K1") = vArr
  n = InputBox("How many months?", , 12)
  Set oTable = Range(Cells(2, 5), Cells(1 + n, 11))
  With oTable
    .Columns(1).Formula = "=INDEX($A:$C,COUNTA($A:$A)-ROW(A1)+1,1)"
    .Columns(2).Formula = "=INDEX($A:$C,COUNTA($A:$A)-ROW(B1)+1,2)"
    .Columns(3).Formula = "=INDEX($A:$C,COUNTA($A:$A)-ROW(C1)+1-3,2)"
    .Columns(4).Formula = "=F2/G2-1"
    .Columns(5).Formula = "=INDEX($A:$C,COUNTA($A:$A)-ROW(A1)+1,3)"
    .Columns(6).Formula = "=INDEX($A:$C,COUNTA($A:$A)-ROW(A1)+1-3,3)"
    .Columns(7).Formula = "=I2/J2-1"
    For i = 2 To .Columns.Count
      .Columns(i).Cells.NumberFormat = "0.00"
    Next i
    .Columns(1).Cells.NumberFormat = "m/d/yy"
    .BorderAround , xlThick
    .Cells.Font.Bold = True
  End With
End Sub
```

	A	B	C	D	E	F	G	H	I	J	K	L
1	Month	Traditional	S&P 500		Month	Traditional	Trad-3mo	BenchMark	S&P500	S&P-3mo	BenchMark	
2	1/1/04	51.50	65.90		12/1/06	68.38	64.10	0.07	87.16	81.68	0.07	
3	2/1/04	52.17	66.81		11/1/06	67.41	62.48	0.08	85.95	79.63	0.08	
4	3/1/04	51.37	65.80		10/1/06	66.18	61.04	0.08	84.35	77.78	0.08	
5	4/1/04	50.60	64.77		9/1/06	64.10	60.99	0.05	81.68	77.30	0.06	
6	5/1/04	51.29	65.66		8/1/06	62.48	60.52	0.03	79.63	77.20	0.03	
7	6/1/04	52.26	66.93									
8	7/1/04	50.55	64.72									
9	8/1/04	50.73	64.98									
10	9/1/04	51.29	65.68									
11	10/1/04	52.17	66.68									
12	11/1/04	54.30	69.38									
13	12/1/04	56.12	71.74									

Chapter 83: Stock Volatility

What the simulation does

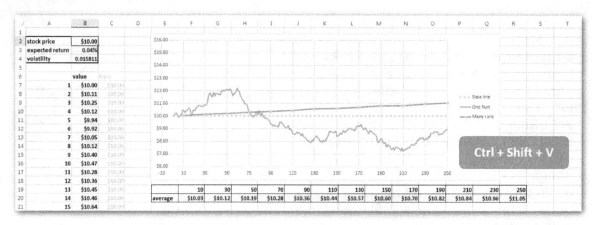

There is much uncertainty on the stock market. Monte Carlo simulations are a great tool to get a bit more certainty in the midst of numerous uncertainties.

The information needed is in the left top corner. The expected return in cell B3 is based on history: an expected return of 10% divided by 250 trading days per year. The volatility in cell B4 is also based on past performance: an annualized volatility of 25% divided by the square root of trading days per year.

The simulation plots in column B the changes in stock value up to a maximum of 250 trading days. To harness our uncertainty a little better, the macro runs at least 1,000 to 10,000 iterations to beat volatility. This is to ensure that we have a statistical chance of getting sufficient outliers (extreme values) to make the variance analysis meaningful.

The simulation does all of this without a *Data Table*—which saves us some "overhead costs." Instead it uses a VBA array of 10,000 entries. It finds the value after the first 10 days, repeats this 10,000 times, and stores these 10,000 values in the array; the average of these values is entered in cell F20. Then it does this again, but now for 30 days (G20), and so on, up to 250 days at the most. The chart shows the results of one run (columns A:C) and of 10,000 runs (F20:R20).

What you need to know

The sheet itself has only formulas in rows A:C (column C is solely for a baseline in the chart). The formulas from row 7 down are generated by the macro.

	A	B	C
1			
2	stock price	10	
3	expected return	=10%/250	
4	volatility	=25%/SQRT(250)	
5			
6		value	base
7	=ROW(A1)	=B2	=$B$7
8	=ROW(A2)	=B7+B7*($B$3+$B$4*NORMINV(RAND(),0,1))	=$B$7
9	=ROW(A3)	=B8+B8*($B$3+$B$4*NORMINV(RAND(),0,1))	=$B$7
10	=ROW(A4)	=B9+B9*($B$3+$B$4*NORMINV(RAND(),0,1))	=$B$7

What you need to do

```
Option Explicit

Sub Volatility()
   Dim oRange As Range, i As Long, n As Long, c As Integer, j As Integer
   Dim arrVals() As Double, oTotals As Range
   Set oRange = Range("A7").CurrentRegion
   oRange.ClearContents
   n = InputBox("How many days ahead (10-250)?", , 250)
   If n > 250 Then Exit Sub Else n = n + 1
   Range("B2").Activate
   With oRange
      .Cells(1, 2) = "value":  .Cells(1, 3) = "base":   .Cells(2, 2).Formula = "=B2"
      .Range(Cells(2, 1), Cells(n, 1)).Formula = "=ROW(A1)"
      .Range(Cells(3, 2), Cells(n, 2)).Formula =
"=B7+B7*($B$3+$B$4*NORMINV(RAND(),0,1))"
      .Range(Cells(2, 3), Cells(n, 3)).Formula = "=$B$7"
   End With
   Set oTotals = Range(Cells(20, 6), Cells(20, 18))
   oTotals.ClearContents
   With oTotals
      For c = 10 To n Step 20
         ReDim arrVals(0 To 9999)
         For i = 0 To 9999
            oRange.Calculate
            arrVals(i) = WorksheetFunction.VLookup(c, oRange.Range(Cells(2, 1),
Cells(n, 2)), 2, True)
         Next i
         j = j + 1
         .Cells(1, j) = WorksheetFunction.Average(arrVals)
         Calculate
         DoEvents
      Next c
   End With
End Sub
```

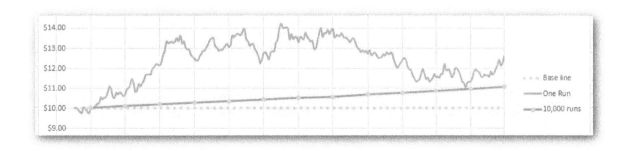

Chapter 84: Return on Investment

What the simulation does

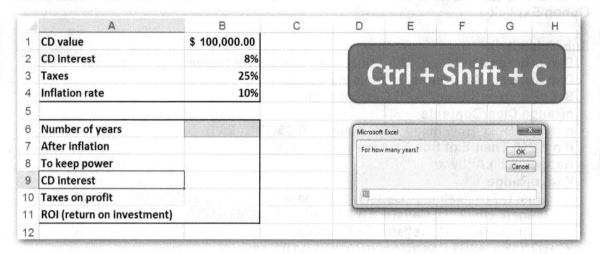

In this simulation, we want to calculate our return on an investment, but also take into consideration the cost of inflation and taxes for our investment.

The sheet simulates the return on investment (ROI) when buying bank CDs for a certain amount of money (B1), with the assumption that these have a fixed interest rate (B2), a certain fixed inflation rate (B4), and that we are taxed at 25% for CD profits (B3). We also assume that we want to keep our CD value at its original power by, at least theoretically, putting in more money each year (B8). We do all of this for a certain number of years (B6).

The core part of this simulation is calculating the return on investment (ROI) in cell B11, based on all the cells above it. The macro also creates a *Data Table* to be placed in D6:K13. This table shows at what return rates and inflation rates our investment becomes profitable. It uses a link to that calculation in B11. Based on this calculation, the two-dimensional *Data Table* shows what the ROI is for a range of changes in CD interest and in inflation rate.

What you need to know

	A	B	C	D	E	F	G	H	I	J	K	L
1	CD value	$ 100,000.00										
2	CD interest	8%										
3	Taxes	25%										
4	Inflation rate	10%										
5												
6	Number of years	10		-3.11%	4.00%	5.00%	6.00%	7.00%	8.00%	9.00%	10.00%	CD interest
7	After inflation	$ 34,867.84		4.00%	-2.63%	2.98%	8.60%	14.22%	19.84%	25.45%	31.07%	
8	To keep power	$ 65,132.16		5.00%	-7.23%	-1.87%	3.48%	8.83%	14.18%	19.54%	24.89%	
9	CD interest	$ 80,000.00		6.00%	-11.04%	-5.91%	-0.78%	4.35%	9.49%	14.62%	19.75%	
10	Taxes on profit	$ 20,000.00		7.00%	-14.25%	-9.30%	-4.35%	0.59%	5.54%	10.49%	15.43%	
11	ROI (return on investment)	-3.11%		8.00%	-16.97%	-12.17%	-7.38%	-2.59%	2.20%	6.99%	11.78%	
12				9.00%	-19.28%	-14.63%	-9.97%	-5.31%	-0.66%	4.00%	8.66%	
13				10.00%	-21.28%	-16.73%	-12.19%	-7.65%	-3.11%	1.43%	5.98%	
14				inflation rate								
15												

What you need to do

```
Option Explicit

Sub CDReturn()
  Dim i As Integer, oTable As Range
  Range("B6:B11").ClearContents
  Range("D6").CurrentRegion.Clear
  i = InputBox("For how many years?", , 10)
  Range("B6") = i
  Range("B7").Formula = "=B1*(1-B4)^B6"
  Range("B8").Formula = "=B1-B7"
  Range("B9").Formula = "=B1*B2*B6"
  Range("B10").Formula = "=B9*B3"
  Range("B11").Formula = "=(B9-B8-B10)/(B1+B8)"
  Set oTable = Range(Cells(6, 4), Cells(13, 11))
  With oTable
    .Cells(1, 1).Formula = "=B11"
    .Range(Cells(1, 2), Cells(1, 8)).Formula = "=COLUMN(D1)/100"
    .Range(Cells(1, 2), Cells(1, 8)).Borders(xlEdgeBottom).Weight = xlMedium
    .Range(Cells(2, 1), Cells(8, 1)).Formula = "=ROW(A4)/100"
    .Range(Cells(2, 1), Cells(8, 1)).Borders(xlEdgeRight).Weight = xlMedium
    .Table Range("B2"), Range("B4")
    .Cells.NumberFormat = "0.00%;[Red] -0.00%"
    .Cells(8, 1).Offset(1, 0) = "inflation rate"
    .Cells(1, 8).Offset(0, 1) = "CD interest"
  End With
End Sub
```

	A	B	C	D	E	F
1	CD value	100000				
2	CD Interest	0.08				
3	Taxes	0.25				
4	Inflation rate	0.1				
5						
6	Number of years	10		=B11	=COLUMN(D1)/100	=COLUMN(E1)/100
7	After inflation	=B1*(1-B4)^B6		=ROW(A4)/100	=TABLE(B2,B4)	=TABLE(B2,B4)
8	To keep power	=B1-B7		=ROW(A5)/100	=TABLE(B2,B4)	=TABLE(B2,B4)
9	CD interest	=B1*B2*B6		=ROW(A6)/100	=TABLE(B2,B4)	=TABLE(B2,B4)
10	Taxes on profit	=B9*B3		=ROW(A7)/100	=TABLE(B2,B4)	=TABLE(B2,B4)
11	ROI (return on investment)	=(B9-B8-B10)/(B1+B8)		=ROW(A8)/100	=TABLE(B2,B4)	=TABLE(B2,B4)
12				=ROW(A9)/100	=TABLE(B2,B4)	=TABLE(B2,B4)
13				=ROW(A10)/100	=TABLE(B2,B4)	=TABLE(B2,B4)
14				inflation rate		
15						

Chapter 85: Value at Risk

What the simulation does

	A	B	C	D	E	F	G
1	Portfolio	$25,000.00					
2	Avg return	0.152					
3	SD	0.135		Ctrl Shift T			
4	Confidence	95%					
5							
6	Confidence	Min. return	New value	Value at risk	Monthly VaR		
7	95%	-0.07	$23,248.62	$1,751.38	$8,214.71		
8	90%	-0.02	$24,474.76	$525.24	$2,463.58		
9	85%	0.01	$25,302.04	($302.04)	($1,416.68)		
10	80%	0.04	$25,959.53	($959.53)	($4,500.59)		
11	75%	0.06	$26,523.60	($1,523.60)	($7,146.30)		
12	70%	0.08	$27,030.15	($2,030.15)	($9,522.24)		
13	65%	0.10	$27,499.54	($2,499.54)	($11,723.90)		
14	60%	0.12	$27,944.95	($2,944.95)	($13,813.06)		
15	55%	0.14	$28,375.89	($3,375.89)	($15,834.34)		
16	50%	0.15	$28,800.00	($3,800.00)	($17,823.58)		
17							

Value-at-Risk, or *VaR*, is the potential maximum loss in a portfolio (and a certain standard deviation) at a given confidence interval over a given period of time (which could be a day, a month, or a year). We calculate the minimum expected return, which is done with the function NORMINV in B7 (although investments do not always follow a normal distribution!).

What you need to know

The *VaR* is for a single time period (say, one trading day). To convert that value to a longer range, simply multiply the *VaR* by the square root of the number of single periods within the longer period. Say, you calculated the *VaR* for one day and want it for a month, use the number of trading days in a month, say 22, and multiply your *VaR* with $\sqrt{22}$.

VaR is not your worst case loss. At a confidence level of 95%, the *VaR* is your minimum expected loss 5% of the time—not your maximum expected loss. So don't be surprised.

5					
6	Confidence	Min. return	New value	Value at risk	Monthly VaR
7	0.95	=NORM.INV(1-B4,B2,B3)	=B1*($B$7+1)	=B1-$C$7	=$D$7*SQRT(22)
8	0.9	=TABLE(,B4)	=TABLE(,B4)	=TABLE(,B4)	=TABLE(,B4)
9	0.85	=TABLE(,B4)	=TABLE(,B4)	=TABLE(,B4)	=TABLE(,B4)
10	0.8	=TABLE(,B4)	=TABLE(,B4)	=TABLE(,B4)	=TABLE(,B4)
11	0.75	=TABLE(,B4)	=TABLE(,B4)	=TABLE(,B4)	=TABLE(,B4)
12	0.7	=TABLE(,B4)	=TABLE(,B4)	=TABLE(,B4)	=TABLE(,B4)
13	0.65	=TABLE(,B4)	=TABLE(,B4)	=TABLE(,B4)	=TABLE(,B4)
14	0.6	=TABLE(,B4)	=TABLE(,B4)	=TABLE(,B4)	=TABLE(,B4)
15	0.55	=TABLE(,B4)	=TABLE(,B4)	=TABLE(,B4)	=TABLE(,B4)
16	0.5	=TABLE(,B4)	=TABLE(,B4)	=TABLE(,B4)	=TABLE(,B4)
17					

What you need to do

```
Sub TableBox()
  Dim cPort As Currency, pAvg As Double, pSD As Double, pConf As Double
  Dim sStart As String, i As Integer, oRange As Range
  Range("A6").CurrentRegion.ClearContents
  cPort = InputBox("Portfolio", , Cells(1, 2)):    Cells(1, 2) = cPort
  pAvg = InputBox("Average", , Cells(2, 2)):    Cells(2, 2) = pAvg
  pSD = InputBox("Standard Deviation", , Cells(3, 2)):    Cells(3, 2) = pSD
  pConf = InputBox("Confidence Level", , 0.95):    Cells(4, 2) = pConf
  sStart = InputBox("Start table in", , "A6")
  If Range(sStart) <> "" Then Range(sStart).CurrentRegion.Delete
  With Range(sStart)
    .Offset(0, 0) = "Confidence":        .Offset(0, 1) = "Min. return"
    .Offset(0, 2) = "New value":        .Offset(0, 3) = "Value at risk"
    .Offset(0, 4) = "Monthly VaR"
    For i = 1 To 10
      .Offset(i, 0) = FormatPercent(pConf - (i - 1) * 0.05, 0)
    Next i
    .Offset(1, 1).Formula = "=NORM.INV(1-B4,B2,B3)"
    .Offset(1, 2).Formula = "=B1*(" & .Offset(1, 1).Address & "+1)"
    .Offset(1, 3).Formula = "=B1-" & .Offset(1, 2).Address
    .Offset(1, 4).Formula = "=" & .Offset(1, 3).Address & "*SQRT(22)"
    Set oRange = Range(.Offset(1, 0), .Offset(10, 4)) ;   oRange.Table , Range("B4")
    oRange.Columns(2).NumberFormat = "0.00"
    oRange.Columns(3).NumberFormat = "$#,##0.00_);[Red]($#,##0.00)"
    oRange.Columns(4).NumberFormat = "$#,##0.00_);[Red]($#,##0.00)"
    oRange.Columns(5).NumberFormat = "$#,##0.00_);[Red]($#,##0.00)"
    Cells.Columns.AutoFit
  End With
  'Conditional Formatting with Bars (only in later versions of Excel)
  With oRange.Columns(5)
    Dim oBar As Databar
    .Select
    Set oBar = Selection.FormatConditions.AddDatabar
    oBar.MinPoint.Modify newtype:=xlConditionValueAutomaticMin
    oBar.MaxPoint.Modify newtype:=xlConditionValueAutomaticMax
    oBar.BarFillType = xlDataBarFillGradient
    oBar.Direction = xlContext
    oBar.NegativeBarFormat.ColorType = xlDataBarColor
    oBar.BarBorder.Type = xlDataBarBorderSolid
    oBar.NegativeBarFormat.BorderColorType = xlDataBarColor
    oBar.AxisPosition = xlDataBarAxisAutomatic
  End With
  Range("B1").Select
End Sub
```

Chapter 86: Asian Options

What the simulation does

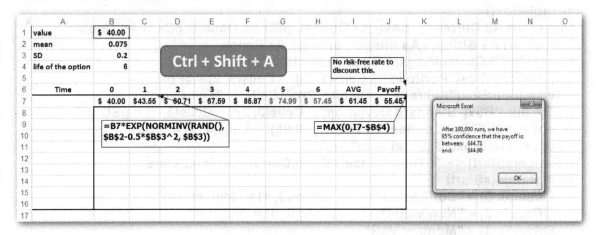

This simulation concerns an Asian option, which is valued by determining the average underlying price over a period of time. Simply put, an option contract is an agreement between two people that gives one the right to buy or sell a stock at some future date for some preset price. To price an Asian option by its mean, we need to know, at least to some degree, the path that the stock will take as time progresses.

An Asian option (or "average value option") is a special type of option contract. The payoff is determined by the average underlying price over some pre-set period of time. This is different from the usual European options and American options which are valued at the expiration of the contract.

One advantage of Asian options is that these reduce the risk of market manipulation. Another advantage is the relatively low cost of Asian options. Because of the averaging feature, Asian options reduce the volatility inherent in the option; therefore, Asian options are typically cheaper than European or American options.

What you need to know

To simplify things, we will track the stock over 5 years in yearly increments (B7:H7). To derive the average value in I7, we multiply the initial stock price (column B) by the first randomly generated log-normal number (with the functions EXP and NORMINV in C7:H7) to obtain a value for year 1 (I won't go into further explanations). The result must be multiplied by the second randomly generated number (column C), and so on.

To make the predictions more reliable, we give it 10,000 runs in this simulation. This is done with a VBA array (so we won't need a *Data Table*). For each trial, the simulation recalculates row 7 and stores the payoff amount (J7) for each run in an array of 10,000 elements. Then the simulation calculates the average payoff and its standard deviation in the array.

The Standard Error of the mean (SE) is the Standard Deviation (SD) divided by the square root of the number of cases. A confidence level of 95% evaluates to the mean ± (1.96 * SE).

The macro reports in a *MsgBox* what the payoff amount would be with 95% confidence.

What you need to do

```
Option Explicit

Sub AsianOption()
    Dim arrPayoffs() As Double, i As Long
    Dim pAvg As Double, pSD As Double, pSE As Double
    Dim sLower As String, sUpper As String, sAvg As String, sSD As String
    ReDim arrPayoffs(0 To 99999)
    For i = 0 To 99999
        Range("B7:J7").Calculate
        arrPayoffs(i) = Range("J7")
    Next i
    pAvg = WorksheetFunction.Average(arrPayoffs)
    pSD = WorksheetFunction.StDev(arrPayoffs)
    pSE = pSD / Sqr(100000)
    sLower = FormatCurrency(pAvg - (1.96 * pSE), 2)
    sUpper = FormatCurrency(pAvg + (1.96 * pSE), 2)
    MsgBox "After 100,000 runs, we have " & vbCr & "95% confidence that the payoff
is:" & _
        vbCr & "between:" & vbTab & sLower & vbCr & "and:" & vbTab & sUpper
End Sub
```

VIII. MISCELLANEA

Chapter 87: Cracking a Password

What the simulation does

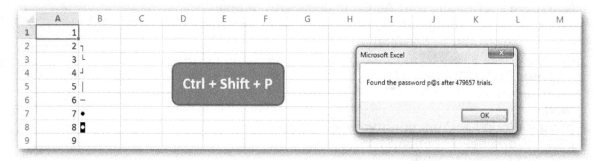

This is not a real password cracker, of course, but we can still mimic part of the process. First of all, in real life you don't know the password yet. Second, the password can be, and should be, rather long. Neither condition can be met in this simulation.

Let us assume that the password is "p@s." This is a 3-letter word, so even if we only use the characters a-z (no capitals), then we would still have 26^3 possible combinations—which amounts to 17,576 different arrangements. But we would like to use other characters as well. So don't make the password longer than 3 characters, for that could take an enormous amount of processing time. Even in the simple example shown above, we were "lucky enough" to find one matching combination after 479,657 trials. Run times may vary considerably, of course.

What you need to know

There is a VBA function called *Chr* (in Excel it's the CHAR function) which returns the character that comes with a certain *asci* number. To find out what the *asci* number of a certain key is, we could use the VBA function *Asc* (in Excel it's the CODE function); for instance, Chr("a") would give us the number 97.

The sheet shows 125 asci numbers in column A and the corresponding characters in B, just for your information. To limit ourselves to "readable" characters, we use the Excel function RANDBETWEEN to get a random character between the asci-numbers 33 and 122

The macro also uses the *Application.StatusBar* property to report progress on the status bar after every 1,000 runs.

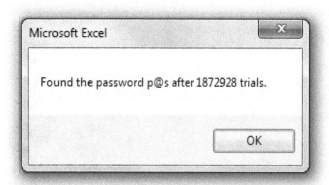

What you need to do

```
Option Explicit

Sub Password()
   Dim i As Long, j As Integer, sPass As String, sGuess As String
   sPass = InputBox("Which password?", "Watch the Status Bar", "p@s")
   'More than 3 chars could take very long
   If Len(sPass) > 3 Then MsgBox "No more than 3 chars": Exit Sub
   Range("A1").Select
   Do
      For j = 1 To Len(sPass)
         sGuess = sGuess & Chr(WorksheetFunction.RandBetween(33, 122))
      Next j
      If sGuess = sPass Then Exit Do
      i = i + 1
      DoEvents
      If i Mod 1000 = 0 Then Application.StatusBar = i & " runs"
      sGuess = ""
   Loop
   MsgBox "Found the password " & sPass & " after " & i & " trials."
End Sub
```

Chapter 88: Encrypting Text

What the simulation does

	A	B	C	D	E	F	G	H	I	J	K	L	M
1	Name	SSN		Encrypted	Decrypted					1	=CHAR(J1)	=CODE(K1)	
2	Avery, G.	157933429		MFHGGMKIE	157933429					2	⌐	2	
3	Babcock, C.	198964226		JFFHJMLME	198964226					3	∟	3	
4	Brown, G.	751296322		FFGJMFEIK	751296322					4	⌐	4	
5	Bucca, P.	467349145		IHEMHGKJH	467349145					5	∣	5	
6	Carrel, M.	547195212		FEFIMEKHI	547195212					6	−	6	
7	Donaldson, S.	476173168		LJEGKEJKH	476173168					7	•	7	
8	Frommer, F.	387671515		IEIEKJKLG	387671515					8	◘	8	
9	Gary, S.	494589555		IIIMLIHMH	494589555					9		9	
10	Josephs, P.	963427969		MJMKFHGJM	963427969					10		10	
11	Lively, S.	338639296		JMFMGJLGG	338639296					11	♂	11	
12	Matthews, J.	188886695		IMJJLLLLE	188886695					12	♀	12	
13	Piazza, L.	893754524		HFIHIKGML	893754524					13		13	
14	Rice, R.	237655466		JJHIIJKGF	237655466					14	♫	14	
15	Smith, J.	419654867		KJLHIJMEH	419654867					15	☼	15	
16	Smithers, S.	692117613		GEJKEEFMJ	692117613					16	►	16	
17	Stevens, J.	223935571		EKIIGMGFF	223935571					17	◄	17	
18	Stevens, M.	925929699		MMJMFMIFM	925929699					18	↕	18	
19	Stevens, P.	917499325		IFGMMHKEM	917499325					19	‼	19	
20	Johnson, A.	652448919		MEMLHHFIJ	652448919					20	¶	20	
21	White, M.	925579926		JFMMKIIFM	925579926					21	⊥	21	
22	Green, S.	971141551		EIIEHEEKM	971141551					22	T	22	
23										23	⊣	23	

Ctrl + Shift + C
Ctrl + Shift + E

This file has two sheets. It uses two different macros: one for the 1st sheet, and the other for the 2nd sheet. They both encrypt and decrypt cells—in this case cells with Social Security numbers (SSN). Both macros use a costom function that I gave the name *Encrypt* (the first code on the next page). This function has been given two arguments, the second of which is *Boolean* and determines whether to encrypt the SSN or decrypt the encrypted SSN. In the former case, it shifts asci numbers up by 20 (or so); in the latter case it shifts them down by that amount. Obviously, it is one of the simplest algorithms one could think of.

The difference between macros (*Sub*) and functions (*Function*) is a bit semantic. Functions return something—a word, a value—just like the function SUM returns the total of values. Subs, on the other hand, change things. Let's leave it at that.

The first macro (the second code on the next page) places in column D of the 1st sheet an encrypted SSN, and then decrypts it again in column E. It does so by setting the *Formula* property of those cells that uses the function *Encrypt*.

The second macro (the third code on the next page) does something similar, but this time by directly calling the *Encrypt* function.

What you need to know

To make the encrypted version a bit harder to crack, we used the VBA function *StrReverse*, which puts the text, a *String*, in a reversed order.

What you need to do

```
Option Explicit
'A simple algorithm, so if law enforcement detects illegal use of it, the code can be
cracked easily

Function Encrypt(sInput As String, bEncrypt As Boolean) As String
   Dim i As Integer, sChar As String, sNew As String
   sInput = StrReverse(UCase(sInput))
   For i = 1 To Len(sInput)
     sChar = Mid(sInput, i, 1)
     sChar = Chr(Asc(sChar) + IIf(bEncrypt, 20, -20))
     sNew = sNew & sChar
   Next i
   Encrypt = sNew 'OR: = LCase(sNew)
End Function

Sub CreateFormulas()
   Dim iRows As Long
   Sheet1.Activate: Range("A1").Select
   iRows = Range("A1").CurrentRegion.Rows.Count
   Range("D1").Range(Cells(2, 1), Cells(iRows, 1)).ClearContents
   Range("E1").Range(Cells(2, 1), Cells(iRows, 1)).ClearContents
   If MsgBox("Encrypt and decrypt with formula?", vbYesNo) = vbNo Then Exit Sub
   Range("D1").Range(Cells(2, 1), Cells(iRows, 1)).Formula = "=Encrypt(B2,TRUE)"
   Range("E1").Range(Cells(2, 1), Cells(iRows, 1)).Formula = "=Encrypt(D2,FALSE)"
End Sub

Sub Encrypting()
   Dim sText As String, i As Long
   Sheet3.Activate
   Columns("D:E").ClearContents
   MsgBox "Encrypting and decrypting column B"
   For i = 2 To Range("A1").CurrentRegion.Rows.Count
     Cells(i, 4) = Encrypt(Cells(i, 2), True)
     Cells(i, 5) = Encrypt(Cells(i, 4), False)
     Cells.EntireColumn.AutoFit
   Next i
End Sub
```

Chapter 89: Encrypting a Spreadsheet

What the simulation does

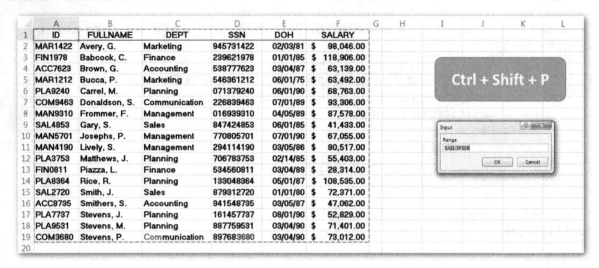

With an *Application.InputBox*, the user can indicate which part of a sheet to encrypt. Then the macro uses the function *Encrypt* (the same function as used in the previous chapter) to encrypt each cell in this selected range and place it on a new sheet. This is done with a *For-Each*-loop.

Next the macro asks the user whether they want to create a CSV-file of this encrypted sheet (see below). If the user says yes, another *Sub* is called, *SaveAsText*, which opens NotePad and copies the encrypted text onto it.

What you need to know

	A	B	C	D	E	F	G	H	I	J	K	L
1	]X	Zi``bUaY	XYdh	ggb	Xc\	gU`Ufm						
2	aUfEHFF	UŠyŤ@4[B	auŤ[y^},{	MHIKGEHFF	FCGCEMLE	MLDHJ						
3	Z]bEMKL	Vuvwfwl@4WB	Z},u,wy	FGMJFEMKL	ECECEMLI	EELMDJ						
4	UWWKJFG	VŤf‹,@4[B	Uwwf‰,^},{	IGLKKKJFG	GCHCEMLK	JGEGM						
5	aUfEFEF	V‰wwu@4dB	auŤ[y^},{	IHJGJEFEF	JCECEMKI	JGHMF						
6	d`UMFHD	WuŤŤy€@4aB	d€u,,},{	DKEGKMFHD	JCECEMMD	JLKJG						
7	WcaMHJG	Xf,u€x‡f,@4gB	Wf‰,}wu^}f,	FFJLGMHJG	KCECEMLM	MGGDJ						
8	aUbMGED	ZŤfyŤ@4ZB	au,u{yy,^	DEJMGMGED	HCICEMLM	LKIKL						
9	gU`HLIG	[uŤ@4gB	gu€yŤ	LHKHFHLIG	JCECEMLI	HEHGG						
10	aUbIKDE	^fŤy„|‡@4dB	au,u{yy,^	KKDLDIKDE	KCECEMMD	JKDII						
11	aUbHEMD	`}Šy€@4gB	au,u{yy,^	FMHEEHEMD	GCICEMLJ	LDIEK						
12	d`UGKIG	au^^|y‹‡@4^B	d€u,,},{	KDJKLGKIG	FCEHCEMLI	IIHDG						
13	Z]bDLEE	d}uŽŽu@4`B	Z},u,wy	IGHIJDLEE	GCHCEMLM	FLGEH						
14	d`ULGJH	f]wy@4fB	d€u,,},{	EGGDHLGJH	ICECEMLK	EDLIGI						
15	gU`FKFD	g}^|@4^B	gu€yŤ	LKMGEFKFD	ECECEMLD	KFGKE						
16	UWWLKGI	g}^|yŤ‡@4gB	Uwwf‰,^},{	MHEIHLKGI	GCICEMLK	HKDJF						
17	d`UKKGK	g^yŠy,‡@4^B	d€u,,},{	EJEHIKKGK	LCECEMMD	IFLFM						
18	d`UMIGE	g^yŠy,‡@4aB	d€u,,},{	LLKKIMIGE	GCHCEMMD	KEHDE						
19	WcaGJLD	g^yŠy,‡@4dB	Wf‰,}wu^}f,	LMKJLGJLD	GCHCEMMD	KGDEF						
20												

It is thanks to a global variable, *bEncrypt*, that the macro *Processing* "knows" whether to encrypt or decrypt.

What you need to do

```
Option Explicit
Dim bEncrypt As Boolean

Sub Processing()
  If bEncrypt = False Then
    bEncrypt = True: Encrypting
  Else
    bEncrypt = False: Encrypting
  End If
End Sub


Sub Encrypting()
  Dim oWS1 As Worksheet, oWS2 As Worksheet, oCell As Range, oSelect As Range,
sAddr As String
  Set oWS1 = ActiveSheet
  Set oSelect = Application.InputBox("Range", ,
Range("A1").CurrentRegion.Address, , , , , 8)
  Set oWS2 = Sheets.Add(, oWS1)
  For Each oCell In oSelect
    sAddr = oCell.Address ;   oWS2.Range(sAddr) = Encrypt(oCell.Value, bEncrypt)
  Next oCell
  oWS2.Cells.EntireColumn.AutoFit
  If MsgBox("Do you want an encrypted CSV file?", vbYesNo) = vbYes Then
SaveAsText
  If bEncrypt = False Then Exit Sub
  If MsgBox("Do you want to decrypt next?", vbYesNo) = vbYes Then bEncrypt =
False: Encrypting
End Sub

Function Encrypt(sTxt As String, bEncr As Boolean)
  Dim i As Long, sChar As String, sNew As String
  For i = 1 To Len(sTxt)
    sChar = Mid(sTxt, i, 1) :  sChar = Chr(Asc(sChar) + IIf(bEncr, 20, -20))
    sNew = sNew & sChar
  Next
  Encrypt = sNew
End Function

Sub SaveAsText()
  Dim vExe As Variant, oSelect As Range
  Set oSelect = Application.InputBox("Range", ,
Range("A1").CurrentRegion.Address, , , , , 8)
  oSelect.Copy :   vExe = Shell("notepad.exe", vbNormalFocus)
  AppActivate vExe ;   SendKeys "^V", True
End Sub
```

Chapter 90: Numbering Records

What the simulation does

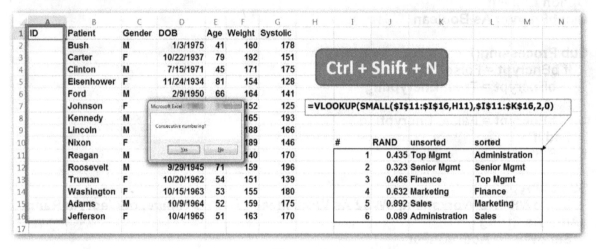

This macro automatically "numbers" each record in a database by inserting a column before the first column and then populating it with various options:

- Consecutive numbering
- With leading zeros
- Starting at a specific number
- Repeating from 1 to n
- Repeating each number n times

At the end of all these options, the macro lets the user sort range (J11:J16) in a randomly sorted way. The sorting is based on random numbers in column I. The randomly sorted list uses the Excel functions VLOOKUP and SMALL as shown in the comment of cell L11.

What you need to know

The Excel functions that can be used here are ROW, RIGHT, MOD, QUOTIENT, VLOOKUP, and SMALL.

QUOTIENT returns the integer portion of a division; its 1st argument holds the numerator, the 2nd argument the divisor.

	ID	Patient
1	ID	Patient
2	001	Bush
3	002	Carter
4	003	Clinton
5	004	Eisenhower
6	005	Ford
7	006	Johnson
8	007	Kennedy
9	008	Lincoln
10	009	Nixon
11	010	Reagan
12	011	Roosevelt
13	012	Truman
14	013	Washington
15	014	Adams
16	015	Jefferson

	ID	Patient
1	ID	Patient
2	1001	Bush
3	1002	Carter
4	1003	Clinton
5	1004	Eisenhower
6	1005	Ford
7	1006	Johnson
8	1007	Kennedy
9	1008	Lincoln
10	1009	Nixon
11	1010	Reagan
12	1011	Roosevelt
13	1012	Truman
14	1013	Washington
15	1014	Adams
16	1015	Jefferson

	ID	Patient
1	ID	Patient
2	1	Bush
3	2	Carter
4	3	Clinton
5	4	Eisenhower
6	5	Ford
7	1	Johnson
8	2	Kennedy
9	3	Lincoln
10	4	Nixon
11	5	Reagan
12	1	Roosevelt
13	2	Truman
14	3	Washington
15	4	Adams
16	5	Jefferson

	ID	Patient
1	ID	Patient
2	1	Bush
3	1	Carter
4	1	Clinton
5	1	Eisenhower
6	1	Ford
7	2	Johnson
8	2	Kennedy
9	2	Lincoln
10	2	Nixon
11	2	Reagan
12	3	Roosevelt
13	3	Truman
14	3	Washington
15	3	Adams
16	3	Jefferson

What you need to do

```
Option Explicit

Sub Numbering()
  Dim oRange As Range
  Range("A1").EntireColumn.Insert
  Range("A1") = "ID"
  Set oRange = Range("A1").CurrentRegion
  Set oRange = oRange.Offset(1, 0).Resize(oRange.Rows.Count - 1, 1)
  With oRange
    MsgBox "Consecutive numbering."
    .Formula = "=ROW(A1)"
    .Formula = .Value
    MsgBox "With leading zeros."
    .Formula = "=RIGHT(""000"" & ROW(A1),3)"
    .Copy: .PasteSpecial xlPasteValuesAndNumberFormats
    Application.CutCopyMode = False: Range("A1").Select
    MsgBox "Starting at 1001."
    .Formula = "=ROW(A1001)"
    .Formula = .Value: Application.CutCopyMode = False
    MsgBox "Repeating from 1 to 5."
    .Formula = "=MOD(ROW(A1)-1,5)+1"
    .Formula = .Value
    MsgBox "Repeating each number 5 times."
    .Formula = "=QUOTIENT(ROW(A1)-1,5)+1"
    .Formula = .Value
  End With
  MsgBox "The last step deletes column A"
  Range("A1").EntireColumn.Delete
  Do While MsgBox("In H11:K16, we sort data randomly. Again?", vbYesNo) = vbYes
    Calculate
  Loop
End Sub
```

#	RAND	unsorted	sorted	
1	0.731	Top Mgmt	Sales	
2	0.993	Senior Mgmt	Marketing	
3	0.813	Finance	Top Mgmt	
4	0.611	Marketing	Finance	
5	0.538	Sales	Administration	
6	0.955	Administration	Senior Mgmt	

Chapter 91: Sizing Bins for Frequencies

What you need to know

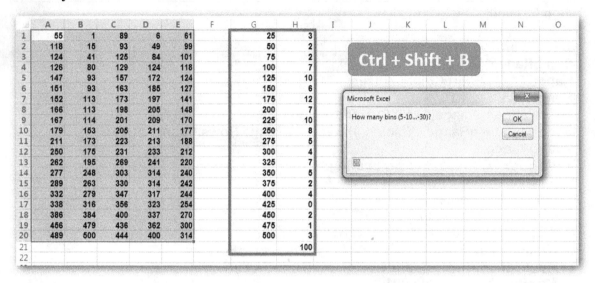

In this macro, an *Application.Inputbox* asks the user which values from A1:E20 should be covered in the frequency table of columns G:H. The macro also checks how many bins the user wants to create, so the VBA code can properly calculate the bin sizes.

What the simulation does

The VBA code creates a *Range Name* for the range that has been selected, so that this *Name* can be used in formulas. At the beginning of the code, a previously assigned *Name* has to be deleted, if there is one. But if this *Name* did not exist yet, the code would run into trouble for it cannot delete what is not there—that's what the line *On Error Resume Next* tries to prevent.

An alternative would be to declare a variable of the *Name* type: *Dim oName as Name*. And then make a loop like this: *For Each oName in Names | If oName = "data" then oName.Delete | Next oName.*

The FREQUENCY function returns the frequencies for each bin, but also returns one additional value for what we could call the "left-overs." If that extra bin is not 0, then some or more values have been left out. That is a final check that not all values have been covered.

The formula in the bins range that creates the bins would look like this: =INT(MIN(data)+(ROW(A1)*(MAX(data)-MIN(data))/" & iBin & ")).

What you need to do

```
Option Explicit

Sub BinSizing()
   Dim iBin As Integer, oData As Range, oBins As Range, oFreqs As Range
   On Error Resume Next
   Sheet1.Names("data").Delete
   Set oData = Application.InputBox("Range", , Range("A1").CurrentRegion.Address, , , , , 8)
   oData.Name = "data"
   iBin = InputBox("How many bins (5-10...-30)?", , 20)
   If iBin > 30 Then Exit Sub
   Columns("G:H").ClearContents
   Set oBins = Range(Cells(1, 7), Cells(iBin, 7))
   oBins.Formula = "=INT(MIN(data)+(ROW(A1)*(MAX(data)-MIN(data))/" & iBin & "))"
   Set oFreqs = Range(Cells(1, 8), Cells(iBin + 1, 8)) '+1 for the left-overs
   oFreqs.FormulaArray = "=FREQUENCY(data," & oBins.Address & ")"
   oData.Select
End Sub
```

Chapter 92: Creating Calendars

What the simulation does

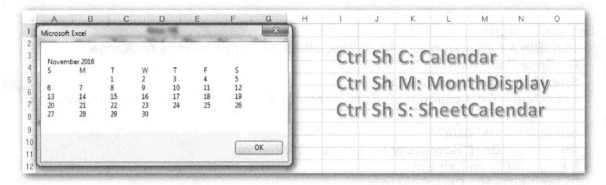

This macro creates a calendar for the month and year of your choosing, either in a *MsgBox* (picture above) or on the sheet itself (picture below)

What you need to know

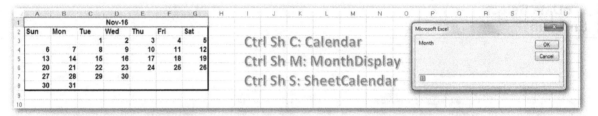

The VBA function *DateSerial* returns a date based on 3 arguments (year, month, day). The VBA function *WeekDay* returns the day of the week from 1 (Sunday) to 7 (Saterday). So the VBA expression *WeekDay*(2) would return "Monday."

What you need to do

```
Sub Calendar()
    Dim dStart As Date, dDay As Date
    Dim i As Integer, sCal As String
    dStart = InputBox("Start", , Date)
    For i = 0 To 30
        dDay = dStart + i
        If Weekday(dDay) <> 1 And Weekday(dDay) <> 7 Then
            sCal = sCal & vbCr & Format(dDay, "ddd" & vbTab & "mm/dd/yy")
        Else
            sCal = sCal & vbCr
        End If
    Next i
    MsgBox sCal
End Sub
```

```vba
Sub MonthDisplay()
  Dim dDate As Date, sCal As String, i As Integer, iMonth As Integer, iYear As Integer
  iMonth = InputBox("Month", , Month(Now()))
  iYear = InputBox("Year", , Year(Now()))
  sCal = MonthName(iMonth) & " " & iYear & vbCr
  sCal = sCal & "S" & vbTab & "M" & vbTab & "T" & vbTab & "W" & vbTab & "T" &
vbTab & "F" & vbTab & "S" & vbCr
  dDate = DateSerial(iYear, iMonth, 1 :   dDate = dDate - Weekday(dDate) + 1
  Do
    For i = 1 To 7
      If Month(dDate) = iMonth Then sCal = sCal & Day(dDate)
      sCal = sCal & vbTab
      dDate = dDate + 1
    Next i
    sCal = sCal & vbCr
  Loop While Month(dDate) = iMonth
  MsgBox sCal
End Sub


Sub SheetCalendar()
  Dim dDate As Date, iMonth As Integer, iYear As Integer
  Dim sRange As String, r As Integer, i As Integer
  sRange = Application.InputBox("Start in cell", , "A1")
  iMonth = InputBox("Month", , Month(Now()))
  iYear = InputBox("Year", , Year(Now()))
  With Range(sRange)
    .Value = MonthName(iMonth) & " " & iYear
    .Range(Cells(1, 1), Cells(1, 7)).Merge
    .HorizontalAlignment = xlCenter
    r = 2
    For i = 1 To 7
      .Cells(r, i) = Left(WeekdayName(i), 3)
    Next i
    dDate = DateSerial(iYear, iMonth, 1)
    dDate = dDate - Weekday(dDate) + 1
    Do
      r = r + 1
      For i = 1 To 7
        If Month(dDate) = iMonth Then .Cells(r, i) = Day(dDate) Else .Cells(r, i) = ""
        dDate = dDate + 1
      Next i
    Loop While Month(dDate) = iMonth
    .CurrentRegion.BorderAround , xlThick
  End With
End Sub
```

Chapter 93: Populating a Jagged Array

What the simulation does

	A	B	C	D	E	F	G	H	I	J	K	L	M	N	O	P
1	$83.83	$867.08	$921.04	$975.55	$844.34	$96.55	$951.67	$988.54	$5,730.60							
2	$743.31	$91.72	$577.43	$214.97	$955.85	$960.20	$703.68	$891.13	$12.56	$784.46	$497.74	$958.42	$7,391.47			
3	$230.34	$774.61	$534.31	$15.16	$480.27	$799.48	$385.72	$932.85	$561.41	$303.38	$882.09	$5,899.62				
4	$923.77	$748.76	$198.53	$12.47	$268.34	$845.16	$768.95	$972.37	$625.22	$314.81	$989.15	$6,667.53				
5	$681.72	$908.26	$169.98	$498.28	$360.50	$670.00	$740.47	$469.67	$647.72	$454.10	$700.91	$6,301.61				
6	$671.12	$689.82	$326.04	$277.92	$28.17	$397.23	$118.09	$408.83	$364.19	$452.88	$10.01	$806.57	$200.50	$105.34	$4,856.71	
7	$333.52	$12.48	$740.91	$947.16	$91.29	$557.78	$899.21	$339.70	$561.39	$454.37	$538.79	$682.92	$995.83	$7,155.35		
8	$552.78	$552.78														
9	$57.76	$293.85	$534.50	$653.32	$712.09	$477.59	$793.10	$698.09	$366.11	$400.56	$619.15	$685.00	$260.10	$6,551.22		
10	$800.33	$813.58	$108.00	$409.76	$386.99	$495.27	$987.99	$4,001.92								
11	$707.79	$306.54	$483.14	$222.31	$1,719.78											
12	$192.03	$72.03	$969.55	$101.90	$917.67	$769.37	$504.72	$864.78	$773.81	$16.63	$5,182.49					
13	$522.21	$528.33	$822.65	$189.13	$778.84	$629.78	$154.30	$536.24	$961.39	$5,122.87						
14	$577.05	$973.29	$784.28	$39.71	$145.67	$398.53	$365.25	$976.74	$544.79	$820.57	$5,625.88					
15	$674.03	$479.54	$186.49	$132.71	$780.32	$316.19	$459.98	$211.90	$3,241.16							
16	$972.78	$949.44	$1,922.22													
17	$515.06	$59.71	$886.15	$463.18	$250.57	$270.42	$252.33	$619.76	$265.45	$21.94	$3,604.57					
18	$464.05	$986.74	$345.60	$675.71	$902.83	$256.57	$27.58	$405.40	$636.87	$535.19	$999.59	$315.79	$676.46	$7,228.38		
19	$979.46	$315.87	$107.12	$19.43	$361.79	$284.37	$2,068.04									
20	$564.54	$358.54	$923.08													
21	$203.43	$953.65	$389.71	$208.90	$806.70	$534.71	$723.91	$224.13	$957.53	$742.61	$5,745.28					
22	$732.44	$351.80	$52.26	$212.76	$133.06	$604.29	$2,086.61									
23	$413.44	$13.69	$764.40	$1,191.53												
24	$40.44	$228.64	$81.69	$957.06	$964.91	$226.96	$21.56	$583.01	$0.39	$1,104.66						
25	$530.84	$145.25	$293.43	$62.19	$553.45	$374.54	$964.21	$223.94	$795.99	$713.57	$4,657.41					
26	$224.96	$743.38	$270.08	$381.59	$159.78	$924.50	$19.95	$502.34	$936.44	$427.77	$260.36	$780.37	$354.55	$666.85	$312.91	$6,965.83
27														GrandTotal	$115,498.60	

Ctrl + Shift + J

This simulation creates random sales per row—which could be per day, per week, or whatever. Since the number of sales per row can vary, a simulation like this can best be done with a so-called jagged array.

The "main" array has 26 elements (0 to 25). But each one of these 26 elements holds another array of elements. So we end up with an array of arrays—a 1-dimensional "main array" with 1-dimensional "subarrays." The dimension of each subarray is determined randomly.

What you need to know

The simulation loops through the 26 elements of the main array and starts each time a subarray with a random amount of (random) elements, the sales. Once the subarray is finished, the simulation stores it in the main array: *arrMain(i) = arrSub*. Make sure the main array is of the *Variant* type, for only a *Variant* can store another array.

To populate the cells on the sheet, you need to address each element in the main array as well as in the subarray. This is done as follows: *arrMain(i)(j)*—with *j* refering to a subarray element, and *i* to a main array element.

On the last line, the simulation calculates the total sales amount.

In case you want to create the jagged array on a new sheet, the VBA code has also a *Sub* called *InsertSheet*.

What you need to do

```
Option Explicit

Sub JaggedArray()
  Dim arrMain(25) As Variant, arrSub() As String
  Dim i As Integer, j As Integer, iRand As Integer
  Dim cSubTotal As Currency, cGrandTotal As Currency
  Range("A1").CurrentRegion.Cells.Interior.ColorIndex = 0
  Range("A1").CurrentRegion.ClearContents
  'Loop thru Main Array and create Sub arrays of random length
  For i = 0 To UBound(arrMain)
    iRand = Int(Rnd() * 15)
    ReDim arrSub(iRand)
    For j = 0 To UBound(arrSub)
      arrSub(j) = FormatCurrency(Rnd() * 1000)
    Next j
    arrMain(i) = arrSub
  Next i
  'Call InsertSheet below if you like
  For i = 0 To UBound(arrMain)
    For j = 0 To UBound(arrMain(i))
      ActiveCell.Offset(i, j) = arrMain(i)(j)
      cSubTotal = cSubTotal + arrMain(i)(j)
    Next j
    ActiveCell.Offset(i, j) = cSubTotal
    cGrandTotal = cGrandTotal + cSubTotal: cSubTotal = 0
    ActiveCell.Offset(i, j).Interior.ColorIndex = 15
  Next i
  ActiveCell.Offset(i, j) = cGrandTotal
  ActiveCell.Offset(i, j - 1) = "GrandTotal"
  Cells.EntireColumn.AutoFit
End Sub

Sub InsertSheet()
  Dim oWS As Worksheet, sName As String
Again:
  sName = InputBox("Which name?")
  If sName = "" Then Exit Sub
  For Each oWS In Worksheets
    If LCase(oWS.Name) = LCase(sName) Then GoTo Again
  Next oWS
  Set oWS = Worksheets.Add(, ActiveSheet)
  oWS.Name = sName
End Sub
```

Chapter 94: Filtering a Database

What the simulation does

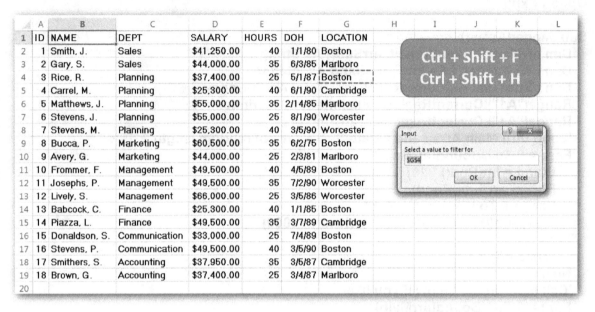

The first macro creates an *AdvancedFilter* on a new sheet. It loops through all the headers and asks the users if they want a filter for label1, label2, etc. (see next picture).

The second macro asks users to select the item they want to filter for (bottom picture).

What you need to know

	ID	NAME	DEPT	SALARY	HOURS	DOH	LOCATION
1	ID	NAME	DEPT	SALARY	HOURS	DOH	LOCATION
2				>35000			Boston
3							
4	ID	NAME	DEPT	SALARY	HOURS	DOH	LOCATION
5	1	Smith, J.	Sales	$41,250.00	40	1/1/80	Boston
6	3	Rice, R.	Planning	$37,400.00	25	5/1/87	Boston
7	8	Bucca, P.	Marketing	$60,500.00	35	6/2/75	Boston
8	10	Frommer, F.	Management	$49,500.00	40	4/5/89	Boston
9	16	Stevens, P.	Communication	$49,500.00	40	3/5/90	Boston
10							

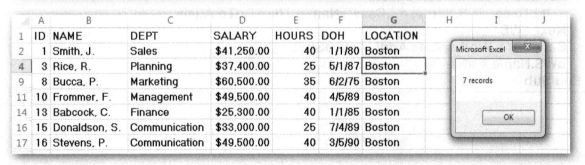

What you need to do

```
Option Explicit

Sub FilterDB()
  Dim oData As Range, oFilter As Range, i As Integer, sSet As String, oWS As
Worksheet
  Set oData = ActiveCell.CurrentRegion
  oData.Rows(1).Copy
  Set oWS = Worksheets.Add(, ActiveSheet)
  ActiveCell.PasteSpecial
  For i = 1 To oData.Columns.Count
    sSet = InputBox("Set filter (or leave empty) " & oData.Cells(1, i))
    If sSet <> "" Then ActiveCell.Offset(1, i - 1) = sSet
  Next i
  Set oFilter = ActiveCell.CurrentRegion
  oData.AdvancedFilter xlFilterCopy, Range(oFilter.Address), Range("A4")
  oFilter.EntireColumn.AutoFit
End Sub

Sub HideRows()
  Dim col As Integer, r As Long, i As Long, iCount As Long, oSelect As Range
  With ActiveCell.CurrentRegion
    r = .Rows.Count
    Set oSelect = Application.InputBox("Select a value to filter for", ,
Range("G4").Address, , , , , 8)
    oSelect.Select: col = ActiveCell.Column
    For i = 2 To r
      If .Cells(i, col) <> ActiveCell Then
        .Cells(i, col).EntireRow.Hidden = True
      Else
        iCount = iCount + 1
      End If
    Next i
    MsgBox iCount & " records"
    If MsgBox("Unhide rows?", vbYesNo) = vbYes Then .EntireRow.Hidden = False
  End With
End Sub
```

Chapter 95: Formatting Phone Numbers

What the simulation does

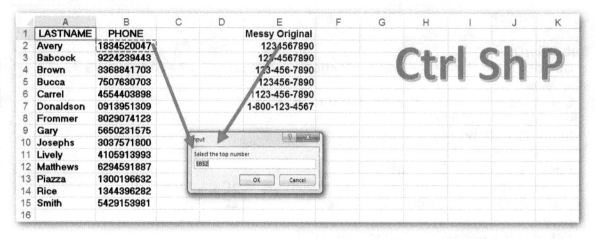

This macro formats "messy" phone numbers so they look properly formatted. It works even for seriously mutilated numbers (see column E). The macro is based on the format that the USA uses for its phone numbers. You may have to adjust the VBA code to your country's format.

Through *an Application.InputBox*, the users can select the top phone number in a column. The macro will insert a new column to the right of it and produce the formatted version of all the numbers in the preceding column.

What you need to know

	A	B	C	D	E	F	G	H
1	LASTNAME	PHONE				Messy Original		
2	Avery	1834520047	(183)-452-0047			1234567890	(123)-456-7890	
3	Babcock	9224239443	(922)-423-9443			123-4567890	(123)-456-7890	
4	Brown	3368841703	(336)-884-1703			123-456-7890	(123)-456-7890	
5	Bucca	7507630703	(750)-763-0703			123456-7890	(123)-456-7890	
6	Carrel	4554403898	(455)-440-3898			1123-456-7890	(123)-456-7890	
7	Donaldson	0913951309	(091)-395-1309			1-800-123-4567	(800)-123-4567	
8	Frommer	8029074123	(802)-907-4123					
9	Gary	5650231575	(565)-023-1575					
10	Josephs	3037571800	(303)-757-1800					
11	Lively	4105913993	(410)-591-3993					
12	Matthews	6294591887	(629)-459-1887					
13	Piazza	1300196632	(130)-019-6632					
14	Rice	1344396282	(134)-439-6282					
15	Smith	5429153981	(542)-915-3981					
16								

The macro *PhoneColumn* does the heavy work, but it does so in the new column by creating formulas that use the custom function *PhoneFormat*. This function does the cobbling together of the numbers by using VBA functions such as *Len*, *Right*, *Mid*, and *IsNumeric*. They all speak for themselves. To determine the number of characters in a string, we use the *Len* function. Perhaps *Mid* needs a bit more information. It has 3 arguments: string, start (the character position in a string), and length (the number of characters to return).

Another new VBA element is the *Select Case* statement. In this macro, it specifies the length of the string we have reached so far in the process.

What you need to do

```
Option Explicit

Function PhoneFormat(Phone As String) As String
   Dim i As Integer, sFormat As String, sCur As String, sTrunc As String, n As Integer
   sTrunc = Phone
   For i = 1 To Len(sTrunc)
      If IsNumeric(Mid(sTrunc, i, 1)) Then n = n + 1
   Next i
   If n > 10 Then sTrunc = Right(sTrunc, Len(sTrunc) - 1)
   For i = 1 To Len(sTrunc)
      sCur = Mid(sTrunc, i, 1)
      If IsNumeric(sCur) Then
         Select Case Len(sFormat)
            Case 0: sFormat = "(" & sCur
            Case 3: sFormat = sFormat & sCur & ")-"
            Case 8: sFormat = sFormat & sCur & "-"
            Case Else: sFormat = sFormat & sCur
         End Select
      End If
   Next i
   PhoneFormat = sFormat
End Function

Sub PhoneColumn()
   Dim r As Long, c As Integer, i As Long, iLast As Long, oSelect As Range
   Set oSelect = Application.InputBox("Select the top number", ,
Range("B2").Address, , , , , 8)
   oSelect.Select
   r = ActiveCell.Row
   c = ActiveCell.Column
   iLast = ActiveCell.CurrentRegion.Rows.Count
   ActiveCell.Offset(0, 1).EntireColumn.Insert
   Range(Cells(2, c + 1), Cells(iLast, c + 1)).NumberFormat = "General"
   Range(Cells(2, c + 1), Cells(iLast, c + 1)).FormulaR1C1 = "=PhoneFormat(RC[-1])"
End Sub
```

Chapter 96: Creating Gradients

What the simulation does

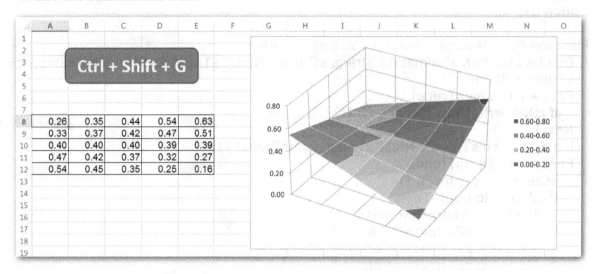

This simulation creates gradients between the four corner cells of range A8:E12. At each run the four corner cells change randomly. All the other cells have to be adjusted so they form a smooth gradient with gradual transitions.

What you need to know

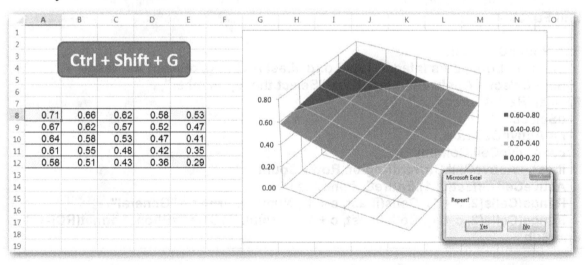

The "trick" to achieve this is using the AVERAGE function, but in such a way that the formula refers to two neighboring cells plus itself—for instance, in cell B8: =AVERAGE(A8:C8). Since the formula in such cells uses a reference to itself, it causes circular reference. Excel does not allow this, unless you temporarily turn *Iteration* on.

Once the formulas are "settled," the macro replaces them with the values found, so it can turn *Iteration* back off.

If the matrix would have more cells, you may have to increase *MaxIterations* in the VBA code, to make sure each cells reaches a stable value.

What you need to do

```
Option Explicit

Sub Gradients()
  Application.Iteration = True
  Application.MaxIterations = 1000
  Application.Calculation = xlCalculationAutomatic
  Do
    Range("A8") = Rnd:    Range("A8").Formula = Range("A8").Value
    Range("E8") = Rnd:    Range("E8").Formula = Range("E8").Value
    Range("A12") = Rnd:    Range("A12").Formula = Range("A12").Value
    Range("E12") = Rnd:    Range("E12").Formula = Range("E12").Value
    'Fill the outer ranges first and then the center
    Range("B8:D8").Formula = "=AVERAGE(A8:C8)"
    Range("E9:E11").Formula = "=AVERAGE(E8:E10)"
    Range("B12:D12").Formula = "=AVERAGE(A12:C12)"
    Range("A9:A11").Formula = "=AVERAGE(A8:A10)"
    Range("B9:D11").Formula = "=AVERAGE(A8:C10)"
    'Replace formulas with values
    Range("A8:E12").Formula = Range("A8:E12").Value
  Loop Until MsgBox("Repeat?", vbYesNo) = vbNo
  Application.Iteration = False
End Sub
```

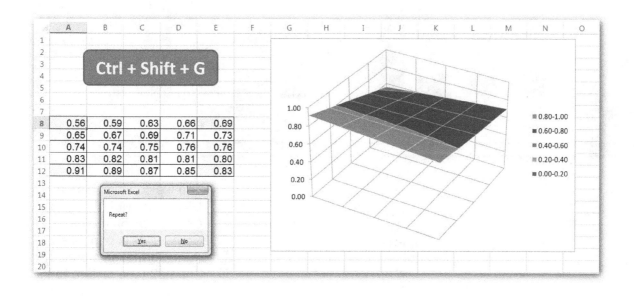

Chapter 97: Aligning Multiple Charts

What the simulation does

	A	B	C	D	E	F	G	H	I	J	K	L
1	**2010**	Qtr1	Qtr2	Qtr3	Qtr4							
2	Location1	$81,146.00	$53,993.00	$58,631.00	$85,241.00							
3	Location2	$70,153.00	$72,777.00	$67,987.00	$89,929.00							
4	Location3	$95,683.00	$79,376.00	$65,265.00	$96,282.00							
5	Location4	$96,694.00	$85,584.00	$81,543.00	$53,927.00							
6												
7	**2011**	Qtr1	Qtr2	Qtr3	Qtr4							
8	Location1	$66,617.00	$91,839.00	$84,354.00	$89,384.00							
9	Location2	$56,890.00	$56,111.00	$87,324.00	$65,549.00							
10	Location3	$63,447.00	$70,792.00	$85,567.00	$63,911.00							
11	Location4	$64,535.00	$97,190.00	$75,648.00	$66,033.00							
12												

Ctr Shift C: creates charts

Ctr Shift T: changes type

This sheet has multiple *Areas*—that is, sections separated by empty rows (or columns). The macro loops through the collection of *Areas* and creates charts next to each other of a new sheet.

What you need to know

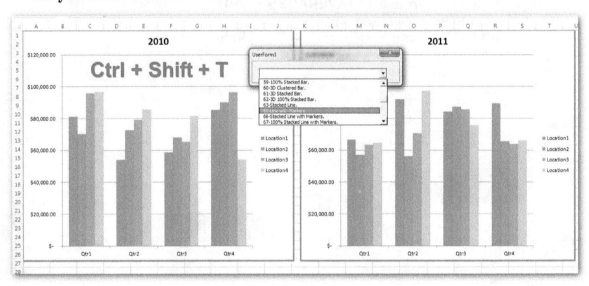

	A	B	C	D
1	1	Area	xlArea	
2	4	Line.	xlLine	
3	51	Clustered Column.	xlColumnClustered	
4	52	Stacked Column.	xlColumnStacked	
5	53	100% Stacked Column.	xlColumnStacked100	
6	54	3D Clustered Column.	xl3DColumnClustered	
7	55	3D Stacked Column.	xl3DColumnStacked	
8	56	3D 100% Stacked Column.	xl3DColumnStacked100	
9	57	Clustered Bar.	xlBarClustered	
10	58	Stacked Bar.	xlBarStacked	
11	59	100% Stacked Bar.	xlBarStacked100	
12	60	3D Clustered Bar.	xl3DBarClustered	
13	61	3D Stacked Bar.	xl3DBarStacked	

The file contains also a *UserForm* with a *ComboBox* on it. The *ComboBox* is populated with information stored on Sheet22 (see picture to the left). With the settings in column C, the user can regulate through the *ComboBox* which type of chart to display. The user can activate the form with the *Sub Types* (Ctrl+Sh+T).

What you need to do

```vba
Private Sub UserForm_Activate()  'code in a UserForm with a ComboBox
   Dim i As Integer
   With Sheet22.Range("A1").CurrentRegion
      For i = 1 To .Rows.Count
         ComboBox1.AddItem .Cells(i, 1) & "-" & .Cells(i, 2)
      Next i
   End With
End Sub

Private Sub ComboBox1_Click()
   Dim oWS As Worksheet, i As Integer
   On Error Resume Next
   Set oWS = ActiveSheet
   For i = 1 To oWS.ChartObjects.Count
      oWS.ChartObjects(i).Chart.ChartType = Left(ComboBox1.Text, InStr(1,
ComboBox1.Text, "-") - 1)
   Next i
End Sub
```

```vba
Sub CreateCharts() 'this code is in a Module
   Dim oRange As Range, i As Integer, oChart As Chart, oWS As Worksheet
   Set oWS = Worksheets.Add(, ActiveSheet)
   Set oRange = Sheet1.Columns(1).SpecialCells(xlCellTypeConstants).Cells
   For i = 1 To oRange.Areas.Count
      Set oChart = Charts.Add
      With oChart
         .SetSourceData oRange.Areas(i).CurrentRegion
         .ChartArea.Border.Weight = xlThick :    .ChartType = xlColumnClustered
 :       .HasTitle = True :            .ChartTitle.Caption = oRange.Areas(i).Cells(1, 1)
         .Location xlLocationAsObject, oWS.Name
      End With
   Next i
   oWS.Activate
   For i = 1 To oWS.ChartObjects.Count
      With oWS.ChartObjects(i)
         .Width = ActiveWindow.Width * 0.4 :     .Height = ActiveWindow.Height * 0.6
         .Left = ((i - 1) Mod oWS.ChartObjects.Count) * ActiveWindow.Width * 0.41
         .Top = Int((i - 1) / oWS.ChartObjects.Count) * 150
      End With
   Next i
End Sub

Sub Types()
   UserForm1.Show vbModeless     'see code above
End Sub
```

Chapter 98: Temperature Fluctuations

What the simulation does

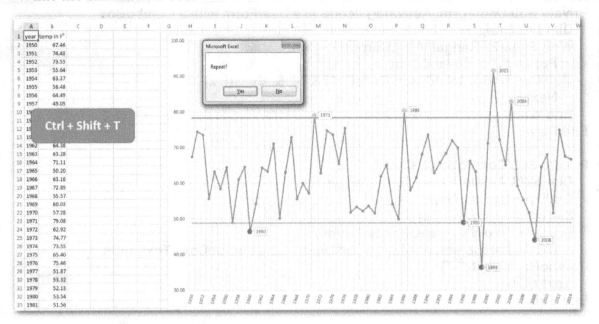

As they say, nothing is as fickle as the weather. We will simulate this for temperature, having it oscillate around a mean of 65° F and a standard deviation of 10 during a period of 65 years.

As to be expected, there will be some relatively extreme values below the 5th percentile mark or above the 95th percentile mark by mere randomness. Sometimes we might hit more "peaks" or more extreme "peaks" than usual.

What you need to know

	A	B	C	D	E
1	year	temp in F°	0.95	0.05	
2	1950	=NORMINV(RAND(),65,10)	=PERCENTILE($B$2:$B$66,$C$1)	=PERCENTILE($B$2:$B$66,$D$1)	=IF(B2>C2,B2,NA())
3	1951	=NORMINV(RAND(),65,10)	=PERCENTILE($B$2:$B$66,$C$1)	=PERCENTILE($B$2:$B$66,$D$1)	=IF(B3>C3,B3,NA())
4	1952	=NORMINV(RAND(),65,10)	=PERCENTILE($B$2:$B$66,$C$1)	=PERCENTILE($B$2:$B$66,$D$1)	=IF(B4>C4,B4,NA())
5	1953	=NORMINV(RAND(),65,10)	=PERCENTILE($B$2:$B$66,$C$1)	=PERCENTILE($B$2:$B$66,$D$1)	=IF(B5>C5,B5,NA())
6	1954	=NORMINV(RAND(),65,10)	=PERCENTILE($B$2:$B$66,$C$1)	=PERCENTILE($B$2:$B$66,$D$1)	=IF(B6>C6,B6,NA())
7	1955	=NORMINV(RAND(),65,10)	=PERCENTILE($B$2:$B$66,$C$1)	=PERCENTILE($B$2:$B$66,$D$1)	=IF(B7>C7,B7,NA())
8	1956	=NORMINV(RAND(),65,10)	=PERCENTILE($B$2:$B$66,$C$1)	=PERCENTILE($B$2:$B$66,$D$1)	=IF(B8>C8,B8,NA())
9	1957	=NORMINV(RAND(),65,10)	=PERCENTILE($B$2:$B$66,$C$1)	=PERCENTILE($B$2:$B$66,$D$1)	=IF(B9>C9,B9,NA())

Dramatic swings in temperature can be quite common because of pure randomness. The 5th and 95th percentile lines in the chart are based on the "hidden" columns C and D. The markers for extremes outside that range are based on hidden columns E and F. The VBA code changes the font color in these four columns to white, and it can protect these columns from manual changes.

The chart plots the series of values in columns B:F. The horizontal axis is based on the first column. Columns E and F plot only the positive and negative peaks; the other cells in those two columns contain the function NA and do not show.

What you need to do

```vba
Option Explicit

Sub Temps()
    Dim oRange As Range, r As Long
    'to protect the "hidden" columns
    Sheet1.Unprotect
    Columns("C:F").Cells.Font.Color = vbWhite
    Sheet1.Protect , False, , , True  'True allows VBA to work
    Set oRange = Range("A1").CurrentRegion
    r = oRange.Rows.Count: r = r - 1
    Set oRange = oRange.Offset(1, 0).Resize(r, oRange.Columns.Count)
    Do
        oRange.Columns(3).Formula = "=PERCENTILE($B$2:$B$66,$C$1)"
        oRange.Columns(4).Formula = "=PERCENTILE($B$2:$B$66,$D$1)"
        oRange.Columns(5).Formula = "=IF(B2>C2,B2,NA())"
        oRange.Columns(6).Formula = "=IF(B2<D2,B2,NA())"
    Loop Until MsgBox("Repeat?", vbYesNo) = vbNo
    If MsgBox("Protect the formulas in columns A:E?", vbYesNo) = vbYes Then
        Cells.Locked = False
        Columns("A:F").Locked = True
        Sheet1.Protect , , , , True, True
    End If
End Sub
```

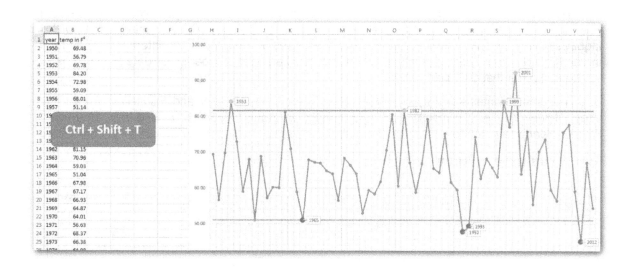

Chapter 99: Working with Fiscal Years

What the simulation does

Excel has great functions to extract the year, month, and day part of a date—but amazingly enough, it has no function to find out to which *quarter* of the year such a date belongs. For data analysis and summary overviews, that is quite a limitation. This problem can be solved, though, with a simple formula of nested functions such as *ROUNDUP(MONTH(any date)/3,0)*.

However, finding the correct quarter becomes much harder when your company does not have a regular fiscal year. That's where a macro comes in handy. On this sheet, an *InputBox* inquires in which month your fiscal year starts and stores that number in an internal variable (and in cell K2). Based on that information, the macro calculates for any particular date to which fiscal year and quarter that date belongs.

The sheet contains two macros: *RegularYear* for a regular year and *FiscalYear* for a fiscal year. However, the 2nd macro can also handle a regular year by calling the 1st macro, *RegularYear*, when needed.

What you need to know

	K	L	M	N	O	P
1	starts in		1	January	=INT(1+MOD(M1-$K$2,12)/3)	=YEAR(TODAY())+COUNTIF($M$1:M1,$K$2)
2	10		2	February	=INT(1+MOD(M2-$K$2,12)/3)	=YEAR(TODAY())+COUNTIF($M$1:M2,$K$2)
3			3	March	=INT(1+MOD(M3-$K$2,12)/3)	=YEAR(TODAY())+COUNTIF($M$1:M3,$K$2)
4			4	April	=INT(1+MOD(M4-$K$2,12)/3)	=YEAR(TODAY())+COUNTIF($M$1:M4,$K$2)
5			5	May	=INT(1+MOD(M5-$K$2,12)/3)	=YEAR(TODAY())+COUNTIF($M$1:M5,$K$2)
6			6	June	=INT(1+MOD(M6-$K$2,12)/3)	=YEAR(TODAY())+COUNTIF($M$1:M6,$K$2)
7			7	July	=INT(1+MOD(M7-$K$2,12)/3)	=YEAR(TODAY())+COUNTIF($M$1:M7,$K$2)

The table to the right is only for comparison purposes so you can check whether your calculations in the left table are correct. Conditional formatting in the range M1:P24 does the rest: =AND(ROW()>=$K$2,ROW()<$K$2+12)

What you need to do

```
Option Explicit

Sub RegularYear()
  Dim i As Long, dDate As Date, pQtr As Double, oStart As Range
  Columns("D:E").ClearContents
  Set oStart = Application.InputBox("Select the top date", , Range("C2").Address, , , , 8)
  With oStart
    Do While .Offset(i, 0) <> ""
      dDate = .Offset(i, 0)
      .Offset(i, 1) = Year(dDate)
      pQtr = Month(dDate) / 3
      .Offset(i, 2) = IIf(pQtr - Int(pQtr) = 0, pQtr, Int(pQtr) + 1) 'Instead of RoundUp
      i = i + 1
    Loop
  End With
End Sub

Sub FiscalYear()
  Dim i As Long, dDate As Date, iFiscMonth As Integer, iMonth As Integer, oStart As Range
  Columns("D:E").ClearContents
  Set oStart = Application.InputBox("Select the top date", , Range("C2").Address, , , , 8)
  iFiscMonth = InputBox("In which month does your fiscal year start?", , 10)
  Range("K2") = iFiscMonth
  If iFiscMonth = 1 Then RegularYear: Exit Sub
  With oStart
    Do While .Offset(i, 0) <> ""
      dDate = .Offset(i, 0)
      .Offset(i, 1) = Year(dDate) + IIf(Month(dDate) >= iFiscMonth, 1, 0)
      iMonth = Month(.Offset(i, 0)) - iFiscMonth + 1
      If iMonth <= 0 Then iMonth = iMonth + 12
      .Offset(i, 2) = IIf(iMonth / 3 - Int(iMonth / 3) = 0, iMonth / 3, Int(iMonth / 3) + 1)
      i = i + 1
    Loop
  End With
End Sub
```

Chapter 100: Time Calculations

What the simulation does

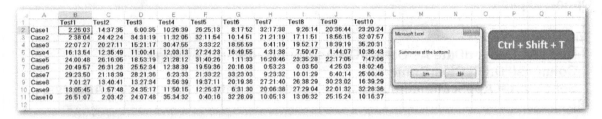

In Excel, time is a value that ranges from 0 to 0. 999988425925926, representing the times from 0:00:00 (12:00:00 AM) to 23:59:59 (11:59:59 PM). You can see the value of a particular time under *General Format* or by using *Ctrl + ~* (the tilde is just below the *Esc* key). The advantage of using decimal values for time is that you can then easily add and subtract them. You can even use functions such as SUM, AVERAGE, and so on.

When the difference in time values or their total is more than 24 hours, the decimal time values go beyond 0.9999999. This causes trouble, for time values beyond 0.9999999 get truncated when forced into the *h:mm:ss* format. If the sum is 1.5, for example, Excel shows only its decimal part, 0.5, which is 12:00:00 AM. To solve this problem, you must change the format of this number from *h:mm:ss* to *[h]:mm.ss*. Then a number such as 1.5 will indeed show up as 1.5 (in the proper time format, of course: 36:00:00). Thanks to the *[h]:mm:ss* format, you can calculate with time values beyond the duration of 1 day, which is usually necessary for sum operations.

What you need to know

	Test1	Test2	Test3	Test4	Test5	Test6	Test7	Test8	Test9	Test10		Sum	Mean					
Case1	2:26:03	14:37:35	6:00:35	10:26:39	26:25:13	8:17:52	32:17:38	9:26:14	20:36:44	23:20:24		153:54:56	15:23:30					
Case2	2:38:04	24:42:24	34:31:19	11:32:05	32:11:54	10:14:51	21:21:19	17:11:51	18:56:15	32:07:57		205:28:00	20:32:48					
Case3	22:07:27	20:27:11	15:21:17	30:47:55	3:33:22	18:55:59	6:41:19	19:52:17	18:39:19	35:20:31		191:46:39	19:10:40					
Case4	16:13:54	12:35:49	11:00:41	12:03:13	27:24:23	16:49:55	4:31:38	7:50:47	1:44:07	10:36:43		120:51:09	12:05:07					
Case5	24:00:48	26:16:05	18:53:19	21:28:12	31:40:26	1:11:33	16:20:46	23:35:28	22:17:05	7:47:06		193:30:49	19:21:05					
Case6	20:49:57	26:31:28	25:52:34	12:38:39	19:59:36	20:16:08	0:53:23	0:03:50	4:25:03	18:02:46		149:33:22	14:57:20					
Case7	29:23:50	21:18:39	28:21:36	6:23:33	21:33:22	33:23:03	9:23:32	10:01:29	6:40:14	25:00:46		191:30:02	19:09:00					
Case8	7:01:27	13:40:41	13:27:34	3:56:39	19:37:11	20:19:36	27:21:40	26:38:29	30:23:02	16:39:29		179:05:47	17:54:35					
Case9	13:05:45	1:57:48	24:35:17	11:50:15	12:26:37	6:31:30	20:06:38	27:29:04	22:01:32	32:28:36		172:33:01	17:15:18					
Case10	26:51:07	2:03:42	24:07:48	35:34:32	0:40:16	32:28:09	10:05:13	13:06:32	25:15:24	10:16:37		180:29:21	18:02:56					
Sum	164:38:22	164:11:22	202:12:00	156:41:41	195:32:20	168:28:35	149:03:08	155:16:02	170:58:42	211:40:54								
Mean	16:27:50	16:25:08	20:13:12	15:40:10	19:33:14	16:50:52	14:54:19	15:31:36	17:05:52	21:10:05								

This is basically all the macro does for summaries below the table, if needed, and also to the right, if so desired. On the next run it will delete those summaries first.

Some people prefer to use hours with decimals—where, for example, 13.50 (with a decimal point) is 13 hours and 30 minutes, as opposed to 13:50 (with a colon), which is 13 hours and 50 minutes. To convert these decimals to Excel's time decimals, you need to divide by 24 because Excel works with day units of 24 hours, 60 minutes, and 60 seconds.

What you need to do

```
Option Explicit

Sub TimeCalc()
    Dim oSum As Range, oTable As Range, oAvg As Range, r As Long, c As Long
    Set oTable = Range("B2").CurrentRegion
    r = oTable.Rows.Count: c = oTable.Columns.Count
    oTable.Rows(r).Offset(2, 0).ClearContents
    oTable.Rows(r).Offset(3, 0).ClearContents
    oTable.Columns(c).Offset(0, 2).ClearContents
    oTable.Columns(c).Offset(0, 3).ClearContents
    If MsgBox("Summaries at the bottom?", vbYesNo) = vbYes Then
        Cells(r + 2, 1) = "Sum"
        Set oSum = Range(Cells(r + 2, 2), Cells(r + 2, c))
        Cells(r + 3, 1) = "Mean"
        Set oAvg = Range(Cells(r + 3, 2), Cells(r + 3, c))
        oSum.FormulaR1C1 = "=SUM(R[-" & r & "]C:R[-2]C)"
        oSum.NumberFormat = "[h]:mm:ss"
        oAvg.FormulaR1C1 = "=AVERAGE(R[-" & r + 1 & "]C:R[-3]C)"
        oAvg.NumberFormat = "h:mm:ss"
    End If
    If MsgBox("Also summaries to the right?", vbYesNo) = vbYes Then
        Cells(1, c + 2) = "Sum"
        Set oSum = Range(Cells(2, c + 2), Cells(r, c + 2)): oSum.ClearContents
        Cells(1, c + 3) = "Mean"
        Set oAvg = Range(Cells(2, c + 3), Cells(r, c + 3)): oAvg.ClearContents
        oSum.FormulaR1C1 = "=SUM(RC[-" & r & "]:RC[-2])"
        oSum.NumberFormat = "[h]:mm:ss"
        oAvg.FormulaR1C1 = "=AVERAGE((RC[-" & r + 1 & "]:RC[-3]))"
        oAvg.NumberFormat = "h:mm:ss"
    End If
End Sub
```

IX. APPENDIX

Data Tables

A *Data Table* is a range of cells that shows how changing one or two variables in your formulas will affect the results of those formulas. A *Data Table* provides a powerful way of calculating multiple results in one operation and a way to view and compare the results of all the different variations together on your worksheet.

	A	B	C	D	E	F	G
1	AMOUNT	$ 5,000.00					
2	APR	4%					
3		$200.00	4%	5%	6%	7%	APR
4		$ 5,000.00	$ 200.00	$ 250.00	$ 300.00	$ 350.00	
5		$10,000.00	$ 400.00	$ 500.00	$ 600.00	$ 700.00	
6		$15,000.00	$ 600.00	$ 750.00	$ 900.00	$1,050.00	
7		$20,000.00	$ 800.00	$1,000.00	$1,200.00	$1,400.00	
8		$25,000.00	$1,000.00	$1,250.00	$1,500.00	$1,750.00	
9		$30,000.00	$1,200.00	$1,500.00	$1,800.00	$2,100.00	
10		$35,000.00	$1,400.00	$1,750.00	$2,100.00	$2,450.00	
11		$40,000.00	$1,600.00	$2,000.00	$2,400.00	$2,800.00	
12		$45,000.00	$1,800.00	$2,250.00	$2,700.00	$3,150.00	
13		$50,000.00	$2,000.00	$2,500.00	$3,000.00	$3,500.00	
14		AMOUNT					

To implement a *Data Table*, you select the entire range, including its point of origin with a formula in it—so that is B3:F13 in the example above. Then you go through the following menus: Data | What-If Analysis | Data Table. In the dialog box, set the row input to cell B2 and the column input to cell B1.

Once you click OK, Excel replaces all empty cells (in the shaded area) with an array formula like this: {=TABLE(B2,B1)}. Or more in general, *{=TABLE(row-input-cell, column-input-cell)}*. Sometimes, one or both of the two arguments are missing. Do not type the braces—Excel creates them automatically when you hit the *Data Table* button. And do not type the formula!

Why use a *Data Table*? There are several reasons. First, it might be easier to implement one than working with locked and unlocked cell references. Second, no part of the array can inadvertently be deleted or changed, because the array acts as one entire unit. Third, a *Data Table* has much more extra potential, as you can see in many of the simulations we use in this book.

However, there is one drawback. Because there may be many operations involved in a *Data Table*, Excel may run into speed problems. There are two ways to get around this speed issue. Method #1 is to stop automatic recalculation—at least for Data Tables. Do the following: File | Options | Options | Formulas | Automatic Except for Data Tables (you can even set all calculations to manual). If you ever need to recalculate a *Data Table*, just use *Sh + F9*, and that will recalculate only the particular sheet you are on (whereas *F9* alone would recalculate the entire file).

Method #2 is that, after you run a specific what-if analysis, you copy the *Data Table* section—that is, the area between the top row and the left column—and then paste it as values over itself. Move on to the next *Data Table*, run it, and paste values again. Whenever you need to run a pasted table again, quickly reimplement the *Data Table*.

One more limitation: A Data Table cannot accommodate more than two variables. So they are at best two-dimensional but never three-dimensional. There are ways to get around this limitation as shown in some simulations (e.g. Chapter 69).

In VBA, it is actually very easy to implement a *Data Table* by using a range's *Table* method followed by a space and two arguments, one for the row input and one for the column input.

Simulation Controls

Controls such as spin buttons and scroll bars are great tools for many kinds of what-if analysis. They quickly reset specific hard-coded values and then show you the impact of such operations.

In order to create such controls, you need the *Developer* tab in your menu, which may not be present on your machine. To add it to the ribbon, you do the following, depending on your Excel version. Pre-2010: File | Options | General | Enable the Developer Tab. In 2010 and 2013: File | Options | Customize Ribbon | in the far right list: Developer. From now on, the tab can be found in the menu on top.

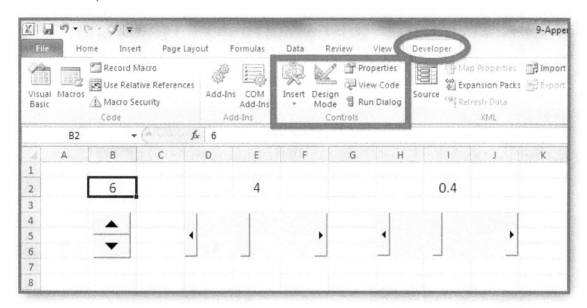

On the above sheet, we placed three controls. You do so by clicking on the *Insert* button and then on one of the options in the lower section of the list (Active-X Controls). Draw the control you have chosen on your sheet.

Then click on the *Properties* menu (make sure the control you want to set the properties for is still selected, or select it). Set at least the properties *Min*, *Max*, and *LinkedCell* (that is, the cell where you want the control's value to appear).

Once you are done, do not forget to click the *Design Mode* button OFF, so you can go back to your sheet!!! Be aware, though, that when you change a control and calculation is not automatic, you need to activate the sheet first before you can hit the "run" keys *Sh F9*.

You probably noticed already that the properties *Min* and *Max* can only hold integers. So if you want to regulate decimals with your control (like in the scroll bar to the far right), you need an intermediate cell. I happened to choose a *LinkedCell* reference located behind the control (e.g. cell I5). In the cell where you want the decimal number visibly displayed, you need to place a formula like =I5/10 (or I5/100, etc.).

Controls like these are fantastic. I used them for several simulations in this book. They are not only fun, but also very informative and revealing. I think you will love them more and more, if you did not al- ready.

If Statements

Either one-liners:

If ..... Then .....
If ..... Then ..... [Else .....]
If ..... Then ..... [ElseIf ..... Then .....] [Else .....]

Or multi-liners:

If ..... Then	**If ..... Then**	**If ..... Then**
.....	.....	.....
End If	**Else**	**ElseIf ..... Then**
	.....	.....
	End If	**Else**
		.....
		End If

Value Type Variables

Data type	Storage size		Range
Byte	1 byte		0 to 255
Boolean	2 bytes	b	True or False
Integer	2 bytes	i	-32,768 to 32,767
Long (long integer)	4 bytes	l	-2,147,483,648 to 2,147,483,647
Single (single-precision floating-point)	4 bytes	f	-3.402823E38 to -1.401298E-45 for negative values; 1.401298E-45 to 3.402823E38 for positive values
Double (double-precision floating-point)	8 bytes	p	-1.79769313486231E308 to -4.94065645841247E-324 for negative values; 4.94065645841247E-324 to 1.79769313486232E308 for positive values
Currency (scaled integer)	8 bytes	c	-922,337,203,685,477.5808 to 922,337,203,685,477.5807
Decimal	14 bytes		+/-79,228,162,514,264,337,593,543,950,335 with no decimal point; +/-7.9228162514264337593543950335 with 28 places to the right of the decimal; smallest non-zero number is +/-0.0000000000000000000000000001
Date	8 bytes	d	January 1, 100 to December 31, 9999
String (variable-length)	10 bytes + string length	s	0 to approximately 2 billion
String (fixed-length)	Length of string	s	1 to approximately 65,400
Variant (with numbers)	16 bytes	v	Any numeric value up to the range of a Double
Variant (with characters)	22 bytes + string length	v	Same range as for variable-length String

Ranges vs. Cells

	Which Cell
Range("A1")	A1
Range("A1:A7")	A1:A7
Range("A1, A5")	A1 + A5
Range("A1","A5")	A1:A5
Cells(1, 1)	A1
Cells(5, 2)	B5
Cells()	All cells

		Which Cell
Range("A1:A5").Cells(1, 1)		A1
Range("B1:C5").Cells(1, 1)		B1
Range("A1:A5").Cells(5, 1)		A5
Range("A5").Range("A2")	OR: .Offset(1,0)	A6
Range(Cells(1, 1), Cells(5, 1))		A1:A5
Range(Cells(1, 1), Cells(5, 3))		A1:C5
Range(Cells(2, 2), Cells(5, 5)) .Range("A1")		B2

FormulaR1C1

FormulaR1C1	
The ActiveCell is B11	**Result**
R1C1	A1
RC	B11
R[1]C	B12
R[-1]C[-1]	A10
=SUM(R2C:R[-1]C)	SUM(B2:B10)

Arrays

Dim arr(1 To 10) As String	**Can hold 10 *Strings***
Dim arr(0 To 4) As Integer	**Can hold 5 *Integers***
Dim arr(4) As Variant	**Can hold 5 items of anything**
Dim arr() As String ReDim arr(9)	**Reset to hold 10 *Strings***

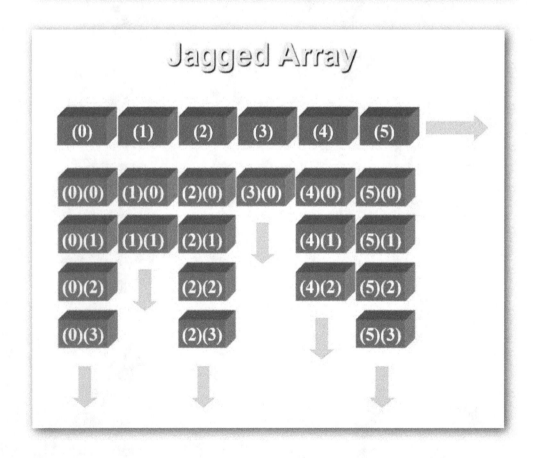

Error Handling

Error Handling

On Error 0	Switches off error handling (until next *On Error* statement)
On Error Resume Next	Execution continues with the line following the error line
On Error GoTo *myLabel*	Execution jumps to line starting with the specified label (+ colon)
Resume	Execution resumes with the statement that caused the error
Resume Next	Execution resumes with the line following the error line
Resume *myLabel*	Execution resumes at the line starting with a specified label

This would make a very general error handler:

```
Sub AnySub()
    On Error GoTo ErrTrap
    ....
    Exit Sub
ErrTrap:
    MsgBox "Number: " & Err.Number & vbCr & _
           "Description: " & Err.Description & vbCr & _
           "Source: " & Err.Source, vbCritical, "Call 1-800-123-4567"
```

X. INDEX

About the Author

Dr. Gerard M. Verschuuren is a human geneticist who also earned a doctorate in the philosophy of science. He studied and worked at universities in Europe and the United States and wrote several biology textbooks in Dutch. During this time, he also used and programmed computer software, including Excel, to simulate scientific problems.

Currently, he is semi-retired and spends most of his time as a writer, speaker, and consultant on the interface of science and computer programming.

His most recent computer-related books are:

1. From VBA to VSTO (Holy Macro! Books, 2006).
2. Visual Learning Series (MrExcel.com).
3. VBScript (CD)
4. Excel 2013 for Scientists (CD)
5. Excel 2013 for Scientists (book)
6. 100 Excel Simulations (book)
7. Excel 2013 VBA (CD)
8. Excel Video Medley (double DVD)

For more info see: http://en.wikipedia.org/wiki/Gerard_Verschuuren

For his YouTube videos on Excel and VBA: http://www.genesispc.com/links.htm#videos

All his books, CDs, and DVD's can be found at http://www.genesispc.com

Visual Learning Series (CD or DVD)

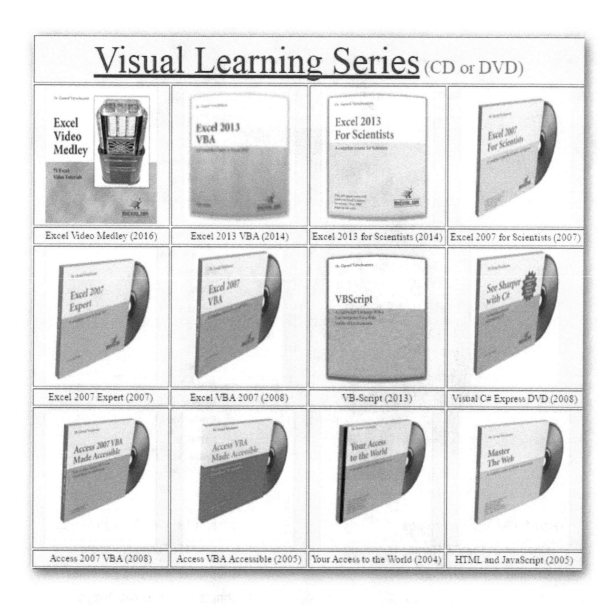

Excel Video Medley (2016)	Excel 2013 VBA (2014)	Excel 2013 for Scientists (2014)	Excel 2007 for Scientists (2007)
Excel 2007 Expert (2007)	Excel VBA 2007 (2008)	VB-Script (2013)	Visual C# Express DVD (2008)
Access 2007 VBA (2008)	Access VBA Accessible (2005)	Your Access to the World (2004)	HTML and JavaScript (2005)

**All by the same author,
Dr. Gerard M. Verschuuren**

"Excel for Scientists gave me the key skills I needed to have for working with Excel in a scientific profession. Dr. Verschuuren has an easy to understand teaching approach, covering both the basics and more in-depth tasks. It's highly informative with great reference material and is great for the beginner and the more advanced user. Step by step instructions will have you up to speed in no time." -Erin Best, Wyeth BioPharma

Designed by Scientists for Scientists

Graphs
Transformations
Error Bars
Secondary Axis
Histograms
Chart Formulas
Record Keeping
IF & Nested IF
VLOOKUP
Frequency
DSUM
Filtering
Solving
Array Formulas
Sampling
Distributions
Regression
Analysis

EXCEL 2013 for SCIENTISTS
REVISED & EXPANDED 3RD EDITION
Dr. Gerard Verschuuren

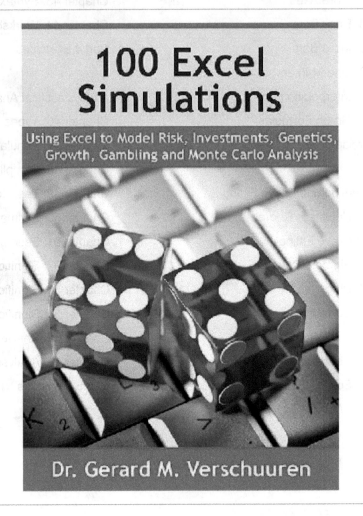

100 Excel Simulations:
very similar to the ones in this book
but all done with formulas (no VBA)

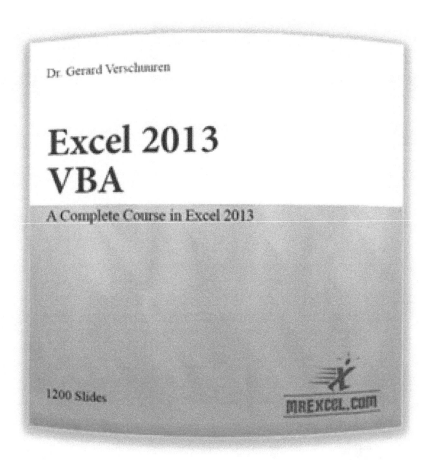

Part 1: Basic Essentials	Part 2: Formulas and Arrays	Part 3: Buttons and Forms
Object Oriented	Dates and Calendars	Importing and Exporting
Recording Macros	The Current-Region	Buttons, Bars, Menus
Branch Statements	WorksheetFunction	Application Events
Interaction	Property Formula	User Forms
Variables (Value Type)	Property FormulaR1C1	Data Entry + Mail Merge
Variables (Object Type)	Custom Functions	Custom Objects (Classes)
Collections	Array Functions	Class Collections
Loop Statements	1D- and 2D-Arrays	Error Handling
Variables as Arguments	Customized Arrays	Distributing VBA code
Pivot Tables and Charts	Variant Arrays	VBA Monitoring VBA

www.ingramcontent.com/pod-product-compliance
Lightning Source LLC
Chambersburg PA
CBHW060551060326
40690CB00017B/3671